Anguilla: Tranquillity Wrapped in Blue

Edited by Arif Ali

HANSIB

First published in Great Britain in 2003
by Hansib Publications Limited
London: PO Box 34621, London E17 4GL
Hertfordshire: Orchard Road, Royston, Hertfordshire SG8 5HA

www.hansib-books.com

ISBN 1 870518 68 3

Cover design by Graphic Resolutions, Hertfordshire, UK

Production by Books of Colour, Hertfordshire, UK

Printed and bound in Great Britain by Woolnough's of Irthlingborough, UK

Photos on cover by Chris Mason, and background image by Jessica Bensley

Photo on title page by Jessica Bensley

CAP JULUCA

"Three Great Reastaurants One Great Destination"

"Pimm's" restaurant

photo bill milne

THIS BOOK WOULD NOT HAVE BEEN POSSIBLE WITHOUT THE SUPPORT OF THE FOLLOWING:

All Island Cable Television
Tel: 497-3600
Email: alisland@anguillanet.com

Alloyd's Enterprises Ltd
Tel: 497-5622 / Fax: 497-5220

Altamer Resort
Tel: 498-4000
Email: info@altamer.com

American Eagle
Tel: 497-3501
Email: eagleaa@anguillanet.com

Anguilla Block and Sand Co. Ltd / Anguilla Masonary Products Ltd
Tel: 497-5600
Email: laker@anguillanet.com

Anguilla Development Board
Tel: 497-2595
Email: adb@anguillanet.com

Anguilla Drug Store
Tel: 497-2738 / Fax: 497-5656

Anguilla Electricity Company Ltd
Tel: 497-5200
Email: info@anglec.com

Anguilla Garden Centre Ltd
Tel: 497-8362 / Fax: 497-3773

Anguilla Great House Beach Resort / Olde Caribe Restaurant
Tel: 497-6061
Email: flemingw@anguillanet.com

Anguilla National Council for Women / Anguilla Arts & Craft Shop
Tel: 497-2200
Email: ernie@anguillanet.com

Anguilla Rums Ltd
Tel: 497-5003
Email: lyn@anguillanet.com

Anguilla Social Security Board
Tel: 497-2201
Email: angsosec@anguillanet.com

Anguilla Tourist Board
Tel: 497-2759
Email: atbtour@anguillanet.com

Anguilla Vision Center
Tel: 497-3700
Email: axavision@anguillanet.com

Apex Car Rental
Tel: 497-2642
Email: avisaxa@anguillanet.com

Ashley & Sons
Tel: 497-2641
Email: ashleys@anguillanet.com

Audain & Associates / Eden House Villa
Tel: 497-5620
Email: mraudain@candw.com.ai
Email: info@edenhousevilla.com

Bartlett's Collection & Iced & Easy Smoothies
Tel: 497-7293
Email: Bartlett@anguillanet.com

Bennie's Travel
Tel: 497-2788
Email: bennies@anguillanet.com

Blue Waters Beach Apartments
Tel: 497-6292 / Fax: 497-6982

Blues & Blues Ltd
Tel: 497-6334
Email: samcon@anguillanet.com

Cable and Wireless (WI) Ltd
Tel: 497-3100
Email: avon.carty@cw.com

Cap Juluca Hotel
Tel: 497-6666
Toll free: 1-888-852-5822
Email: capjuluca@anguillanet.com

Caribbean Associated Chambers
Tel: 497-5405
Email: abelc@anguillanet.com

Caribbean Commercial Bank (Anguilla) Ltd
Tel: 497-2571
Email: ccbaxa@anguillanet.com

Caribbean Insurers (Anguilla) Ltd
Tel: 497-5610
Email: cial@anguillanet.com

Caribbean Juris Chambers
Tel: 497-3470
Email: caribjur@anguillanet.com

Caribbean Rentals Ltd
Tel: 497-4732 & 4662
Fax: 497-2181

Caribbean Sea View
Tel: 497-4732 & 4662 / Fax: 497-2181

Carimar Beach Club
Tel: 497-6881
Email: carimar@anguillanet.com

Cheddie's Carving Studio
Tel: 497-6027
Email: cheddie@anguillanet.com

Christine Mini Mart
Tel: 497-6309 / Fax: 497-6589

Covecastles Resort
Tel: 497-6801
Toll Free: 1-800-348-4716
Email: covecastles@anguillanet.com

CuisinArt Resort & Spa Anguilla
Tel: 498-2000
Email: cuisinartresort@anguillanet.com

D-3 Enterprises Ltd
Tel: 497-3525
Email: d-3ent@anguillanet.com

Deluxe Ferry Service
Tel: 497-6289

Devonish Art Gallery / Something Special
Tel: 497-2949
Email: cperry@anguillanet.com

Dolphin Fantaseas
Email: apape@dolphinfantaseas.com

Elegant Retreats
Tel: 497-2596
Email: prems@anguillanet.com

Elodias Beach Resort
Tel: 497-3363
Email: elodias@anguillanet.ai

English Rose Restaurant
Tel: 497-5353

Fairplay Management / Royal Caribbean
Tel: 497-2976
Email: fairplay@anguillanet.com

Flag Luxury Properties
Tel: 212-407-9181
Email: jonathan.stern@flagluxury.com

Flavours Restaurant
Tel: 497-0629 / Fax: 497-8804

Frangipani Beach Club
Tel: 497-6442
Email: frangipani@anguillanet.com

General Post Office
Tel: 497- 2528
Email: angstamp@gov.ai

Georgiana's
Tel: 497-8360

Gorgeous Scilly Cay
Tel: 497-5123
Email: gorgeous@anguillanet.com

Government House
Tel: 497-3312
Email: govthouse@anguillanet.com

Government of Anguilla Treasury Department
Tel: 497-3235 / Fax: 497-5011

Hair World Accessories
Tel: 497-0052

Highway Rent-A-Car
Tel: 497-2183 / Fax: 497-2306

Hughes Medical Centre
Tel: 497-3053 / Fax: 497-3083

J.W. Proctors Ltd
Tel: 497-2445
E:mail: jwproctors@anguillanet.com

Judicial Department
Tel: 497-2377 / Fax: 497-5420

Keene Enterprises
Tel: 497-2544
Email: keene-ent@anguillanet.com

Keithley Lake & Associates
Tel: 497-2069
Email: lakelaw@anguilla-attorney.com

Lake & Kentish
Tel: 497-2582
Email: laken@anguillanet.com

Lake's World
Tel: 497-8414
Email: lakear@anguillanet.com

Lloyd's Guest House
Tel: 497-2351 / Fax: 497-3028

M & R Corporate Services Ltd
Tel: 497-5621
Email: mraudain@anguillanet.com

Meads Bay Hideaway
Tel: 498-5555
Email: healthdream@anguillanet.com

Ministry of Finance
Tel: 497-2547
Email: mofgoa@anguillanet.com

Ministry of Social Development
Tel: 497-3930 / Fax: 497-5695

Ministry of Works
Tel: 497-2651 / Fax: 497-3651

National Bank of Anguilla Ltd
Tel: 497-2101
Email: nbabankl@anguillanet.com

Nico's Restaurant
Tel: 497-2844

Offshore Finance Companies Registry
Tel: 497-3881 / Fax: 497-8053

Palm Grove Bar & Grill
Tel: 235-6582 & 4224

Paradise Cove
Tel: 497-6603
Email: para-cove@anguillanet.com

Paramount Pharmacy
Tel: 497-2366 / Fax: 497-3866

Professional Realty Services (Anguilla) Ltd
Tel: 497-3575
Email: shauser@profgroup.com

Ranny & Jo's Anguilla Ice Cream
Tel: 497-8357 / Fax: 497-0024

Rendezvous Bay Hotel & Villas
Tel: 497-6549
Toll Free: 1-800-274-4893
Email: rendezvous@anguillanet.com

Richards Architecture Development & Survey Co. Ltd
Tel: 497-4333
Email: rads@anguillanet.com

Sandy Hill Villas
Tel: 497-4043

Savannah Gallery
Tel: 497-2263
Email: savannah@anguillanet.com

Scotiabank (Anguilla) Ltd
Tel: 497-3333
Email: scotia@anguillanet.com

Serenity Cottage
Tel: 497-3328
Fax: 497-5229

Shoal Bay Beach Hotel
Tel: 497-2011 & 498-6020
Email: shoalbaybeach@anguillanet.com

Shoal Bay Villas
Tel: 497-2051
Email: sbvillas@anguillanet.com

Summer Set Car Rental
Tel: 497-5278
Email: summerset@anguillanet.com

Syd-An's Inn & Villas
Tel: 497-3180
Email: sydans@hotmail.com

Tasty's Café
Tel: 497 2723

TCL Trading Ltd
Tel: 497-3593
Email: tcltrade@anguillanet.com

Temenos
Tel: 222-9000
Fax: 498-9050
Email: reservations@temenos

The Anguilla Professional Co
Tel: 497-1212 & 1213
Email: jaggumbs_co@anguilla

The Office of the Chief Minist
Tel: 497-2518
Email: chief-minister@gov.ai

The Old House Restaurant &
Tel: 497-2228 / Fax: 497-5229

Tropical Sunset / Uncle Ernie's
Tel: 235-7991
Email: tropicalsunsetue_2@hotmail.com

Two Sons Funeral Home
Tel: 497-3249
Fax: 497-2903

Valda's T-Shirt Shop
Tel: 772-2172
Fax: 497-6586

Villa Coyaba
Tel: 497-3400
Email: Coyaba@anguillanet.com

Wallblake Airport
Tel: 497-2384 / 3510
Email: wallblakeairport@anguillanet.com

Weblinks Limited
Tel: 497-1265
Email: griff@weblinks.ai

Ronald Webster
Tel: 497-4100

Wendell Connor's Anguilla Taxi Service & Car Rental
Tel: 497-6894
Fax: 497-8305

Wigley & Associates
Tel: 497-8129
Email: wigleyj@anguillanet.com

World Art & Antiques Gallery
Tel: 497-5950
Email: worldart1@yahoo.com

Contents

Acknowledgements

Anguilla: Tranquillity Wrapped in Blue, was made possible because of the contribution and support of scores of individuals and organisations. Special thanks are given to Chief Minister, Osborne Fleming, Minister of Finance, Victor Banks, and their colleagues for commissioning the project.

Thanks are also due to the following: Donna Banks, Special Assistant Tourism, and Amelia Vanterpool-Kubisch, Director of Tourism, both of whom encouraged and supported the project from its inception. Amelia's commitment and hands-on support inspired her team's co-operation far beyond the call of duty; the members of the Anguilla Tourist Board, collectively and individually, and especially John Benjamin, the Chairman; Deputy Director of Tourism, Candis Niles, whose sterling effort in getting the endorsement of the private sector meant that the project would get on its way; the Anguilla Tourist Board personnel, James Harrigan, Marion John, Desserie Brooks, Brenda Gumbs, who arranged my meetings, and all the others who made working in Anguilla such a pleasure; The Director of the Anguilla Hotel and Tourism Association, Mimi Gratton, and her assistant, Mercia Smith; The people at Hansib in the UK and their support network, Kash Ali, Isha Persaud, Shareef Ali of Graphic Resolutions, Richard Painter of Print Resources, Alan Cross of Lancross, and our printers, Woolnough's of Irthingborough; Walton Fleming, Wilbert Fleming and all the staff at Anguilla Great House, where I spent some inspiring and memorable weeks, in an environment congenial to peace and harmony; Eustace Guishard, Phyllis Fleming-Banks and the staff at Cap Juluca, a hotel that is, most definitely, 'a touch of class'; Keithly Benjamin, Commissioner of Police, Ensor Gumbs, Chief Immigration Officer and Kenrick Richardson, Comptroller of Customs and their officers nationwide, Anguilla Lions Club and the Anguilla Chamber of Commerce; Ronald Webster, Sir Emile Gumbs, Herbert Hughes, Chief Statistician, Penny Hope-Ross, Ministry of Education, Claude Brooks, Jessica Bensley, Mitch Lake, Paj McLaren Poulter, Bob Green, Shannon Davies, Luke Niles, Sir Ronald Sanders, Ella Barnes, for your thoughtfulness, Jim Graham of JJ Travel, Fidel Persaud, Cecil Wade and the staff at Amaryllis Hotel in Antigua, Moti Persaud, Christi Douglas, Rafina Rahaman, Chris Rink, Eudoxie and Sandra Wallace, LaToya Scarborough, Chandani Persaud, Arindell Sauderland, Alkin Rogers, Rodney Rey, Samuel Connor, Moran Rey, Dennis Sheehan, and Pamela Mary for caring so much;

The writers and photographers especially Chris Mason, Ivor Hodge, Nik Douglas and Ken Hodge.

And the following writers and photographers: Writers - Ken Banks, Dr Oluwakemi M Linda Banks, Dr Louis Bardfield, John Benjamin, Whaldama 'Ras B' Brooks, Brenda Carty, David Carty, Jacqueline Cestero, Ijahnya Christain, Courtney Devonish, Tara Douglas, Marcel Fahie, Michael Faligant, Phyllis Fleming-Banks PhD, Mimi Gratton BA, Josephine A G Gumbs-Connor LLB, LEC, Sir Emile Gumbs, Aiden A Harrigan PhD, James R Harrigan, Karim Hodge, Nathaniel Hodge MBE, Joanne Mason, Nazma Muller, Candice Niles, Amber Olson-Pape, Colville L Petty OBE, Alex Richardson LLM, Ronnie Richardson, Foster Rogers, Aileen Smith, and Iain K N Smith; Photographers - Dean L Barnes, Jessica Bensley, Jacqueline A Cestero, Linda Lake, Carol Lee, Bill Milne, Penny Slinger, Iain Smith, and Mary Woodruff.

Arif Ali

Thank you to the following governmet departments, businesses and organisations in Anguilla without whose support this book would not have been possible. Their advance orders made it possible for us to add more pages to the book, increase the print run, and include four non-English language synopses. The statement, "We'll back it as long as it promotes Anguilla", is now very familiar.

All Island Cable Television
Alloyd's Enterprises Ltd
Altamer Resort
American Eagle
Anguilla Arts & Craft Shop
Anguilla Block & Sand Co Ltd
Anguilla Development Board
Anguilla Drug Store
Anguilla Electricity Co Ltd
Anguilla Garden Centre Ltd
Anguilla Great House Beach Resort
Anguilla Masonary Products Ltd
Anguilla National Council for Women
Anguilla Rums Ltd
Anguilla Social Security Board
Anguilla Vision Center

Apex Car Rental
Ashley & Sons
Audain & Associates
Bartlett's Collections
Bennie's Travel
Blue Waters Beach Apartments
Blues & Blues Limited
Cable and Wireless (WI) Ltd
Cap Juluca Hotel
Caribbean Associated Chambers
Caribbean Commercial Bank (Anguilla) Ltd
Caribbean Insurers (Anguilla) Ltd
Caribbean Juris Chambers
Caribbean Rentals Ltd
Caribbean Seaview Hotel
Carimar Beach Club
Cheddie's Carving Studio
Christine Mini Mart
Covecastles Resort
CuisinArt Resort & Spa
D-3 Enterprises Ltd
Deluxe Ferry Service
Devonish Art Gallery
Dolphin Fantaseas
Eden House Villa
Elegant Retreats
Elodias Beach Resort
English Rose Restaurant
Fairplay Management
Flag Luxury Estate

Flavours Restaurant
Frangipani Beach Club
General Post Office
Georgiana's
Gorgeous Scilly Cay
Government House
Hair World Accessories
Highway Rent-A- Car
Hughes Medical Centre
J W Proctors Ltd
Judicial Department
Keene Enterprises
Keithley Lake & Associates
Lake & Kentish
Lake's World
Lloyd's Guest House
M & R Corporate Services Ltd
Meadsbay Hideaway
Ministry of Finance
Ministry of Social Development
Ministry of Works
National Bank of Anguilla Ltd
Nico's Restaurant
Offshore Finance Companies Registry
Old House Restaurant & Bar
Olde Caribe Restaurant
Palm Grove Bar & Grill
Paradise Cove
Paramount Pharmacy
Professional Realty Services

(Anguilla) Ltd
Ranny & Jo's Ice Cream / Island in the Sun Co
Rendezvous Bay Hotel &Villas
Richards Architecture Development & Survey Co Ltd
Ronald Webster
Royal Caribbean
Sandy Hill Villas
Savannah Gallery
Scotiabank (Anguilla) Ltd
Serenity Cottage
Shoal Bay Beach Hotel
Shoal Bay Villas
Something Special
Summer Set Car Rental
Syd-An's Inn & Villas
TCL Trading Ltd
The Anguilla Professional Complex
The Office of Chief Minister
Tropical Sunset
Two Sons Funeral Home
Uncle Ernie's
Valda's T'Shirt Shop
Villa Coyaba
Wallblake Airport
Weblinks Ltd
Wendell Connor's Anguilla Taxi Service & Car Rental
Wigley & Associates
World Art & Antiques Gallery

Foreword

The idea for this book started in the late 1990s when I was approached by Claude Brooks, a fellow executive colleague of the UK-based West Indian Standing Conference. Anguillian-born Claude, who was our then Chairman, suggested a meeting with Hubert Hughes, Chief Minister of Anguilla. Several meetings followed, including a trip to Anguilla, but it seemed that the time had not arrived for us to begin the project.

In November 2001, at the World Travel Market in London, we approached Donna Banks, Special Assistant Tourism to the new Chief Minister, Osbourne Fleming, who encouraged us to persevere with our negotiations. A year later, once again at the World Travel Market in London, our team had further meetings with Donna Banks and Anguilla's Director of Tourism, Amelia Vanterpool-Kubisch. I was invited for a meeting in Anguilla with the Chief Minister, the Finance Minister, Victor Banks, and other ministers and government officials.

It was the general consensus at the meeting, that the book would be an important addition to the country's efforts to increase investment and tourism. The government was aware of its financial limitations, and it was agreed that the publishers and the Anguilla Tourist Board approach the private sector for their support. Between the Tourist Board representatives and the Hansib team, we made presentations to over one hundred and fifty organisations and businesses.

The end result was a commitment from the private sector to support the Government's initiative - over one hundred businesses and organisations had placed advanced orders ensuring that the Tourist Board and Hansib could adequately fund the project.

The more than 100,000 visitors to Anguilla, from November 2003 onwards, will find a treasure trove of information in Anguilla: Tranquillity Wrapped in Blue. It will be available in their hotel rooms and gift shops, and is the perfect souvenir for themselves and their friends. It will also help to encourage others to visit this welcoming, friendly and tranquil destination. Anguillians will, no doubt, use the book as gifts for family and friends overseas to remind them of the beauty of this country and the progress of the nation.

I have been honoured with many new friendships and rekindled several others during the past year in Anguilla. It is my wish that the experience and struggle of yesteryear that inspired Marcel Fahie's poem, 'The Rock' (featured in this book), will live on forever in this land of pleasant people and tranquillity wrapped in blue.

Arif Ali
Anguilla Great House, Rendezvous Bay
September 2003

Message from the Chief Minister

Welcome to *Anguilla: Tranquillity Wrapped in Blue*. As you read through our 25th Anniversary of Tourism commemorative book I hope you will begin to sense the pride we as Anguillians feel to call this tranquil island home.

It was in 1967 that we gained the world's attention because of our bold move to secede from an unsatisfactory political union thereby signalling our free and independent spirit. I believe that as you journey through this book you will experience the sense of freedom we enjoy in this safe and tranquil island. History shows that Anguilla was not considered a prized possession for any of the colonial powers, for our land was not fertile enough to grow crops for export.

We are proud of this heritage; for that which our land lacked, our waters adequately compensated for and we are proud to boast of our thirty-three pristine white sand beaches rated as some of the best in the world. Even as you leaf through the pages of this book and are lured into dreaming of the powdery white sand between your toes, you will realize that Anguilla is more than its famous azure waters, boat racing, lobster and coral reefs.

Our warm and friendly people, quality accommodations and fine cuisine provide the backdrop against which the discerning traveller can etch his/her perfect vacation. Our many art galleries, Arawak ceremonial sites and other cultural interests, as well as boutiques for the discriminating shopper, offer a special dimension to our visitors.

And still Anguilla offers more than a vacation choice. Anguilla provides an excellent base for business and commerce, a stable political environment, advanced telecommunications, sound professional infrastructure and easy access from anywhere in the world. Anguilla is continuing to define its place as a well-regulated jurisdiction in the Financial Services Industry.

Twenty-five years after this tiny, eel-shaped island entered the world's tourism stage, Anguilla is no longer known as the mouse that roared. Anguilla's tourism brand of quality at all levels of the destination product is the desire of discriminating travellers and the standard others seek to attain.

I sincerely hope that this book gives you a glimpse into the heart of Anguilla and the Anguillians who will welcome your visit.

Hon. Osbourne B. Fleming
Chief Minister

Message from the Minister of Finance

Congratulations to Hansib Publications for an excellent job in meeting the challenge of publishing an informative, colourful and attractive book on Anguilla appropriately entitled *Anguilla: Tranquillity Wrapped in Blue*.

We have for a number of years marketed Anguilla as "the best kept secret in the Caribbean". Our quest for sustainable development, however, requires that we become well known to discerning visitors and investors seeking unique and exciting opportunities in an emerging and politically stable small island economy. This publication will assist considerably in raising Anguilla's profile.

The section on the economy should stimulate potential investors seeking viable business opportunities as well as those seeking a highly reputable financial services jurisdiction.

Tourism continues to be the driver of our economy. The industry will experience a period of exciting new growth and diversification in the immediate future. Current projects include an ultra luxurious golf resort, other significant new hotel and luxury villa projects and a world class championship tennis facility. Future projects include a mega yacht marina and a second ultra luxurious golf resort. The expansion of Wallblake Airport to 6,000 feet will greatly improve the air transportation infrastructure and facilitate this new period of expansion in tourism.

Government is committed to diversification of the economy to achieve sustainability. Financial services and e-commerce have been identified as two additional pillars of the economy over the long run. The legal, institutional and technological arrangements in financial services are undergoing constant improvement to ensure that Anguilla maintains the highest standards.

An E-commerce Policy Framework, setting out Government's intentions to promote a vibrant e-commerce sector was recently published. The nucleus of this sector has been quietly established in recent years and it is poised to experience rapid growth.

The telecommunications market will be fully opened up to competition in the near future, following agreement on market liberalization between the Government and Cable and Wireless and the passage of a new Telecommunications Act in May 2003.

We are geared up and ready to do business.

Victor F. Banks
Minister of Finance, Economic Development, Investment and Commerce

Message from the Director of Tourism

We congratulate Hansib Publications on the production of this book, an extensive visual and informative journey through our small island of beautiful beaches, unique accommodations, world-renowned dining experiences and exciting boat races. Most of all, we welcome the opportunity for you to learn about the gracious citizens of our country, our culture and our unique and fascinating history. You'll find that Anguilla truly is 'tranquillity, wrapped in blue.'

Though there is nothing quite the same as exploring Anguilla in person, this book will introduce you to the many advantages and charms of our island. Anguilla offers a haven for replenishing your body, relaxing your mind, and rejuvenating your spirit. A plethora of choices await you - quiet days basking in the sun on one of our 33 beaches; a tour of our many art galleries; a fascinating excursion to our undersea world; history and museum tours; sailing; snorkelling; horseback riding; dancing to island beats; and the simple enjoyment of sunrise and sunset strolls on our powder soft, white sand beaches.

Anguilla is an island retreat for couples, families and singles. We value our visitors, as much as our visitors value the time they spend on Anguilla. So enjoy this book, and as soon as you can, visit us, if you haven't already done so!

Amelia Vanterpool Kubisch
Director of Tourism

SYMBOLS OF THE NATION

The Anguilla flag has an interesting history. Prior to 1967 the only flags flown on the island were the Union Flag and the flag of the West Indies Federation from 1958 to 1962.

When St Kitts, Nevis and Anguilla became an Associated State in February 1967, the Anguillians refused to recognise the statehood flag. The flag was flown on Government House in Anguilla, but only a few hours before it was torn down by the people who vehemently opposed their new status.

Their opposition to statehood led to the Anguilla Revolution and in July 1967, the island acquired its own flag referred to as the "Mermaids Flag". It was designed by a small group of friends of Anguilla, resident in San Francisco, USA, and carried the words REPUBLIC OF ANGUILLA. The red field symbolised the blood of patriotism and the dark blue, in the centre, the magnificent waters of the Caribbean. The mermaids represented the island's maritime heritage. The olive branch held by one of them stood for peace, for which Anguillians strived, while the spear in the hand of the other symbolised self-defence. The seashell represented the natural beauty and tranquillity of the island.

But the Anguillian people found it difficult to identify with the flag and it quickly went into disuse. It was replaced in September 1967 by the "Three Dolphins Flag", designed by Marvin Oberman and Lydia Gumbs, which became the rallying symbol of the Anguillian Revolution. The white symbolised peace and tranquillity and the three orange dolphins placed thereon, in a circular manner, represented unity, strength and endurance. The turquoise-blue at the bottom symbolised the surrounding sea and also faith, youth and hope.

Following the British invasion in March 1969, and the setting up of a British administration, the Union Flag replaced the "Three Dolphins Flag". However, the fact that the "Three Dolphins Flag" was so much a part of the people ensured that it was flown alongside the Union Flag. But the situation was an affront to Anguillian nationalism. The people wanted their own flag and Governor Brian Canty, after consultations with a committee set up to make recommendations for its design, eventually sent design proposals to London for approval.

Approval was granted and Anguilla's national flag was hoisted for the first time on 30th May 1990. It is a combination of the "Three Dolphins Flag" and the Union Flag.

The flag has a dark blue background with the Union Flag filling the upper hoist quarter. In the centre of the fly end is the shield of the national seal. The shield, which includes the symbols of the "Three Dolphins Flag", is divided horizontally with white at the top and turquoise-blue at the bottom. Three orange dolphins figure in the centre of the white.

Meaning of the flag

The Union Flag symbolises the island's colonial status, the three orange dolphins represent strength and endurance, the turquoise-blue signifies the Caribbean Sea and faith, youth and hope, and the white stands for peace and tranquillity.

The National Seal

Anguilla has no coat of arms. It has a national seal which comprises a shield with the symbols of the "Three Dolphins Flag" divided horizontally: white at the top and turquoise-blue at the bottom. Three orange dolphins figure in the centre of the white. The shield has a double circle around it with the words "Anguilla: Strength and Endurance."

The National Bird

The turtle dove

The National Flower

The white cedar

The National Song

God Bless Anguilla

God bless Anguilla,
Nurture and keep her,
Noble and beauteous
She stands midst the sea.
O land of the happy,
A haven we'll make thee,
Our lives and love
We give unto thee.

Chorus
With heart and soul,
We'll build a nation,
Proud, strong and free.
We'll love her,
Hold her dear to out hearts,
For eternity.
Let truth and right our banner be!
We'll march ever on.
Let truth and right our banner be!
We'll march ever on.

Mighty we'll make her,
Long may she prosper.
God grant her leaders
Wisdom and grace.
May glory and honour
Ever attend her,
Firm shall she stand
Throughout every age.

Written by Alex Richardson
Musical arrangements by Ronnie Richardson

ALEX RICHARDSON

In January 1981, celebrations were held to mark the official separation of Anguilla from St Kitts-Nevis. The celebrations included a competition to select a National Song for Anguilla. Alex Richardson, a seventeen-year-old Sixth Form student at the Valley Secondary School, wrote the winning entry, "God Bless Anguilla". Today, the National Song is performed at functions, including official ceremonies, and is taught to all school children.

Mr Richardson went on to become the keyboardist and captain of North Sound International, one of Anguilla's premiere musical bands. North Sound made several recordings and toured extensively in the Caribbean and the USA.

Today, Alex Richardson is a Barrister and Solicitor and heads the Anguillian office of the law firm Harney Westwood & Riegels. He pursued his legal career in the Caribbean and the United Kingdom and holds a Master of Laws degree in Corporate and Commercial Law from the University of London. He commenced his legal career at the Attorney General's Chambers and during that time also acted as Magistrate and Registrar of the High Court. Later he was the Deputy Director of Financial Services in the Government of Anguilla and was deeply involved in the world-wide marketing of Anguilla as an offshore financial services centre.

Mr Richardson is Vice-President of the Anguilla Bar Association, Immediate Past-President of the Anguilla Financial Services Association and Chairman of the Anguilla branch of the Society of Trust and Estate Practitioners (STEP).

Mr Richardson maintains a keen interest in music and is the manager of one of Anguilla's foremost musical groups, the Xtreme Band.

The National Song

Leaders of the Nation

Colville Petty

Ronald Webster

RONALD WEBSTER – Father of the Nation

Ronald Webster was Anguilla's man of the twentieth century. He was the greatest of its revolutionary leaders. Of course there were other outstanding leaders but few of them were in his class when it came to sheer guts, determination and courage. He was a man of steel.

Webster was a charismatic leader who easily attracted followers and won their respect, confidence and support. Most of them trusted his judgment and had faith in his leadership. He gave courageous leadership at a time when it was badly needed and had instilled in his people's minds that their goals were achievable whatever the odds. He enkindled hope in their hearts and had come to be regarded as the Father of the Anguillian nation. Under his dogged leadership the people refused to succumb to the myriad obstacles which confronted them in their struggle for self-determination.

Webster's leadership role in the 1967 Anguilla Revolution contributed immeasurably to its success. He harnessed the energies of the Anguillian people with whom he laid the foundation on which all of them could now build. Once the struggle was over, Anguilla experienced a complete social, economic and political metamorphosis. The removal of the 'choke-hold' from St Kitts allowed the laying of the foundation for economic takeoff and Anguillians now enjoy one of the highest standards of living in the Caribbean.

Webster holds the distinction of being Anguilla's first Chief Minister (1976-1984). History will remember him as the man who brought Anguilla through the wilderness and across the Red Sea. He has left it to present and future generations to take it to the Promised Land.

ATLIN HARRIGAN – Campaigner for Democracy

Atlin Harrigan is one of the founders of modern Anguilla. Writing in *The Democrat* newspaper of St Kitts, 6th August 1966, he called on Anguillians to break all ties with St Kitts and "stay colonial" – stay with Mother England.

Harrigan not only provided the idea which gave rise to the Revolution, he was in the vanguard of the struggle and one of its principal strategists, tacticians and planners.

Following the expulsion of the St Kitts policemen from Anguilla on 30th May 1967, he became a member of the Peace-keeping Committee charged with the responsibility for managing the island's affairs until representative institutions were established. The Committee was later replaced by the Anguilla Council of which Harrigan was a member from 1968 to 1972.

Atlin Harrigan

Harrigan was a staunch believer of democracy and ensured that its seeds were planted in the course of the Revolution. To this end, he established *The Beacon*, Anguilla's first newspaper, on 27th September 1967. The paper became the principal medium through which Anguillian people, of all shades of political opinion, were free to make their views known and make suggestions on the way forward. At times, *The Beacon* came in for much criticism from others in the leadership of the Revolution, but Harrigan was determined that freedom of expression was one of those fundamental rights which should not be suppressed and he therefore kept on publishing his paper despite the odds. In fact, *The Beacon*'s press was confiscated by some of his political detractors. It was subsequently returned and the paper remained a symbol of hope for, and a guardian of, democracy in Anguilla.

With the gradual legalisation of Anguilla's constitutional and political situation, Atlin became a Nominated Member of the Legislative Assembly. The highpoint of his outstanding political career came in 1985 when he assumed the office of Speaker of the Anguilla House of Assembly. He served in that capacity for nine years with distinction and was later appointed an Officer of the Most Excellent Order of the British Empire (OBE) by Her Majesty the Queen, in recognition of his outstanding contribution to Anguillian society.

Albena Lake Hodge

ALBENA LAKE-HODGE – Educator and Politician

Albena Lake-Hodge, better known as Teacher Albena, was one of Anguilla's foremost educators. Her area of specialisation was primary education in which she was involved until her retirement in 1975 (She once acted as Education Officer). Following her retirement, Teacher Albena entered the political arena. She won a seat in the Legislative Assembly in 1976, and was appointed Minister of Social Services in a Ronald Webster-led government. She was the first woman in Anguilla to hold an appointment as a minister of government.

A woman of tremendous moral strength and courage, Teacher Albena was one the driving forces behind the founding of the Anguilla National Alliance (ANA) in 1980. When the ANA, under the leadership of Emile Gumbs, won the 1984 general elections she was appointed Minister of Education and Tourism. It was in that capacity that Teacher Albena helped in laying the foundation of the island's tourism industry and continued to focus on programmes for the advancement of Anguilla's youth, to which she was emotionally attached. Unfortunately, failing health caused her to resign her ministerial responsibilities. She passed away on 19th October 1985.

In recognition of her phenomenal contribution to education, the Anguilla House of Assembly passed a Resolution in 1987, changing the name of the Valley Secondary School to the Albena Lake-Hodge Comprehensive School.

EMILE GUMBS – Anguilla's longest-serving politician

Emile Gumbs occupied leadership positions in politics in Anguilla for twenty-seven years, from 1967 to 1994 when he retired from active politics. That is a record by any politician in Anguilla. He never lost an election since he first contested them in 1968.

Anguilla acquired a ministerial system of government in 1976 and Gumbs became Minister of Communications of Works in a Ronald Webster-led government. When Webster lost the support of his political colleagues in 1977, Gumbs was appointed Chief Minster by the British Commissioner (now called Governor).

Emile Gumbs

Hubert Hughes

In 1980, he helped to found the Anguilla National Alliance (ANA) of which he became leader. The ANA, which is a major force in Anguilla's politics, was elected to office in 1984 and 1989 with Gumbs as Chief Minister. He was a conscientious leader and during his tenure of office, noted for its political stability, the island experienced significant economic growth with the take off of the tourism industry.

Emile Gumbs was knighted by Her Majesty Queen Elizabeth II during her visit to Anguilla in 1994. He is the only Anguillian, to date, to have received such an honour.

HUBERT HUGHES – Steadfast in Opposition

Hubert Hughes is one of the most flamboyant of Anguilla's political leaders. He is outspoken and controversial. His anti-colonist stand is well-known and, as a consequence, he has been a thorn in the side of British Governors with whom he never seemed able to work.

Hughes was first elected to the Legislative Assembly in 1976 as an Independent. He was in and out of governments (as a minister) between 1980 and 1985, until 1994 when he became Chief Minister after his Anguilla United Party had formed a coalition with the Anguilla Democratic Party. The coalition won the general elections in 1999 but if fell apart shortly after and Hughes assumed the position of Leader of the Opposition.

Hughes has a good grasp of political and economic issues, is a quick thinker and an excellent orator. He has spent most of his political life on the opposition benches and has done a commendable job in holding governments accountable.

The Rock – Anguilla
By Marcel Fahie

Our fathers chose to starve
Than give up this rock
for the moist promise of Demerara
and the sweat of sugar.

And when things were rough
We ate the dust
Held on to our boats,
Our land …
Left God to work his plan.

We did not need 'Mother Country'
To teach us to sail
The salt seas to survive:
Macoris southward to Port-of-Spain,
Bridgetown leeward to Willemsted
With everything in our heads.

Independence, pride,
Struggle to keep alive,
Scrimp and save
Wife and children left behind,
Build a home
To rest the aging frame.

Panama, Cuba
USA, Canada
St Thomas, Puerto Rico
St Maarten, St Kitts
Slough in England
Talk of the salty Caribbean seas
Eternally freshening breeze
On a quiet evening.

Talk of returning home
Of returning soon
Talk of ANGUILLA - our island home.

SYSTEM OF GOVERNMENT

Colville Petty

The Governor and the Executive Council

Anguilla is a British Overseas Territory. Its Constitution provides for, among other things, a Governor, an Executive Council and a House of Assembly (the Legislature). It further provides for the Governor to exercise, on behalf of Her Majesty, the executive authority of Anguilla and confers upon him the necessary powers to do so. He is required to consult with the Executive Council in the formulation of policy for consideration by the Legislature. This Council, over which the Governor presides, comprises the Chief Minister, three other Ministers, two ex-officio members viz the Deputy Governor and the Attorney General.

Under the ministerial system of government, which the island acquired in 1976, only elected members of the House of Assembly are eligible for appointment as Ministers. The Governor appoints as Chief Minister the elected member who, in his judgment, is likely to command the support of a majority of the elected members of the Assembly. The other Ministers are appointed by the Governor on the advice of the Chief Minister. Their responsibilities are assigned by the Chief Minister. Similarly, their appointments could be revoked by the Governor acting in accordance with the advice of the Chief Minister.

House of Assembly and Court House / Photo: Ivor Hodge

In view of Anguilla's dependency status, the Governor is not obliged to consult the Executive Council, nor act on its advice, with respect to matters relating to defence, external affairs, international financial services, internal security (including the Police) and the public service. In addition, he has reserved executive power to act, other than in accordance with the advice of Council, where in his opinion it would be inexpedient in the interest of public order or public faith to act in accordance with that advice.

The House of Assembly

Anguilla has a unicameral legislature called the House of Assembly. It consists of twelve members: The Speaker, seven elected members, two ex-officio members (the Deputy Governor and the Attorney General) and two nominated members. A quorum consists of two-thirds of the members of the Assembly in addition to the person presiding.

Elections for membership of the House are constitutionally due every five years. The island is divided into seven electoral districts each of which elects one member. To be eligible for election a person must belong to Anguilla, be twenty-one years and upwards and registered as a voter in one of the electoral districts. All 'belongers' eighteen years and upwards have the right to vote.

Anguilla is a multi-party democracy in which several political parties, representing a plurality of interests, vie for political power. It has the first-past-the-post electoral system in which a candidate needs to get one vote over his or her nearest rival to win a seat in the House of Assembly.

The Public Service

The execution of government's business is undertaken by the public service. The members are full-time appointments and do not lose their jobs following a change of government. Each ministry has a Permanent Secretary who is the Minister's principal adviser but who "does not" make policy. The Permanent Secretary is the channel through which technical and other advice, necessary for the formulation of policy, reach the Minister. Thereafter the Permanent Secretary ensures the implementation of that policy. He also coordinates the activities and supervises the functioning of the various departments in his ministry.

Judiciary

Anguilla is a member of the Eastern Caribbean Supreme Court. Its law is the English Common Law supplemented by local enacted legislation.

There is a Magistrate's Court which deals with minor offences and small claims and a High Court presided over by a Judge which the island shares with Nevis and Montserrat. Decisions of the High Court are subject to review by the Court of Appeal which sits twice a year. Final appeals are heard by the Privy Council which sits in England.

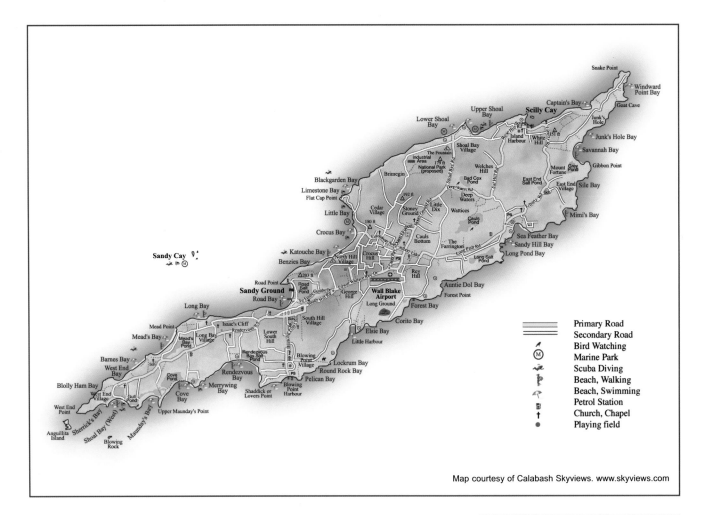

Map courtesy of Calabash Skyviews. www.skyviews.com

Primary Road
Secondary Road
Bird Watching
Marine Park
Scuba Diving
Beach, Walking
Beach, Swimming
Petrol Station
Church, Chapel
Playing field

FACTS AT A GLANCE

Name: Anguilla, British West Indies (pronounced Ann-GWIL-ah)
Capital: The Valley
Size: 16 miles long, 3 miles wide (35 square miles)
Location: The most northerly of the Leeward Islands in the Eastern Caribbean. Latitude 18.2°N, Longitude 63.0°W
Temperature: Mean monthly temperature is 80°F
Language: English
Government: British Overseas Territory
Currency: Eastern Caribbean Dollar (EC$). US currency is accepted throughout the island.
Airport: Wallblake Airport. Served by American Eagle, WINAIR, LIAT, Tyden Air, Trans Anguilla and Caribbean Star. Nearest international airports are St Maarten, San Juan, St Thomas, St Kitts and Antigua.
Flying Times: From St Maarten, 7 minutes; San Juan and Antigua, 1 hour; St Thomas, 45 minutes; St Kitts, 35 minutes.

Entry Requirements: Passport preferred. Official photo ID such as driver's licence plus birth certificate with a raised seal. Return or onward ticket.
Departure Tax: At airport - US$20.00; at ferry port - US$3.00
Seaports: Blowing Point and Road Bay
Ferry Service: From Blowing Point, ferries leave every half hour for St Maarten from 7:30 am to 6:15 pm. Fare is US$10 - day and US$12 at night. (Fares are subject to change).
Driving: On the left. Average speed is 30 mph
Taxi Service: Available from airport, Tel: 497-5054; from ferry port, Tel: 497-6089
Rentals: Car, bike, van and jeep
Air Charters: Trans Anguilla and Tyden Air
Island Tours: Malliouhana Travel & Tours, Bennie's Tours, Anguilla Travel Services and Harry's Taxi Service
Information: Anguilla Tourist Board, The Valley, Anguilla. Tel: 264 497 2759, 800-553-4939. Fax: 264 497 2710
Email: atbtour@anguillanet.com
Website: www.anguilia-vacation.com

The History of Anguilla

Colville Petty

Anguilla, once a lush island with dense rain forest, was settled some 4,000 years ago by an Arawak-speaking Amerindian people who called it Malliouhana, the meaning of which is obscure. There were about 40 Arawak villages on the island the largest of which were at Island Harbour, Sandy Ground, Sandy Hill, Rendezvous Bay and Shoal Bay (east). The Arawaks, who were originally from the Orinoco region of South America, slowly made their way up the chain of Caribbean islands in dugout canoes. They were skilled farmers and fishermen and were also good at pottery making.

By the time the first English settlers arrived in Anguilla, in 1650, there was not a single Arawak on the island. However, in 1656 an Amerindian raid from one of the neighbouring islands wiped out their settlement. The raiders "killed almost all the men, plundered and burnt the houses, but kept the women and children for slaves." Further havoc occurred in 1666 when a French expedition consisting of 300 men attacked the island, terrorised the people and caused them to flee to the woods.

Conditions in Anguilla in the latter part of the seventeenth century were extremely bad. The poor returns from cotton, which had replaced tobacco as the island's cash crop, created considerable hardship. More difficulties were experienced in 1688 when a joint Irish and French attack on the island forced the colonists to seek refuge in Antigua. Several of them emigrated to the Virgin Islands in 1694 in search of a better way of life.

Anguilla had become unattractive. The colonists who chose to remain had to find a new cash crop. By the early eighteenth century, sugar had replaced cotton as the principal cash crop. Sugar transformed a predominantly white society of small farmers into a society of predominantly African slaves labouring on sugar estates. The colonists wanted cheap labour and they got it from Africa.

Anguilla's social and economic development was frequently disrupted by European political conflicts which spilled over into the Caribbean. On 21 May 1745, two French frigates, under M de la Touche, landed some 700 men at Crocus Bay in an attempt to take the island, but the Anguillian militia forced them to retreat. The French attacked Anguilla again towards the end of the eighteenth century, when the Revolutionary Government in France declared war on England. In 1796, 400 men from two warships, Le Desius and La Vaillante, destroyed the island's main settlements at South Hill and The Valley. The French were forced to withdraw when a British frigate, the HMS Lapwing, came to Anguilla's rescue. They lost their two ships in the naval battle which followed.

Life in Anguilla was influenced not only by European conflicts but also by political expediency. In 1825 a legislative union between St Kitts and Anguilla was created when, on the recommendation of the British Government, the St

> Anguilla's social and economic development was frequently disrupted by European political conflicts which spilled over into the Caribbean

Anguilla became a separate British Dependent Territory on 19 December 1980

Kitts House of Assembly passed an Act to allow the freeholders in Anguilla to send a representative to the said Assembly. Although 35 freeholders had initially supported the union, they eventually protested its implementation when they discovered that it was to their disadvantage. Despite their strong protestations the legislative union took effect and the Anguilla Council was replaced by a system of local government called the Vestry.

The legislative union with St Kitts did little to improve the quality of life of the Anguillian people. Furthermore, the prolonged droughts of the 1830s destroyed all food crops and the resultant famine caused much distress especially among the slave population. At the time of emancipation in 1838 there were 2,354 slaves registered in Anguilla but by that time they were virtually free because many of them owned land or rented or occupied plantation land that was abandoned or neglected by the planters.

During the 1840s, the harsh conditions in Anguilla prompted the British Government to propose a plan to abandon the island and send its entire population to Demerara (in British Guiana). Most Anguillians refused to go and the island settled down as a society of peasant farmers, fishermen and seafarers.

It was against all official advice that the Anguillians decided to stay at home and eke out a living but not without difficulties. These difficulties heightened their resentment of the legislative union with St Kitts and in 1872, they wrote to Queen Victoria asking her to dissolve the union and administer Anguilla directly from Britain. Their request went unheeded.

At the close of the nineteenth century, Anguillians endured much suffering because of the great famine which started in 1890. A prolonged drought wiped out all food crops, destroyed most of the animals and caused many people to creep into "the woods and gather berries and herbs for food".

It was in the wake of such difficulties and the depression of the 1920s and

A BRIEF HISTORY OF ANGUILLA'S STAMPS

Anguilla is renowned for its postage stamps which it began issuing in the latter half of the twentieth century. The fact that the island was a political appendage of St Kitts (St Christopher) had prevented it, for nearly a century, from issuing its own postage stamps. In fact, it was not until 1948 that Anguilla appeared on a postage stamp for the first time, in any form, when its map was depicted on two St Kitts-Nevis stamps.

In 1952, following constitutional reforms, the Presidency of St Kitts-Nevis was changed to the Presidency of St Christopher, Nevis and Anguilla. As a consequence, its 1952 definitives carried the inscription 'SAINT CHRISTOPHER NEVIS ANGUILLA'. Anguilla thus appeared as part of the title of the Presidency for the first time.

It was only after the 1967 Revolution, when the Anguillian people took control of their island and declared independence from St Kitts, that the island began to issue its own postage stamps. The first issue comprised the St Christopher, Nevis and Anguilla 1963 definitives from which the inscription 'Saint Christopher Nevis Anguilla' was blocked-out and replaced with 'Independent Anguilla'. Anguilla's first definitive set of postage stamps went on sale in November 1967 and its first commemoratives in May 1968.

On 19 March 1969, Anguilla was invaded by British forces which placed it under the control of a Commissioner but its stamps continued to carry the inscription 'Anguilla'. The political situation changed in 1971 with the coming into force of the Anguilla (Administration) Order. The Order invested executive authority for the island in the Commissioner and therefore the inscription 'Anguilla' was removed from all postage stamps and replaced by 'HM COMMISSIONER IN ANGUILLA', together with the Royal Cypher, 'ER'.

Anguilla was formally separated from the Associated State of St Kitts, Nevis and Anguilla on 19 December 1980. Thereafter, all of its stamps have carried the inscription, 'ANGUILLA' and the Royal Cypher.

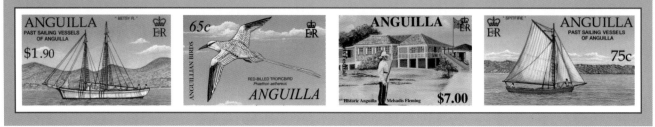

ABOVE: HRH Queen Elizabeth II and HRH Prince Phillip, Duke of Edinburgh, during their visit to Anguilla in 1994
BELOW: Governor, Peter Johnston inspects the Parade during the Queen's Birthday celebrations

1930s that Anguillian men flocked to the Dominican Republic where they found employment in the sugar cane fields. They later took refuge in Aruba and Curacao.

The depression of the 1930s also resulted in a series of labour disturbances throughout the Caribbean. These hastened constitutional reform and limited franchise was introduced in St Kitts, Nevis and Anguilla in 1936. Another consequence of the disturbances was the establishment of the Moyne Commission to study social and economic conditions in the British West Indies. One of its principal recommendations was the granting of universal adult suffrage to all territories. Universal adult suffrage for the Presidency of St Kitts, Nevis and Anguilla came about in 1952.

Further constitutional change affecting the Presidency of the St Kitts, Nevis and Anguilla occurred in 1956 with the dissolution of the Leeward Islands Federation. The Presidency was re-styled as a Colony and was granted a ministerial system of government. When the West Indies Federation was created two years later the Colony was included as a single unit.

Despite the various constitutional changes Anguillians remained powerless. Social and economic conditions continued to be most unsatisfactory. These conditions prompted a petition in 1958 to Governor Williams. The petitioners asked him, "to bring about the dissolution of the . . . political and administrative association of Anguilla with St Kitts." But they were ignored.

After the collapse of the West Indies Federation in 1962, the British Government attempted a federation of the "Little Eight" (non-independent countries). When that failed most of the islands were granted new constitutions which provided for Statehood in association with Britain. The creation of the Associated State of St Kitts, Nevis and Anguilla, on 27 February 1967, and the inclusion of Anguilla against the wishes of its people, sparked off the Anguilla Revolution.

The Revolution was concerned with replacing administration by St Kitts with direct British administration essentially for social and economic reasons. Up until 1967, Anguilla remained relatively poor and undeveloped. There were no industries, electricity, pipe-borne water, paved roads, telephones nor proper port facilities. Health, sanitation and education facilities were grossly inadequate. These conditions and rampant unemployment had turned Anguillians into a nomadic people. The Anguillians placed full blame for their island's plight on the Central Government in St Kitts. They were convinced that St Kitts took the lion's share of all development assistance to the Colony, and that a threat made by Premier Robert Bradshaw in 1967, to put bones in their rice and pepper in their soup, was real.

The highpoint of the Revolution occurred on 30 May 1967 when a hostile

Anguilla Day Celebrations, 35th Anniversary, 30 May 2002. Pictured from top: Hon. Chief Minister, Osbourne Flemming and 'First Lady', Mrs Ruby Fleming; Ministers of the United Front Government, left to right, Hon. Victor Banks, Minister of Finance, Hon. Kenneth Harrigan, Minister of Infrastructure and Communication, and Hon. Eric Reid, Minister of Social Development; James Ronald Webster (Father of the Nation) and Mrs Cleo Webster.

PHOTOS: LINDA LAKE

crowd surrounded the Police Headquarters in the Valley (the capital) and expelled the 13-man contingent of St Kitts policemen which was stationed in Anguilla. Having seized power, the Anguillians established a Peacekeeping Committee to manage the island's affairs until representative institutions could be established. In order to defend the island's newly acquired freedom, the Peacekeeping Committee approved the launching of an armed attack on St Kitts. To this end, an eighteen-man party landed in St Kitts at 2 am on Saturday 10 June, 1967 and attacked the Defence Force Camp, Police Headquarters and Power Station. The attacks fizzled out and five Anguillians were captured.

With a view to legitimising its own authority, and to showing the international community that the Revolution was a popular one, the Peacekeeping Committee held a plebiscite on 11 July 1967. The result was an overwhelming vote in favour of secession and of the establishment of an interim government. However, as Anguillians consolidated their Revolution, the Commonwealth Caribbean Governments sought a peaceful resolution of the crisis by convening a meeting of the interested parties in Barbados in July 1967. "Agreement" was reached on the conditions for Anguilla's return to constitutional rule under St Kitts but it was rejected by the people and the impasse continued.

The impasse was broken in December 1967 when two British parliamentarians worked out an agreement (for an interim settlement) which allowed a British official to "exercise basic administrative authority" over Anguilla, in conjunction with the Anguilla Council, for a period of one year beginning 8 January 1968. Towards the end of 1968, the St Kitts Government and the Anguilla Council failed to agree on an extension of the interim settlement and, following a plebiscite held on 6 February 1969, Anguilla declared itself an "Independent Republic".

This development prompted the British Government to embark on another attempt at finding a solution to the crisis and on 11 March 1969, William Whitlock, a Junior Minister, arrived in Anguilla with proposals for the establishment of an interim British administration. The proposals were unacceptable, and Whitlock was expelled within hours of his arrival. The British Government's reaction was swift. On 19 March 1969, some 400 British troops invaded Anguilla and established an administration under a Commissioner. After several years of negotiations between the British Government and the St Kitts Government, and a series of incremental constitutional changes, Anguilla was given a Ministerial System of Government in 1976 despite strong opposition from St Kitts.

Following the coming to power in St Kitts of a government which sympathised with Anguilla's cause, and which had no objection to its people taking control of their own destiny, Anguilla became a separate British Dependent Territory on 19 December 1980. It was given a new Constitution in 1982. The Constitution increased the number of ministers of government from three to four and removed the Commissioner from the Assembly, the life of which was increased from four years to five years. But most of the changes were cosmetic: "Commissioner", "Legislative Assembly" and "Financial Secretary" were restyled "Governor", "House of Assembly" and "Permanent Secretary for Finance" respectively.

The Constitution underwent further change by way of the Anguilla Constitution (Amendment) Order 1990, which came into force on 30 May 1990. The Order made provision for a Leader of the Opposition and a Parliamentary Secretary; and for a Deputy Governor to replace the Permanent Secretary for Finance in both the House of Assembly and the Executive Council.

Anguilla's constitutional status is now that of British Overseas Territory.

THE HISTORY OF ANGUILLA'S SALT INDUSTRY

Sir Emile R Gumbs

Anguilla's main source of salt has been the Road Salt Pond. With a total area of 130 acres the pond is capable of producing an average of 37,000-40,000 barrels (300 lbs each) yearly. In dry times West End Pond and Long Pond have produced salt but not in significant amounts.

After Anguilla was settled, the English recognized salt as a valuable commodity and the Road Salt Pond was 'held in common'. The salt was harvested each day by slaves and paid labourers for the benefit of the 'free' but after 2.00 pm they were allowed to harvest salt for themselves which they would sell.

Earth works to prevent rain water running into the pond were put in place. This consisted of a dam built to 3-4 feet above pond level on the eastern and southern sides of the pond which, during heavy rains, would channel the flood water into the sea.

An inner 'ring' dam was built inside the perimeter of the pond. This prevented run off rain water from entering the salt making area. Also, the old natural canal at the northern end of Road Bay was opened during high tide to allow the pond to be filled with sea water to produce more salt.

Several attempts by the Crown to commercialise the industry were short-lived and not very successful. In 1908, a lease was granted to Wager Rey, a businessman, who put together a management team to develop the industry. They built the middle dam which divided the pond into two sections - the large salt-making area and a smaller storage and settling area in which sea water was stored. This allowed any impurities (mud and marine flotsam) to settle out of the large volume of sea water which could be let into the salt making area of the pond as needed. This process greatly increased the output of salt as well as improving its quality.

Upon Wagner Rey's death, his son Carter inherited the lease and he continued to manage the industry. Carter Rey later appointed Arthur Carty, the former captain of the schooner, Warspite, as manager of the industry. Carty, upon his retirement, would appoint his son, Elliott, in the same role.

In 1935, a reliable diesel pump was installed resulting in increased production which, in turn, led to salt production becoming a major player in Anguilla's economy. The main market at the time was British Guiana (now Guyana) where salt was required as a dietary additive for working animals.

Large schooners from Saba and the Grenadines shipped the salt to British Guiana and returned with rice for the Windward and Leeward Islands.

When machinery replaced the working animals, the demand for coarse salt fell. However, this down-turn was offset by a new demand for fine salt in Trinidad. The old pump house was enlarged to house a mill and storage area for up to 200 tons of fine salt and the industry continued to prosper. But in the late 1950s, Anguilla lost the fine salt market to cheap iodised fine salt from the United States and Canada. This, coupled with the heavy rains that preceded hurricane Donna in 1960, led to the collapse of the industry.

In late 1962, another son of Arthur Carty, Rupert, who was employed with Texaco in Trinidad, realized that the oil company was increasing its demand for salt. He came to Anguilla to revive the industry and in early 1963, the Anguilla Road Salt Company was registered. The same year, 35,000 barrels of salt were harvested and the industry prospered once more.

In November that year, Elliot Carty passed away and Emile Gumbs retired from being Captain of the famous family schooner, Warspite, and stayed ashore to manage the industry, just as his grandfather, Arthur, had done decades earlier.

The onshore handling of the harvesting process was mechanized and the daily output doubled. The salt company continued to prosper delivering more and more salt to Trinidad. In 1967, during the tense time of Anguilla's break away from St Kitts, a record 71,000 barrels were harvested. But in 1986, when the oil industry suffered a major slump, the salt market crashed and the salt company ceased its operations.

What is left, is a salt pond that has become a bird-watchers paradise. The old pump house is now a favourite night spot which includes a bar and restaurant with live music most nights. The old relics of the salt industry have been preserved by Laurie and Gabi Gumbs, including the mill and its diesel engine which are still in working condition. Many relics of the famous old schooner, Warspite are also on display.

ANGUILLA'S AMERINDIAN HERITAGE

Nik Douglas

Anguilla has a rich Amerindian heritage which has been explored and documented only over the past two decades or so. The first archaeological survey of Anguilla, done by a visiting team of archaeologists in 1979, discovered one pre-ceramic 'archaic' stone-age site and nineteen sites dating to the 'ceramic' period, including The Fountain, a ceremonial cave with fresh water pools and important rock carvings and petroglyphs. The report concluded: "Anguilla has one of the richest archaeological heritages in the region, which it should strive to protect and develop." Largely because of these discoveries, Anguilla's first luxury hotel was called Malliouhana – one of the Amerindian names for the island.

Detail of Amerindian shell 'mask' circa 1050 AD

Founded in 1981, the Anguilla Archaeological and Historical Society organised field trips, looked for additional Amerindian habitations, monitored the existing ones and gathered cultural artefacts from the surface and from recovery digs whenever sites were impacted by tourism development. Within a short time, the known Amerindian sites expanded to more than forty in Anguilla and the offshore keys, including villages, small habitations, cultivated areas, outposts and caves. The array of carvings and petroglyphs at The Fountain was further documented, and test pits dug, which confirmed the Amerindian use of the cave as a sacred sanctuary. A second major ceremonial cave with a water source – 'Big Spring' - was discovered and the petroglyphs and a rock carvings recorded.

Scientists from several US, European and Caribbean institutions have carried out important field-work, including Cuban petroglyph experts who travelled to Anguilla from South America in an Amerindian canoe in November 1987. Over the years, specialists in Caribbean pre-Columbian archaeology made repeated visits, scientific digs and organised field schools, and Anguilla's Amerindian heritage and its regional significance was firmly established. Work done by Dr James Peterson showed that many of the pre-Columbian ceramics found in Anguilla, including many from The Fountain, incorporated materials brought from other islands. Some of these ceramics were possibly used to contain offerings to the Amerindian deities.

More than 60,000 of Anguilla's Amerindian artefacts

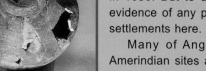

Amerindian ceramic vessels from The Fountain, Corito and Sandy Hill Bay

have now been collected and properly documented through research funded by a grant from UNESCO (United Nations Educational Social and Cultural Organisation). Many components of Anguillian pre-Columbian sites have now been scientifically dated, proving that Amerindians arrived and lived here at least 3200 years ago (the archaic period), and settled here repeatedly, establishing large village communities, seemingly reaching a population peak around 600 years ago. These Amerindians were of Arawak cultures from mainland South America. They were peaceful cultivators, mariners and fisher folk, playful yet spiritually motivated people governed by chiefs whose culture included ballgames, music, art and dance. Their contributions to the world include the development of cotton, corn, cassava, pineapple, and other key crops, as well as the words 'hammock', 'tobacco', 'barbeque' and 'hurricane'. Their settlements were located throughout Anguilla and were in evidence up to the late 15th century – around the time of the arrival of Christopher Columbus. The Caribs were a war-like Amerindian culture whose tribes raided and migrated to some islands in the region about the same time. A Carib raid on Anguilla, from Dominica and St Vincent, occurred in 1656. But to date there is no evidence of any permanent Carib settlements here.

Many of Anguilla's Arawak Amerindian sites are much larger than those on most other islands in the region. For such a small island, this is remarkable. Recently, John Crock from the University of Pittsburgh, was awarded a doctorate from his work on Anguillian pre-Columbian archaeology and his thesis that in Amerindian times Anguilla was a regionally significant ceremonial centre and a hub in a cultural, economic and political network. The evidence he assembled suggested that Amerindians who lived in Anguilla traded high status ceremonial artefacts, made here from imported raw materials, to communities in other Caribbean islands. Many pyramidical-shaped 'zemi' spirit power images, made from extremely hard stones, were produced in Anguilla and exported throughout the region, as well as axes made from imported green stones. Anguillian Amerindians also made wooden idols with shell inlays, bone snuff tubes,

Amerindian canoe

sophisticated shell jewellery and exquisite shell 'masks' – symbols of chiefly power and authority.

In 1985, the Government of Anguilla acquired The Fountain and the adjoining land for development as a show cave and National Park. Since then, numerous surveys and studies have firmly established the importance of this resource, which includes a large carved stalagmite representing 'Jocahu', the Arawak Indian creator deity. Dr C. Dubelaar, one of the foremost specialists in Amerindian petroglyphs of the Caribbean, states that Anguilla's Fountain cave is "the best petroglyph cave in the whole area".

The Fountain cavern is now awaiting formal inclusion as one of UNESCO's World Heritage sites. Additional adjoining lands have been acquired which increases the park to almost fifteen acres, and now fully protects the cave itself and allowing space for proper development which will include a tunnel entrance, museum building, workshop, Arawak garden and Marine Park, and visitor parking. A recently completed feasibility study, and a publication from the National Speleological Society of the

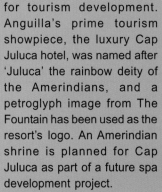

Petroglyphs in The Fountain, including the 'Juluca' petroglyph, far right

United States, have endorsed the project, as does the Government of Anguilla.

Interestingly, most of Anguilla's pre-Columbian sites were located behind beaches, on land with nice views and good breezes – locations which have since been selected for tourism development. Anguilla's prime tourism showpiece, the luxury Cap Juluca hotel, was named after 'Juluca' the rainbow deity of the Amerindians, and a petroglyph image from The Fountain has been used as the resort's logo. An Amerindian shrine is planned for Cap Juluca as part of a future spa development project.

In time, the Amerindian heritage will no doubt become a significant ingredient of Anguilla's tourism industry. The establishment of a national museum, The Fountain show cave and national park, and the Big Spring National Park, as well as the development of other Amerindian sites, will soon be available to the public. By then, and as archaeologists continue their work, we may discover enough additional information to fully understand Anguilla's Amerindian heritage, and its significance to the region as a whole.

Culture and Heritage

The Royal Anguilla Police Force during the Queen's Birthday celebrations

Ijahnya Christian

RELIGION

Christianity is the main religion with several denominations breaking the historic dominance of the Anglicans in the east and the Methodists in the west. The Seventh Day Adventist community is quite strong and the Roman Catholic Church has also shown growth in recent years. However, a wide cross-section of residents enjoy worship in Pentecostal and Baptist churches and there is also a vibrant community of Jehovah's Witnesses. The island's only mosque is in Blowing Point and serves the young Muslim community and a small group of Rastafarians meets for worship on Saturday mornings.

CUSTOMS AND TRADITIONS

Several of the island's customs and traditions are linked to religious observations such as Christmas and Easter and to the rites and rituals associated with birth/ christening, marriage and death, each of which involves a special church service followed by a celebratory aspect that includes the provision of food and drink for family, friends and community.

Traditional customs such as serenading at Christmas time are being replaced with more modern forms of community involvement such as the decorative lighting of trees and entertainment at central points in the island's main communities. Kite-flying and non-meat diets are still associated with the Lenten season, and the Easter cantata has regained popularity as a high point of church tradition.

Anguillians use every possible occasion to hold a boat race, as this is the national sport which also helps to keep boat-building and other aspects of the island's maritime heritage alive and well. Customs such as the pouring of libation when launching a boat and watching the sky for 'turtle tracks' are still practiced.

A baptism at Crocus Bay

NATIONAL EMBLEMS

Three dolphins in a circle symbolising endurance, unity and strength, have become Anguilla's most popular national symbols. The dolphins can be found on the Anguilla Revolution flag as well as on the official Anguilla Flag.

The turtle dove, *zenaida aurita*, has been formally declared the national bird. Informally, the national flower is the white cedar and the national fish is the red snapper, which is served with the national dish of pigeon peas and rice.

Anguilla has no official national dress, although various designs that comprise the colours of the Anguilla Revolution Flag - blue, orange and white - are used during the annual Queen's Pageant at the Summer Festival and at other national and tourism marketing events.

LANGUAGE

English is the only language spoken by most Anguillians but it is not always 'standard' English. Though Anguillian language may not be richly endowed with unique words, if someone in Anguilla tells you, "yuh too struck", you are not being paid a compliment and should find a copy of the 'Dictionary of Anguillian Language', which will tell you what the words means and remind you to be more careful about your table manners. A common idiomatic

WORSHIP AND RELIGIOUS SINGING

Like most Caribbean countries, Anguilla is a traditionally religious and God-fearing nation. Although in recent generations religious life has been waning, for the most part much emphasis is placed upon the values of faithfulness to the church and the moral and spiritual dispositions of its people.

The act of jubilant singing plays an essential part in worship during church services. Local choirs and worship teams contribute invaluably to Sunday services, and their renditions resonate lustily while occasionally drawing the attention of curious passers-by. Worship directors also minister in a vital capacity to conduct the various modes of singing during evangelistic services and revival crusades.

Each local congregation shows high regard for their respective teams of worshippers and choir groups. Furthermore, in many cases, the music that accompanies the worship is just as important to the rendering of worship as the worshippers themselves.

Apart from worship in conventional church settings, however, the island features ministering individuals and interdenominational groups who promote frequent gospel concerts, cantatas and "singspirations" throughout the island. Regardless of one's denominational background, such events serve to reflect and celebrate, through constant awareness, a rich religious heritage that is Anguilla's.
James R. Harrigan

Gospel concert group, Melodies From Heaven / Ivor Hodge

Local church choir and concert chorale, Shekinah / Ivor Hodge

PHOTOS: CHRIS MASON

expression such as "aya looka mi wuk" may be interpreted from the context in which it is used but it is clearly not English. There are a few Spanish-speaking enclaves among the population and these reflect historic and family ties established during the first half of the 20th century, when islanders journeyed to find work in the cane fields of the Dominican Republic.

ETHNIC GROUPS

Like the rest of the English-speaking Caribbean (except Trinidad and Guyana), people of African descent form the majority of the population. A small expatriate community comprising people of European descent has been resident on the island for a long time. In more recent years, as Caribbean integration initiatives are strengthened, an East Indian resident population is becoming more visible. The island also has a small Chinese community which is generally associated with the restaurant industry.

FESTIVALS AND CELEBRATIONS

The Cultural Education Festival is held annually in February to value traditional knowledge and highlight declining customs and traditions. The Festival brings community elders and school children together to facilitate the transmission of Anguillian culture

Moonsplash is Bankie Banx's dynamic musical beach-fest which is held every year at The Dune Preserve, in Rendezvous Bay, on the weekend closest to the full moon in March. A rich mix of musical genres, from reggae to rock to string band, the 'Splash' titillates eclectic musical tastes.

The Anguilla Jazz and Art Festival is the nation's contribution to the tradition of Caribbean Jazz Festivals and is organized each March by the Frangipani Beach Club.

PHOTO: CHRIS MASON

PHOTO: IVOR HODGE

PHOTO: CHRIS MASON

ABOVE RIGHT: The Moonsplash stage at the Dune Preserve, which is owned and operated by local celebrity, Bankie Banx ABOVE, FROM TOP: Local musicians, 'Sprocka' and 'Dumpa'

PHOTO: CHRIS MASON

Festival del Mar focuses on Anguilla's marine and maritime heritage, from boat-building and boat-racing to fish fries and fun days on the best beaches in the world. It is usually highlighted by the Anguilla Day Regatta at the end of May.

Summer Festival takes place throughout the first week in August and includes days filled with boat racing and nights filled with carnival shows.

The Tranquillity Jazz Festival was Launched in November 2002. This festival is part of BET Jazz in the Caribbean and attracts jazz-lovers from throughout the region and the world.

Valley Community Christmas Tree Lighting, which takes place from mid-December, is an event where villages throughout Anguilla vie for the most attractive Christmas lighting. All roads lead to The Valley where Coronation Avenue is transformed into a fairy tale scene with musical programmes offered nightly under the tamarind tree by The Trough.

FOOD AND DRINK

Anguilla is one tourism destination that can be boastful of its cuisine whether the meal is prepared by a world-famous chef or by newfound friends who invite you home for potluck or for roadside fare. Traditional foods include roasted corn on the cob, ground corn "fungie" and fish, corn or pigeon pea soup (with a dash of brown sugar), guinea corn porridge and the famous staple, Johnnycake. A simple limeade, a variety of bush teas or wines made from the wild pommeserette, sea grape or Miss Blyden to accompany Christmas cake, are good examples of traditional food and drink. Roadside barbeque grills have become quite popular in recent years and are a meat-lover's delight, while several restaurants claim to serve the best lobster in the world.

FOLKLORE

Island-wide electricity did not become available until the early 1970s, so 'jumbies' ruled those dark Anguilla nights and elders frightened children with 'jumbie'

stories. On moonlit nights, the West African 'Anansi' stories were told, which helped to pass on cultural values and traditions through tales, proverbs and sayings.

Cultural heritage and the recent history of the Anguilla Revolution have also become part of the island's folklore and is documented in the folksongs performed by the Mayoumba Folkloric Theatre, Sleepy and the All Stars and the Happy Hits String Bands. Legendary figures such as Bobo Johnny, smuggler of contraband liquor and master of Anguillian wit; tales of the prophet, "Judge" Gumbs; cultural activist and prankster Florrie of North Side; Tee-Tee the acrobat dancing on the wire; musicians such as Jimmy and Feddie Carty; master mocka jumbie Sonny Petty; and others who have passed on, have all become part of Anguillian folklore. Stories told with the greatest relish are those connected with the drama of the boat race. Famous boats, their builders, captains and races have been captured in David Carty's book, 'Nuttin Bafflin'.

THIS PAGE: The annual Queen's Birthday Parade at Ronald Webster Park

Original bread oven now consigned to history

When set to burn slowly, this pile of wood, known as a koal keel, will produce high quality charcoal

INDIGENOUS HERITAGE

Over twenty years of archaeology, organised by the Anguilla Archaeological and Historical Society and visiting archaeologists, have unearthed a sizeable collection of artefacts housed at the Anguilla National Trust. The most famous site connected with the island's indigenous heritage is The Fountain cavern, a unique Caribbean site where the petroglyph of the chief Arawak god, Jocahu, resides. The site is currently closed to the public but it has been nominated by the United Kingdom for World Heritage listing and the Fountain National Park Corporation is actively seeking funding for its development. The Big Spring Heritage Site in Island Harbour features an overhanging limestone ledge with petroglyphs and a fresh water spring, indicating a sacred place of the island's earliest population.

BUILT ENVIRONMENT

The built environment includes the sole remaining example of wattle and daub architecture in Welches, historic stonewalls, rock ovens, chattel houses, churches and the architecture of the Lower Valley. Wooden shingles, tray ceilings, gabled roofs and fretwork. A walking tour begins at Anguilla's oldest plantation house - Wallblake House, in the compound of the Roman Catholic Church, then goes across the road to the ice-cream parlour that houses the remains of the old cotton ginnery, and ends at the ruins of the Crocus Hill courthouse with a

drink at the Savannah Gallery next to the Loblolly Gallery in the Lower Valley. The Lower Valley boasts several buildings of architectural distinction including the Ebenezer Methodist Church, the Koal Keel Restaurant, and the Hodge's Homestead. The Crocus Hill site is earmarked for major museum development that includes the establishment of a historic village.

SHIPWRECKS

Anguilla's marine heritage includes more than natural eco-systems, such as coral reefs. Sometimes, artificial reefs are created using shipwrecks, as is the case of the MV Sarah, that had sunk in Road Bay in 1984 but was salvaged, towed out to sea and sunk in 1990.

More well known historic shipwrecks are those of the 18th century Spanish warship, El Buen Consejo, off Scrub Island, and the Jesus, Maria Y Jose at Junks Hole. On the night of 7 July, 1772 while en route to Mexico with fifty Franciscan missionaries aboard, El Buen Consejo ran aground and eventually sank. The site of this shipwreck is designated as an Underwater Archaeological Preserve. Some of the artefacts unearthed from El Buen Consejo are shown publicly from time to time and will eventually become part of a permanent museum display.

'Shipwrecks of Anguilla: 1628-1993', published in 1995, is a compendium of the wrecks that have been found in Anguilla's waters.

BETHEL: AN ENDURING METHODIST CHAPEL

Bethel Chapel at South Hill is one of the oldest Methodist Churches in the Caribbean. It has withstood the test of time and the onslaught of a series of severe hurricanes which battered the region. Bethel celebrated its 125th anniversary in June 2003 with a Thanksgiving Service. It was not the first Methodist Church to be built in the area. Fifteen years after the introduction of Methodism on the island by Anguillian John Hodge in 1813, a small chapel, the ruins of which still exist, was erected just across the road. The labour was mainly provided by slaves.

In a letter dated November 20, 1828, the Reverend Henry Britten informed the Methodist Missionary Society in London of the building of Coke Chapel at the Road, as the Methodist area was then called. "The Committee will be glad to hear that we have now completed a most substantial little chapel 36 by 22 feet and there is no debt remaining," he wrote. "Connected with this, is a Society of 200 members and a Sunday School of 100 children. Matters are so arranged that if at any subsequent period a larger chapel be requisite, it may be built on the land we have."

Coke Chapel, which was dedicated in November 12, 1828, was used for fifty years before its replacement by Bethel, the present church building erected in 1878 by Lay Agent and later Minister, Dirk Almair Schouten. It should be noted that the first ever Methodist Church in Anguilla – Ebenezer Chapel - was built at the Valley by John Hodge in 1815.

The walls of the Bethel Chapel were constructed from stone held in place by lime obtained from burnt coral. The stones were dug from a quarry on Scrub Island, an offshore cay north-east of Anguilla. The shutters, shingles and galvanize for the roof were imported. The chapel was dedicated on June 19, 1878 by the Reverend James Horne Darrell of the St Maarten Circuit.

In a letter to the London-based Methodist Missionary

Bethel Methodist Church at South Hill in District 5 / Photo: Ivor Hodge

Society, he wrote: "It is a fine substantial stone structure and will seat about four hundred. It does Mr Schouten great credit, for it is to his personal skill and labour that we are greatly indebted for it."

Bethel Chapel, as it is known today, is bigger than the original structure. Extension work was carried out by the Reverend George Lawrence in 1934. He was assisted by the then Chairman of the Leeward Islands District, Reverend William Sunter, a reputed architect and builder.

Bethel was damaged in January 1955 by Hurricane Alice. In September 1950 it suffered extensive damage to its roof from Hurricane Donna. In September 1961 the renovation work was completed and the chapel was rededicated. The roof was again badly damaged by Hurricane Luis in August 1995, necessitating major repairs.

Throughout its 125 years, Bethel Chapel has given birth to a cadre of Anguillian Methodist Ministers. The list to date in order of ordination comprises Reverends Charles Leonard Carty, Vera Marjorie Richardson; Rev. Dr S. Wilfred Hodge, Rev. Dr H. Clifton Niles, Rev. Dr Wycherley Gumbs, Rev. Dr Neville Buchanan; Reverends Lindsay K. Richardson, Hugo E. Rey, Jefferson C. Niles and Erica Carty-Lewis.

There are six Methodist Churches in Anguilla. In addition to Bethel at South Hill and Ebenezer at the Valley, there are the Sandy Ground congregation (not yet named), Zion at North Hill, Maranatha at Blowing Point and Immanuel at West End.

At the time of the 2001 Census, there were just over 2,700 Methodists in Anguilla, making this denomination the second largest on the island after the Anglican Church which has a following of well over 3,300 members. Other main denominations are Baptist, Church of God, Seventh Day Adventist and Roman Catholic. **Nat Hodge & Rev Joseph Lloyd**

"Eh, eh, it's the language of Anguilla"

Oluwakemi Linda Banks

Anguilla is one of the few islands of the Caribbean which was not juggled among various colonial powers. Our history books tell us that the British successfully defeated all would-be invaders and therefore retained its sovereignty on the island.

The inhabitants of Anguilla, who were brought to the island as slaves from Africa, came with their own languages. However, the colonists strategically minimized the possibility of revolt by separating the tribes so that people who spoke the same languages were generally not on the same island. Consequently, they were forced to learn the language of the colonizers - English. In the process a rich dialect evolved, based on the English language but coloured by some vestiges of African languages.

It is not surprising therefore that the Anguillian dialect bears some similarities to the dialects on some other islands, especially those that were also occupied by the English. In her dictionary of Anguillian Language, Ijahnya Christian notes, "Not all of the words and expressions in this dictionary are peculiar to Anguilla…However, in the ways in which we use language, the inflections, the nuances, the silences, the gestures and expressions, make a whole that is unique and one that cannot adequately be captured on the printed page."

A brief study of this nature can be by no means exhaustive, therefore I will limit myself to first providing the reader with some of the basic rules of Anguillian dialect. I will then provide some actual examples and then finally give you a chance to eavesdrop on a conversation between two Anguillian ladies, which James a visitor has some difficulty understanding. Of course this will be followed by a translation.

In Anguillian dialect the verb 'to be" is not conjugated. The third person "is" is used to refer to everyone. Therefore you would hear : *"I is hungry", "you is…, we is…, dem is…".* In fact very often "is" is left out completely as in this example *"He comin"*. "Is not" is *"ain"* for everyone: *" Oi ain goin" "You ain goin, He ain goin", We ain goin" They ain goin".*

The past tense of the verb "to have" is usually used to place an action in the past tense. Instead of "he came", one would say *"he had come"*.

In the Anguillian dialect the word "does' is used before a verb in order to infer that something is usually done. For example "I *does go school every day"*; "He does listen to Radio Paradise in di morning". "Does" is used for extra emphasis and the verb which follows remains in the infinitive for everyone.

The consonant blend "th" is usually pronounced as "t" or "d" or is omitted altogether. This becomes *"dis"*, "father" becomes *"fadda"*, "mother" becomes *"mudda"*, "don't" becomes *"doh"*.

The consonant "d" is usually left off the ends of words, "and" becomes *"an"*. The final "g" is also omitted. Therefore "coming" is pronounced *"comin"*.

A favourite Anguillian exclamation is *"Awyer"* pronounced *"Aya, awya, or ayer"*. This can be used with different intonations. It can be long and drawn out like *"Aww-yerrr"*, it can be short and sharp like *"aya"* or it can be used in a phrase like *"Away looka wuk!" "Away"* probably came from "All of you".

Anguillians might greet you with *"Mi gyal, how yer goin"*, *"How tings wid ya"* or *"Mi chile, how tis?".* Your answer might be *"So, so tanks", "Oi awright," or "Oi dere"*. When a question is to be asked one might simply use the same phrase and raise one's voice at the end. "*Yer goin church'* would simply become "*Yer goin' church*?

Anguillians use some contradictions which can be confusing to the unsuspecting visitor. *"Lock it off! Now lock it on",* when referring to a tap of water. This means "Turn it off. Now turn it on". Rather than saying "I'm going and I'll be back later", Anguillians would say *"Oi goin' come back".* Meanwhile *"I don't want any"* becomes *"Oiai wah nun"*.

And the villages in Anguilla have the English name and the Angullian name: Blowing Point is *Blun Point*; South Hill is *Sout'll*; Sandy Ground is *Sandy Grung*; The Valley is *Di Wally*; and St Maarten is *Sa Martin, or Si Martin.*

Anguillians are not very good at giving directions in the traditional manner. Because of the nautical history of the island, directional terms are used: "Go east, den go west". The visitor might also be told *" Over dere so so"*… pointing, *"cross dere", "up a long"* or *"not too fud fun here"*. Of course the boat racers have a language of their own, and that is covered in a book by David Carty 'Nuttin' Bafflin'.

Anguillians were historically called *"Bobo Johnny"* in a derogatory way by the people of St Kitts and Nevis. . It is said that historically the first boy in the Anguillian family was named John, and his younger siblings had to call him *"Bobo Johnny"*- a derivative of Brother Johnny. Similarly the first girl in the family was called *"Titter" meaning "*Sister". The oldest brother or sister had a lot of responsibility for helping to raise and discipline the younger children, and therefore commanded a lot of respect in the family.

However, for the Kittitian, who had no knowledge of the importance of the name, *Bobo Johnny* became the name for all Anguillians and was synonymous with the poor relation, the cousin from the country who was backward and had not been exposed to the niceties of town life. One of the many jokes on *Bobo Johnny* claims that when he went to St Kitts and saw lights on electrical poles for the first time, he exclaimed to a fellow Anguillian, "Wuh, Bobo Johnny! Look moonlight pun tick!"

Now that Anguilla's development is equal to, and has in may cases surpassed, that of its former detractors from neighbouring islands, Anguillians accept the name with pride. Being a real Bobo Johnny, however, implies that you were born in Anguilla, and if you rub an Anguillian up the wrong way s/he would be proud to tell you that "Oi "B.H.", You "C.H.", meaning "I was Born Here. You have Come Here". Please *"doh feel no way"* (in other words "don't take it personally"). It is just a defensive way of staking claim on a land about which Anguillians have been ridiculed for many years, and which they now have every reason to be proud to share with others!

Now that you have had some tutoring, do listen to this conversation and see if you share James' predicament. You might need to get hold of the Dictionary of Anguillian English in order to sharpen your vocabulary.

James has come to Anguilla to visit his classmate Joan whom he met at college in Michigan. Joan has told him how wonderful Anguilla is and he is finding it absolutely fantastic. But one thing has him puzzled...the Joan he met at Michigan State was easy to understand, but, in Anguilla, Joan seems to be speaking two languages. James would be conversing quite comfortably with Joan, but then an Anguillian friend would come along and he would find himself lost and left out of the conversation. Joan switches the language so effortlessly from "standard" English to Anguillian English that, although James hears some familiar words, they seem out of context and he is unable to follow the conversation. Joan also seems to be speaking more quickly now. The conversation with a hypothetical friend, Susie, might go as follows:

Susie   Wuh Joan oi clean figet ta tell yu dat Della gorn again.

Joan   Aw ya looka wuk! Ya mean di gyul from out-a-long? She gorn long again?
Jeesum Bread! Wuh oi hear dat she had tie di knot wid Jason buh oi never believe it.

Susie   Chile, doh addle mi brains. You always ketchin' gapsease an keching it wrong. Oi eeblain able to explain it to yuh cos yuh too blame fast. Da ain di *pusson oi mean. Da Della bin hook up wid Jason fun long toime. Oi mean picky head Della who live pun top uh Roaches Hill. She dere wid Tommy.*

Joan   Oh tis you who humbug mi up! Yuh so disgustin! Tain dat oi dotin. Buh when yuh come wid all dese convulutin stories yuh does addle my brain. Now doh get me ammiffted.

Susie   Buddy yuh ain have ti reprihan mi so. Tis jes dat di Della you bring up has been broadpaish for donkey years. Di Della oi mean look like butter can melt in her mout. She from over so. But her mudda always actin nuf. She so full of herself and so cravishin.

Joan   Oh das who yuh mean! She mudda so froughty mout. Oi never mean to downstrive you but yuh had me on a lean. Anyhow, uh losin' mi manners gyul!... Dis mi fren James from America.

Susie   Gyal he looking good.(laughs) Yuh better hole on dere.

Joan   Gyal stop chatting chupidniss. He jus a friend. (laughs) Gyul, oi want ta go up in di east. Oi see Wyclife fuh Punta. Oi want to coop him for a lif. Oi wan ta go by di Chinese ta feed mi face. Yuh comin?

Susie   You go long buddy. You so struck! Oi ain hungry so oi goin limin cross so. Oi go sight yuh later!

Here now is the translation:

Susie   But Joan I completely forgot to tell you that Della is pregnant again.

Joan   What! Do you mean the girl from over there? Is she pregnant again. I heard that she had married Jason but I did not believe it.

Susie   Girl don't get me confused! You are always looking for gossip and getting it wrong. I can't even explain it to you because you are too nosy. That is not the person I mean. That lady Della has been married to Jason for a long time, I mean Della who has the short hair who lives at Roaches Hill. She is in a relationship with Tommy.

Joan   Oh you are the person who has confused me. You are so irritating. It's not that I am stupid. But when you tell all those twisted stories you get me confused. Now, Please don't get me upset.

Susie   My dear, it's not necessary for you to reprimand me like this. It's just that the Della that you were referring to has been a wild girl for many years. The Della I referred to looks very gentle and soft. She lives in North Side. But her mother is very pompous. She is so egotistical and covetous.

Joan   Oh that's who you mean! Her mother talks so much! I did not mean to contradict you but you were pressuring me. Any how, I've lost my manners. This is my friend James from America…

Susie   Girl, he is so handsome. You should try to hold on to him!

Joan   Girl, stop talking nonsense. He is just a friend! Girl, I want to go up to the east. I see Punta's son Wycliffe. I want to catch him to get a lift. I want to go by the Chinese restaurant to get something to eat. Are you going to come?

Susie   You go ahead! You are so greedy! I am not hungry so I am going to hang out over here. See you later!

As you visit our beautiful island you will note that as Anguillians speak, so do their hands and their bodies. The tone of voice can change the meaning of a word or a phrase, a little "cut-eye" can silence an enemy, and a sound in the throat or a movement of the hand can signal serious disapproval. Some of these non-verbals have been traced directly back to the mother land, Africa, and have therefore been parts of our psyche that could not be taken away.

We Bobo Johnnies enjoy our language and regardless of our educational level or position in the workplace, we hold our Anguillian language dear to our hearts. So although we teach our children "standard" English in school and we love to hear them speak "properly", we still ensure that they learn Anguillian, and that they know when it is appropriate to switch codes. In order to be really enjoyed a good joke must be spoken in Anguillian. "Eh, eh! After all man, yer cah really expeck mi ta enjoy a joke when yer spoksin like dah! Awyer looka wuk! Oi b.h. Oi ain c.h."

So we hope that you will enjoy our language and our unique idiosyncrasies, while you immerse yourself in our culture and our beautiful island!

Small Island, Big Heart

Phyllis Fleming-Banks

Friendly and hospitable are the adjectives visitors most often use to describe Anguillians. Of the 11,561 persons (2001 census) that live on the island, about fifty-one percent are female, with just over 3,000 children accounting for about twenty-eight per cent and eight percent considered elderly.

Anguilla's population, historically very small, has increased by more than seventy percent since the development of tourism in the 1980s. This is significant, when compared with an overall growth of just about 1,000 in the twenty years preceding the 1984 census.

Traditionally a close knit society of peasant farmers, fishermen, boat-builders and seafarers, constant emigration in search of employment and further education served to keep the population relatively small. The discovery of the island as a luxury tourist hideaway saw not only a return of Anguillians, but also a surge in the number of immigrants from other Caribbean islands. In the 1990s some 1,682 Anguillians returning home from the US Virgin Islands, St Maarten, the United States and the United Kingdom accounted for a 15 percent increase in the population. Whereas only about 9 percent of the population were non-Anguillian in 1984, this category now accounts for about 25 percent of the population living in Anguilla.

Today, most of the working population is employed in the tourism sector, with the public service/government and construction being the other significant sectors. The growth in the economic sector has also coincided with a decrease in household size (now an average of three persons) and an increase (43 percent since 1992) in the number of households. The extended family household, a traditional element of Anguillian society, now accounts for two percent of all households, while the number of households comprising just elderly (65 years and over) now stands at nine percent.

Although Anguilla's demographic profile has changed significantly, this predominantly Christian society still maintains much of its heritage. This is most apparent in the continued passion for boat racing, the national sport. Historically, Anguillians were known throughout the islands for their boat-building skills. The Anguillian wooden engine-less schooners plied the Caribbean waters transporting workers and supplies. Today's boat racing emerged from the race home by those schooners. While there is currently only one commercial boat building company on the island, there are quite a few boat-builders who, in addition to making fishing boats, dedicate much of their skill to crafting the "perfect sail boat" for the boat race.

Boat racing attracts large numbers to the beaches and good viewing points, especially on public holidays. During the week of August Festivities, hundreds of locals, returning Anguillians and visitors converge on the beaches

Hotel pioneer, Jeremiah Gumbs

'Bullet' the boat-builder

TOP OF PAGE, RIGHT: 'The Barracudas', one of the teams participating in the annual Marine Life Education Programme.

to "root" for their boat. The August Thursday boat race, which ends at Meads Bay, traditionally draws the largest crowds. Visiting Anguillians use this occasion to catch up on old friends and make new acquaintances amidst music, dancing and food.

While young and old enjoy boat racing, with the advent of technology the youth are more interested in computers and video games than other traditional games like "marble shooting", "nut knicking" and "top spinning". There are quite a number of sports clubs, which compete for supremacy in cricket, wind ball and volleyball as well as basketball and softball and athletics. These sporting clubs fall under national associations. With no cinemas on the island, most of the younger population find recreation in organized groups like the Boys and Girls Brigade, Scouts, Girl Guides, Pathfinders, Cadets, the Jaycees, Optimists, Rotarac and Leo Clubs and other church affiliated youth fellowship groups. Several theatre groups, including the "All Ah We Theatre", "APPLE Theatre" and "Sunshine Theatre" also provide outlets for creative energies for Anguillian youth.

Members of the adult population are also involved in a number of community/service organisations. These include women's groups at almost all of the churches and the Soroptimists, which fall under the umbrella organisation, the Anguilla National Council of Women. There are also a few Christian men's fellowship groups, as well as service clubs like Rotary, the Lions and support groups like the Mental Health Association and the Family Hope Network on domestic violence.

Anguillian families have traditionally taken care of their elderly members in their homes. While there are less multi-generational households, this tradition continues and youth still see this as part of their role, although an increasing number may opt to allow them to remain in their homes with hired caretakers. The Miriam Gumbs Senior Citizens' Home established itself as a model option for the elderly. This home has a healthy relationship with most of the youth and other organisations on the island.

Anguilla's small size and population has made it an "intimate" society. The village communities, which are spread across the island, are still largely family-based. A strong sense of patriotism and affiliation with the land still pervades and so does the "jollification" spirit of community caring and sharing. The changing demographic profile has not yet affected these distinctive features and the island consequently maintains its friendly, hospitable character which complements its "tranquillity wrapped in blue".

PHOTO: JESSICA BENSLEY

PHOTO: CHRIS MASON

ABOVE: Local businessman, Albert Lake

PHOTO: CHRIS MASON

PHOTO: DEAN BARNES

Sir Emile Gumbs / Photo: Dean Barnes

PHOTO: IVOR HODGE

Anguilla's oldest resident, Rose Hughes, celebrated her 100th birthday in 2003

PHOTO: CHRIS MASON

Tracy and her daughter, Jessica, excercise 'Coco' and 'Biscuit' / Jacqueline Cestero

'Smitty' of Island Harbour

PHOTO: DEAN BARNES

PHOTO: DEAN BARNES

PHOTO: JESSICA BENSLEY

Nat Richardson of the Palm Grove
Restaurant at Junks Hole / Carol Lee

PHOTO: CHRIS MASON

ANGUILLA – TRANQUILLITY WRAPPED IN BLUE

An Explosion in Sight and Sound

Ijahnya Christian

Anguilla's Summer Festival means the non-stop action of boat racing by day and the Landsome Bowl Cultural Centre by night. For the die-hards there are family reunions, beach 'limes', entertainment spots, and private parties in between. Carnival usually begins at the end of July and continues throughout the first week in August. Shows at the carnival village include the queen show, teen talent competition, prince and princess pageants and three, sometimes four calypso competitions. There is also a parade of troupes and j'ouvert morning when usually conservative Anguillians take to the streets in wild abandon at the break of day. J'ouvert is usually the time when one can see traces of the traditional 'ole mas' that has been replaced by more modern costumes. However, the 'mocka jumbies' are ever present on their tall stilts and nowadays it is the children that keep this traditional art form alive.

More women are participating in the calypso competitions nowadays and in 2002, Lady Messenger defeated all competitors, capturing crowns from the female calypso competition, the national and the Leeward Islands calypso competitions. Fans turn out in high numbers on competition nights and make their own judgments that sometimes do not coincide with the official ones at all. Carnival is also the time to enjoy the sweet music of many bands that release their albums annually hoping to earn the popular road-march title for the street jamming.

"Carnival is Mass! Carnival is Class! Carnival is Colour! Carnival is Flavour! Filled with Activity, Carnival Brings Out Creativity." Over the last decade, Anguilla's carnival has become a regular fixture on the Festival's calendar of the region.

ANGUILLA – TRANQUILLITY WRAPPED IN BLUE

ANGUILLA – TRANQUILLITY WRAPPED IN BLUE

PHOTO: CHRIS MASON

PHOTO: IVOR HODGE

PHOTO: IVOR HODGE

ANGUILLA – TRANQUILLITY WRAPPED IN BLUE

THE PARADE OF TROUPES

There's just something about street parade. It happens at the end of carnival, well almost the end. All the royalty has been crowned, the songs sung and carnival village is about to go into darkness until next August. But there's one final thing, the best thing is saved for last.

Around noon, quiet sleepy troupes wander in from all over the island to the start point behind Ashley's supermarket. It looks like a jumble of colour and sparkle all mixed together in an disorganised mass. Ever-smiling pageant winners draped in red robes with various crowns sit in open vehicles calmly maintaining their dignity despite the heat. Microphones appear as winners chat about how good it is to win and how they intend to serve the island in the coming year. Ominous tractor-trailers covered in huge black silent boxes and draped with plastic streamers pull into side roads to wait for their turn in the line-up. There is no sound except the soft merry chatter of troupe members, organizers and the roadside observers who have started to trickle in at about the same speed.

Everybody looks west … casually. The waiting is good. Gives people time to get their heart rate up-to-speed before the fire gets hot. It takes a long time to get ready. This is no stick of fire. This one is going to burn all afternoon and into the night. But nobody seems to mind. The first street is lined with mahogany trees and shadows fall around big circles of people trying to stay cool. The sunny spots are empty. You don't stand in the sun in Anguilla. It's too hot at noon, and it's still hot at two.

Things happen slowly. Finally the first troupe ambles into line behind the royalty. They are calm, no need to waste energy, not yet, it's gonna be a long day. There are many shifts in the line-up as the band trucks, still silent, pull into their spaces. By now the street is full of spectators all looking west. The shade has been abandoned by many trying to get a look at the first in line. And then it happens. Just a beat, like striking a match.. Again and again. It's loud but no too loud like it's far away. Even if you are close up it still sounds far away, until magic fingers touch steel guitars and a clear sweet voice cries out, "Are you ready!"

And then it catches. The troupes, already moving to the beat, spring across the street like flames on dry wood. Back and forth across the road they wind along the street shooting flames at everything they meet, guzzling water so they don't burn out, but never missing a beat.

The first truck passes … very slowly. By now the heat is so loud you stop thinking, you just listen to the beat. When the big boxes pass close (and that is the only place to be, close to the flame) you feel the heat in your chest. It takes over your heart and for a moment you can't breath. By now you are feeling the fire. The singer commands, "Hands in the air, let me see you wok" and your body wants to obey. You can't help but move. The toes wiggle, the foot taps, your knees bend when you take a step and you just want to jump into the line and hold on to that fire. The heat, what heat? The sun is blazing but it's not as hot as the pulsating stream of flames winding their way around The Valley.

You become part of the parade even if you don't have a costume. And nobody minds. This is a free parade, audience participation required. This is not a store-bought parade; this is a homemade, original Anguilla creation put on by regular people you will see the next day back at their jobs pretending they know nothing about the fire. They will never show you what burns inside except once a year on this special day. **Joanne Mason**

District Guide to Anguilla

Ken Hodge

DISTRICT ONE
ISLAND HARBOUR

Island Harbour is a small fishing village located in the north-eastern sector of the island about eight miles from the capital, The Valley. This village, along with the surrounding areas of the Copse, Pond Ground, Mount Fortune, White Hill and Welches, make up District One with a population of 1,854. A primary school and a pre-school institution are located in this area.

Island Harbour is the home of the Elected Representative for the area, the Hon. Kenneth Harrigan who serves as Minister of Communications, Works, Public Utilities and Housing in the United Front Government.

Among the noted Anguillians from Island Harbour was Walter G. Hodge (1920-1989). He was one of the many talented and resourceful Anguillians whose varied skills contributed significantly to the success of his country's quest in breaking the yoke of political bondage which had for decades denied them economic and social progress. Other freedom fighters from this area include Wilkin Harrigan and Mitchell Harrigan, former Commissioner of Police.

There are a number of churches in this District, among them the St Andrews Anglican Church, the smallest of three parish churches which dates back to the 1950s. Other more recent churches

Albena Lake Hodge School, above, and Scilly Cay, below, an island in the bay at Island Harbour

PHOTOS THIS PAGE: CHRIS MASON

include the Hilltop Baptist Church and the Faith Baptist Church.

The area contains a number of historical sites. One is Big Spring, a limestone sinkhole which provides an overhang to a fresh water source. It contains a large petroglyph, a small carved stalagmite and other interesting artefacts.

A number of tourism establishments are located in Island Harbour. They include Scilly Cay Restaurant, Hibernia Restaurant, Smitty's on the beach and the Arawak Beach Inn which is located on the site of an ancient Arawak village. The ruins of a tourism complex can be found on Scrub Island, an offshore cay about half a mile off the eastern tip of Anguilla.

The coastline of District One is dotted with a number of beaches. They include Island Harbour, Scilly Cay, Captains Bay, Windward Point Bay, Savannah Bay and Junks Hole. The wrecks of two 17th century Spanish ships, the El Buen Consejo and the Jesus Maria y Jose, are located in this area. Many of the beaches here are not suitable for swimming because of the rugged terrain, rocky shores and pounding seas.

DISTRICT TWO
SANDY HILL

The Sandy Hill District is one of the island's smaller districts with a population of 930. The district encompasses the villages of Long Path, Sandy Hill, Seafeathers, East End, the Copse Chalvilles, Bad Cocks and Deep Waters. District Two is separated from District One by the road through the Copse and is about five miles from the capital.

The elected representative for the area is the Hon. Osbourne Berrington Fleming who heads up the United Front Government as Chief Minister and Minister of Home Affairs and Tourism.

Anguilla's Revolutionary Leader, James Ronald Webster, who was born in Island Harbour,

Sandy Ground

The Valley Police Station, below

lives in Sea Feathers. On 10 February 1976, under the new Anguilla Constitution, Webster, referred to as 'the Father of the Nation', became the island's first Chief Minister. Other freedom fighters from this area include Atlin Harrigan and Doreen Duncan.

There are two churches in District Two. St Augustine's Anglican Church is located on the site of an old sugar estate and served a dual purpose of church and school up until 1918. The second is the Seventh Day Adventist Church located to the south west of the Anglican Church.

In the village of East End is found the East End Pond, an area of natural beauty, noted particularly for its rich bird life. The area is being established as a wetland site for conservation. Adjoining the pond is the Old Boy's School which is no longer used for classes. It was one of the early centres of education at a time when Anguilla was extremely depressed. The school has produced a number of prominent Anguillians some of which include: James Ronald Webster, Osbourne Fleming, Felix Fleming, Vivien Vanterpool and Idahlia Gumbs. To the south is located the Morris Vanterpool Primary School.

Beaches in this district include Mimi Bay, a secluded beach protected by an inshore reef, allowing for safe swimming in shallow water, and Sandy Hill Bay, home to a number of fishing boats.

DISTRICT THREE VALLEY NORTH

District Three - Valley North takes in one half of the island's capital. This area, with a population of 2,285, is one of the two largest districts on the island. It comprises the area of Crocus Bay, Roaches Hill, The Valley, North Valley, Upper Valley, The Quarter, North Side, Stoney Ground, Caul's Bottom, The Farrington, Wattices, Little Dicks

PHOTO: IVOR HODGE

St Mary's Road

PHOTO: IVOR HODGE

Crocus Bay

SOMBRERO ISLAND

Sombrero, so called by the Spanish because of its resemblance to a hat, is one of the more interesting of Anguilla's offshore islands. The three-quarter mile long island, with cliffs ranging from 20 to 40 ft above sea level, lies about 40 miles northwest of Anguilla. There is hardly any soil, no fresh water, no beaches and landing by boat is possible only during calm weather. Sombrero is so barren that plant life is negligible, and the animal life is limited to three species of lizard and a large sea-bird population which includes terns, gulls and brown boobies.

However, Sombrero Island was renowned for its significant deposits of phosphate of lime. In 1865, the British Government leased the island to the Sombrero Phosphate Company, which established extensive mining facilities which operated until 1890.

Sombrero is also renowned for its lighthouse, which went into service in 1868.

After nearly one hundred years, and because of structural deterioration, it was replaced in 1962. This lighthouse, like the one before it, succumbed to the salt-laden atmosphere, and was replaced in 2001 by a fibreglass lighthouse powered by solar energy. Unlike the previous lighthouses, this one is unmanned.

and Shoal Bay. This area houses the island's main public health care facility, the Princess Alexandra Hospital. Valley North is also home to a number of educational institutions including Campuses A & B of the Albena Lake-Hodge Comprehensive School and the Stoney Ground Primary School.

The elected representative for this area is the Honourable Eric Leith Reid who serves as Minister of Social Development in the United Front Government.

A number of prominent Anguillians are from this area. They include the late Idahlia Gumbs (1933 – 2000), who was nominated to the Anguilla Council in 1972 and became a Minister of Government in 1976, Collins Hodge (1925 – 1978), who was one of the principal agitators for secession and a member of the Anguilla Council, and Bob Rogers, a member of the Peace Keeping Committee.

This district also contains the island's major sports venue, the Ronald Webster Park which is used for many sporting events throughout the year as well as official functions including the Anguilla Day and Queen's Birthday parades.

A number of the island's best beaches are found in District Three. They include Little Bay which is a marine park area and nursery for many fish; Limestone Bay, a secluded small bay usually good for swimming and snorkelling and Shoal Bay Beach, a major attraction for locals, tourists and day-trippers from neighbouring St Maarten. The one-mile beach is bordered by restaurants, villas and other tourism establishments including La Fontana, Madeariman, Uncle Ernie's, Serenity, Elodias Restaurant and Beach Resort, Millies Inn, Serenity Cottage and Shoal Bay Villas and Hotel. The newly renovated Tourism Department, the Department of Agriculture and the Ministry of Infrastructure, Communications

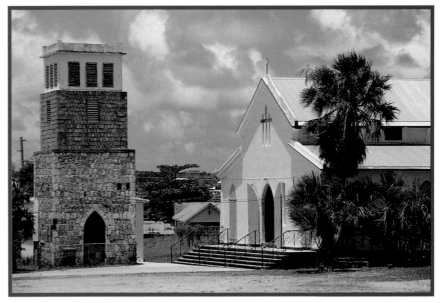

St Mary's Anglican Church

Blowing Point Ferry, above, and the Anguilla Community Foundation fund thermometer

and Utilities are located in the Valley North area. One of the largest and most modern supermarkets – Lakes Marketplace and Wholesale is located on the Stoney Ground Road.

In District Three can be found the Fountain Cavern – one of the most interesting caves in Anguilla and of great archaeological significance. The cave was the ceremonial centre for Arawaks, the earliest known inhabitants of Anguilla. A National Park is being developed on the land surrounding the cave which is temporarily closed to the public while the park is being developed.

A number of churches are located in this area including the Bethany Gospel Hall, Kingdom Hall and the Church of God of Holiness.

DISTRICT FOUR
VALLEY SOUTH

Valley South, the second half of the island's capital - District Four is the largest area with a population of 2,619. It comprises the area of Vieux Fort, Crocus Hill, The Valley, South Valley, Upper Valley, The Quarter, The Farrington, Rey Hill, The Forest, Corito, Long Ground, Statia Valley and George Hill. Valley South is home to the island's business sector. These include the four commercial banks – National Bank of Anguilla, Caribbean Commercial Bank, Scotia Bank and First Caribbean International as well as the Herbert's Commercial Complex, the James Ronald Webster Building and the Fair Play Commercial Complex. All of the island's main administrative buildings are to be found here, including the Government Secretariat and ministerial buildings, the Treasury, the Offshore Finance and Company Registry, the Customs Department, Lands and Surveys Department, the Police Station, House of Assembly/High Court/Magistrate's

PHOTO: CHRIS MASON

PHOTO: IVOR HODGE

Blowing Point Harbour, above, and a solar-powered 'lighthouse' at Windward Point, below

PHOTO: CHRIS MASON

PHOTO: CHRIS MASON

Court and Her Majesty's Prison. Also in this area is the Valley Health Centre, Dental Unit, Primary Health Care and Environmental Health Departments and the Water Lab.

The elected member for this area is the Hon. Victor Franklin Banks who serves as Minister of Finance and Economic Development in the United Front Government.

A number of prominent Anguillians came from this area. They include the Educator and Minister of Government, Albena Lake-Hodge (1920-1985), Edwin Wallace Rey (1906 – 1980), one of the key architects of Anguilla's political reformation, and Captain Clayton Lloyd (1942 -1977), the island's first pilot and one of the island's early pioneers in the establishment of locally-owned airlines.

Churches found in this District include the Ebenezer Methodist Church, the oldest church in Anguilla, St Mary's Anglican Church in the Valley, St Gerard's Roman Catholic Church in Wallblake and the Church of God of Prophecy in the Quarter. The Valley Primary School is located to the west of the Anglican Church and is the island's first primary school, built in the 1960s, to house both male and female students under one roof. Prior to that, boys attended the Old Valley Boys' School located to the North of the Anglican Church while girls attended the Valley Girls' School in the Valley adjacent to the Ebenezer Methodist Church.

Places of Interest in District Four include Koal Keel Restaurant, formerly an old plantation house and used as a residence for island's officials for many years; the ruins of the Old Court House; the Anguilla Museum, which also houses the offices of the Anguilla National Trust which was opened in 1996 and contains many interesting artefacts and information on Anguilla; Wallblake House, Anguilla's oldest plantation house; and the Old

Sandy Ground Police Station and Immigration Department

Home of Marjorie Hodge, The Valley and, below, Church of God of Prophesy pre-school

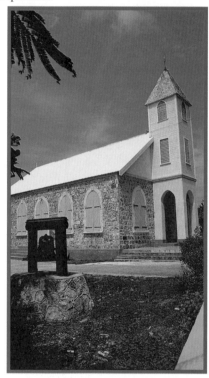

Sydney's Antique Museum, below

Valley Methodist Church, above, and St Gerard's Roman Catholic Church, below, in District 4

ANGUILLA – TRANQUILLITY WRAPPED IN BLUE

Factory, which once housed the island's only cotton ginnery where the cleaning and baling of locally-grown cotton was undertaken in preparation for shipping to England via St Kitts.

At the top of Crocus Hill is located Anguilla's oldest and longest running accommodation establishment, Lloyd's Hotel.

Beaches in this district include the Auntie Dol Bay, Forest Bay, Corito Bay, Elsie Bay and Little Harbour. The two bulk stations, Shell Antilles and Delta Petroleum are located in this area as is the generating station for the Anguilla Electricity Company. Consideration is also being given to this area for the development of the island's main port. Anguilla's Wallblake Airport is also located in this area.

DISTRICT FIVE
ROAD NORTH

The Road North District Five has a population of 1,289. The District takes in the areas of Water Swamp, North Hill, Sandy Ground, part of South Hill lying north of the main road leading from The Valley towards the West End, and the islands of Sombrero, Sandy Island, Dog Island, Upper and Lower Prickly Pear Islands and Seal Island.

The village of Sandy Ground is Anguilla's main port for cargo ships and also night activities. The long curved beach is lined with high cliffs and a salt pond behind.

The elected representative for the area is the Hon. Edison Alva Baird. He served in public office following his success in the March 1994 general elections as Minister of Social Services with responsibility for Health, Education, Welfare and Sports. He is now in opposition.

Noted Anguillians from this district include Sir Emile Gumbs who was Chief Minister of Anguilla for thirteen years and the late

PHOTO: CAROL LEE

Sandy Ground salt pond

PHOTO: IVOR HODGE

Meads Bay

THE ANGUILLA BEAUTIFICATION CLUB

In 1992, Lidia Shave, wife to the Governor at the time, called together a group of about twenty people whose common interest was a love of gardens. They discussed planting trees and flowering shrubs in order to beautify Anguilla. After several meetings, the Anguilla Beautification Club (ABC) was established. In 1999, the organisation was formally constituted and an Executive Committee elected to run its business.

The first major project of the ABC was the planting of ficus benjamina trees along the Queen Elizabeth Avenue in The Valley. Hurricanes destroyed or damaged some of the trees and some were replanted. Despite these setbacks the trees are still flourishing.

Other projects included planting commemorative trees in honour of people such as Diana, Princess of Wales, Mother Teresa, Nurse Miriam Gumbs and Rupert Carty. These plantings can be seen at the junction entering the Secretariat, in the grounds of St Gerard's Church, in the grounds of the Princess Alexandra Hospital and in a garden at the Well in Sandy Ground, respectively. The Anguilla Beautification Club also marked the Golden Jubilee of Her Majesty Queen Elizabeth II with a yellow poinciana, planted on the corner of Queen Elizabeth and Coronation Avenues.

In 1999, the ABC, whose membership currently stands at around fifty volunteers, staged Anguilla's first Flower and Garden Show. The event was a resounding success and has now become an annual event usually held in February or March.

In 2002, the club celebrated its 10th Anniversary, and marked the occasion by landscaping and decorating the South Hill roundabout which it maintains along with most of its other projects. It continues to make a difference and is recognized by the Government and people of Anguilla as a major contributor to the island's beautification. **Lady Josephine Gumbs**

Reverend C. Leonard Carty, MBE (1915 - 1994), who was granted leave by the Methodist Church to serve as Treasurer in Anguilla during the revolution.

Churches in this area include the Bethel Methodist Church which overlooks Sandy Ground, Zion Methodist Church in North Hill, the Gireh Seventh Day Adventist Church and the Church of God of Prophecy, both in Upper South Hill.

Places of interest include the Road Salt Pond, the White House, which is the home of Sir Emile Gumbs, the Mission House, originally a plantation house for the Road Estate where sugar and cotton were grown, and Gavannagh Cave which was mined for phosphate in the late nineteenth century.

DISTRICT SIX
ROAD SOUTH

Road South District Six has a population of 1,848. The area comprises Blowing Point, Sandy Point, Rendezvous and part of South Hill. The main ferry terminal is located in Blowing Point regarded as the island's gateway to St Maarten. A small police outpost is on the second floor of the warehouse. West of the terminal is a very secluded strip of beach that is wonderful for beach picnics and swimming. The area also has several rental villas and restaurants. A modern tennis complex is being earmarked for the village. To the west of Blowing Point can be found Rendezvous Bay, a two-mile stretch of white sand beach. At the eastern end of the bay is Rendezvous Bay Hotel, the island's second oldest hotel. It is owned by Jeremiah Gumbs, who is remembered for his role in securing key contacts in the United States to make the plight of Anguilla known internationally through the United Nations and the news services. His son, Alan, also followed his father's

Meads Bay and Barnes Bay

South Hill, above, and the Court House, below

footsteps into the tourism industry and was a former Chairman of the Anguilla Tourist Board. Jeremiah's wife, the late Lydia Gumbs (1917 – 2002) created the Revolutionary Flag with the three dolphins which later became the emblem of the National Flag. She served on several community groups in Anguilla including the Soroptimist Club, the Mental Health Association and the National Women's Council.

The Anguilla Great House Beach Resort is also located at Rendezvous Bay. It is owned by Walton Fleming, a prominent businessman and real estate developer, who is one of the founding directors of the National Bank of Anguilla.

The elected representative for the area is the Hon. Hubert Benjamin Hughes, a former Chief Minister who serves as the Leader of the Opposition.

A number of sportsmen come from this area. In the field of athletics is Trevor (Ras Bucket) Davis who has represented Anguilla at various championships throughout the world including the Carifta Games in Bermuda and the inaugural World Championships in Helsinki, Finland. In the field of cycling are brothers Charles and Ronnie Bryan and Kris Pradel who participated in the Commonwealth Games in Manchester, England in 2002.

Churches in this district include the Christian Assembly and the Maranatha Methodist Church on the Blowing Point Road, and the Christian Fellowship on the South Hill Main Road.

DISTRICT SEVEN
WEST END

West End District Seven is the smallest district on the island with a population of 736. The district includes Long Bay, Mead's Bay, Maunday's Bay, West End Village and Anguillita Island. Anguilla's first

Beach at Sandy Ground, District 5

cricketer to make the West Indies team, Omari Banks, comes from this district.

The elected representative for the area is Albert Emmanuel Hughes.

The area is referred to as the tourism belt because of the high concentration of resorts and other tourism facilities. These include the Malliouhana Hotel, the first five star resort to be built in Anguilla when the island started its focus on up-market tourism, and the world-renowned Cap Juluca Hotel set on Maunday's Bay, one of the most spectacular beaches in Anguilla. Other tourism establishments include CuisinArt, Altamer Resort, Blue Waters, Paradise Cove, Cove Castles, La Sirena Hotel and Carimar Beach Club; the Sonesta Resort, which was recently demolished to make way for the construction of Temenos Estates which will be a golf course and luxury villas; and the Frangipani Beach Club, whose owner and general manager, Valentine Davis, is a keen jazz enthusiast who has sponsored the Jazz and Art festival since 2001. Some of the island's best beaches can be found in this district including Shoal Bay West, Meads Bay, Maunday's Bay, Long Bay and Barnes Bay.

Places of interest include Cheddie's Art Studio and the Devonish Art Gallery and the Dune Preserve, home of one of the region's acclaimed recording artists, Bankie Banx, and the venue for the annual Moonsplash Music Festival.

One of the churches in this district is the Immanuel Methodist Church which serves the West End and Long Bay area. The other two churches are the Church of God of Prophecy in Lower West End and the Shemei Seventh Day Adventist Church in Long Bay. There is one primary school in this district, the West End Primary School, which was recently rebuilt following damage caused by Hurricane Lenny in 1999.

The ferry port at Blowing Point, above, and opposite, Anguilla's capital, The Valley

Small inlet at the eastern end of Rendezvous Bay, above, and Sandy Ground, below

ANGUILLA – TRANQUILLITY WRAPPED IN BLUE

Tourism in Anguilla

Overlooking Corito Bay

Carimar Beach Resort

Mimi Gratton

In 1978, the Government of Anguilla took the decision to formally pursue tourism as an industry for the island. It was a decision based on sheer economics. The salt industry was in a serious state of decline, having lost the lucrative Trinidad market, and history had shown that Anguilla's dry and arid climatic conditions would not support traditional island crops such as sugar, cotton or bananas. The island lacked natural mineral resources, too. There was no oil, no bauxite, no other precious metals. In fact, the island had precious little, except for 33 pristine white sand beaches, crystal-clear waters, practically non-existent development, and about 6,000 of the friendliest, proudest, most independent and ambitious people that one could ever hope to meet. As assets go, it was really not much to talk about, but when examined in the context of tourism, with all its vagaries and demands for new and unspoiled destinations, it seemed as if Anguilla was sitting on a veritable goldmine.

As the world's largest industry, and Anguilla's principal economic generator, tourism has played, and continues to play, a major role in the island's national and social development, impacting each and every Anguillian in some intrinsic way.

Careful planning, and the determination to pursue policies that would enable the island to develop a quality product, without compromising the unique qualities of Anguilla and its people, have informed the choice of product offering, as well as the type and scale of tourism development. The focus is on quality versus quantity, uniqueness and individuality versus large-scale, conveyor-belt tourism, and a commitment to ensuring that the visitor experience is truly an unforgettable one through the warm hospitality of the island's people. Initiatives have been undertaken to broaden the product offering from a mere sun-sand-sea destination by highlighting aspects of the island's cultural, environmental and eco-heritage, and exploring potential niche markets such as diving, cuisine, honeymoon/romance, art and small meetings.

The industry promotes a tranquil island and quality product: unspoiled and spectacularly beautiful beaches; a small, friendly and hospitable population; and a wide range of ultra-luxurious resorts and villas, moderately priced intimate "hotels de charme", and affordable guesthouses and inns.

Anguilla's cuisine is truly a work of art, with the creative fusion of culinary styles adding to the eclectic flavour of the island's cuisine. There are more than 85 dining experiences available on the island, ranging from glamorous, intimate gourmet restaurants to elegantly casual beachfront bistros, and affordable festive roadside grills. The cosmopolitan cuisine includes menus and specialties from various nationalities and regions, including French, Chinese, Italian, Continental, West Indian and others. Award winning local and international chefs, creative menus complemented by carefully selected choice wines, and efficient and courteous service all come together to create an extraordinary dining experience which is sure to be a highlight of any vacation.

There is a thriving artists' community on the island. Diverse art forms include pottery, sculpture, handcrafts, paintings and woodcraft, and a number of unique, indigenous establishments add their distinctive flavour to the nightlife on the island.

Island activities include swimming, sailing, fishing, day and evening cruises, kayaking, sunfish sailing, parasailing, kite surfing and glass bottom boating. Over the years, the government has sunk nine wrecked ships in order to create habitats for marine life, and complement the natural wrecks and dive sites, the most famous and intriguing wreck being that of El Buen Consejo, a Spanish galleon sunk in the 17th century. Away from the water you can enjoy horseback riding, island tours, art gallery tours and museum tours. Swim with the dolphins or wade with the stingrays at Dolphin Fantaseas, or take a walking tour of the Olde Valley, Sandy Ground or Big Springs and the East End Pond conservation area. Hiking is another option, coupled with bird-watching, nature trailing and a visit to Anguilla's unique rainforest at Katouche Bay. Or simply indulge the spirit and relax the soul with innovative treatment in world-class spa facilities.

Recent tourism developments include the construction of the 18-hole Greg Norman golf course, coupled with a luxurious Five Star resort hotel and villas, a 600-seat conference room facility and hotel, a modern, state-of-the-art Tennis Academy and entertainment complex, and expansions to the existing facilities at the Wallblake Airport.

The Tourism Industry is headed by the Minister of Tourism, who is also the Chief Minister. A Tourist Board administers the day-to-day activities in Anguilla and, internationally, the board has tourist representative offices in New York, London, Germany and Monaco.

PHOTO: CAROL LEE

Cap Juluca, below

PHOTO: BILL MILNE

Anguilla Great House, Rendezvous Bay

Anguilla Great House

Frangipani Beach Resort, above, Malliouhana Resort and Spa on Meads Bay, below left, and Covecastles at Shoal Bay West, below right

Carimar Beach Club

CuisinArt at Rendezvous Bay

'Indigo' is one of Anguilla's luxury villas

Anguilla is unmatched for its collection of magnificently luxurious, yet casually elegant five-star resorts. Here, you'll find the pinnacle of contemporary spa facilities, treatments and services.

Cap Juluca Spa Rituals (pictured)   Massages and skin treatments, and a host of services, some designed especially for two, are enjoyed in the privacy of your own villa or in one of two private spa treatment rooms, located at the Main House, or in a secluded beach space or in the gazebo, located on the sand dune at West Bay.

CuisinArt Resort & Spa A three-story, 7,000 square foot Mediterranean inspired Venus Spa offers a full variety of services including its Wellness Program. This program provides the opportunity not only to transform the nature of your leisure time but also enhance the quality of your life.

Malliouhana Hotel & Spa This is the Caribbean's newest spa and fitness facility, introduced in November 2002. The beachfront centre houses ocean-view, private treatment, day suites and specialty rooms where spa and resort guests can enjoy the attentions of world-class experts providing the latest treatments and using the finest products and remedies. Fitness training experts and advanced equipment are available at the centre.   PHOTO: BILL MILNE

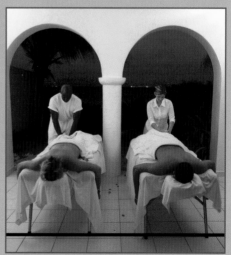

Rendezvous Bay Hotel

Royal Palms Hotel in South Hill

Beach at the Frangipani Beach Hotel, above, and Blue Waters Beach Apartments, Shoal Bay, below

ANGUILLA – TRANQUILLITY WRAPPED IN BLUE

PHOTO: CHRIS MASON

Paradise Cove

PHOTO: CHRIS MASON

Lloyd's Guest House

PHOTO: BILL MILNE

Beach wedding service at Cap Juluca

PHOTO: CHRIS MASON

Temenos Villas in Little Harbour

PHOTO: BILL MILNE

Cap Juluca, Maundays Bay, above and below

PHOTO: CAROL LEE

PHOTO: JACQUELINE CESTERO

Shoal Bay Villas, above

PHOTO: CHRIS MASON

PHOTO: CAROL LEE

La Serena Hotel, Meads Bay

Cafe Paris at the Shoal Bay Beach Hotel, above, and Altamer Resort, below

PHOTO: IVOR HODGE

Anguilla Tourist Board office

PHOTO: CHRIS MASON

Anguilla's Glorious Beaches

Mimi Gratton

What makes a beach the best? According to some of the world's foremost "beachologists" there are a number of criteria to consider in rating the greatness of a beach. There are ecological factors such as year-round weather conditions, the colour, quality and temperature of the water, the size of the waves, softness and colour of the sand and the strength of the water currents. Other aspects are the ease of access, the quality and quantity of the facilities and the prevalence of pests. Finally, safety factors are considered, which include visual obstructions, over-crowdedness and existing security measures.

Anguilla boasts 33 of some of the most stunning beaches in the world each characterized by powder white sand and surrounded by crystal clear turquoise water. Our now-famous Shoal Bay Beach (East) has been ranked as one of the top ten most beautiful beaches in the world, and others, such as Rendezvous Bay and Maundays Bay are regularly cited for their serene beauty.

But whether Anguilla's beaches are ranked among the top in the world or remain largely undiscovered, they are all spectacular natural playgrounds where you can enjoy many recreational activities or private tranquil pleasures. The following is a guide of some of the things to do on Anguilla's beaches and best places to do them.

Meads Bay

SWIMMING Whether you just want a quick dip, a leisurely soak or a vigorous workout, Rendezvous Bay is the spot for you. Sandy Hill Bay is another great swimming beach if you don't mind the occasional pelican or nearby fisherman.

SUNBATHING You'll never have to move your chair or towel to catch the rays if you're at Junks Hole, Savannah Bay. This two-mile long stretch of beach shows off Mother Nature's beauty at her finest. Meads Bay faces the Atlantic Ocean and is dotted by some of Anguilla's top resorts.

The beach at Junkshole

WALKING/JOGGING Take your pick! Most of Anguilla's beaches are ideal for walking or jogging.

BEACHCOMBING Don't expect to find sand pails full of shells or driftwood on Anguilla's beaches. But venture down to Katouche Bay for a vast array of sea rocks and brain coral or Forrest Bay for a collection of interesting shells and other sea artefacts.

FAMILY FUN Road Bay in Sandy Ground offers something for everyone in the family. Wavelets that lap the shore for toddlers and small children to play in, a pier for older kids to jump off, a selection of restaurants and bars for

Barnes Bay

meals and other recreation, lots of boats to admire and friendly people to meet. Shoal Bay East also gets an honourable mention in this category.

WATERSPORTS For snorkelling or scuba diving, your best bet is to stay on the Atlantic side of the island. Popular favourites include Shoal Bay East, Little Bay and Crocus Bay.

PARTYING Get ready to kick off your shoes and hit the dance floor at Road Bay and Shoal Bay East. Both beaches feature popular night (and day) spots that rollick with live calypso, soca and reggae music on a regular basis.

PEOPLE WATCH As one of Anguilla's most popular beaches, Shoal Bay East is a great spot to sit and watch the world, and all its players, go by.

NATURAL BEAUTY For breathtaking natural beauty, plan to spend a day at Captain's Bay, Mimi Bay or Windward Point. Both Captain's Bay and Mimi Bay are designated protected areas and are characterized by their unique indigenous vegetation. Windward Point is located on the eastern-most point of the island and features spectacular crashing waves and a long stranded stretch of powder white sand.

UNFORGETTABLE SUNSETS Secluded and scenic, Limestone Bay is situated close to The Valley and is a favourite spot for picnics and fabulous sunsets. Sunset gazers on Barnes Bay have reported seeing the elusive Green Flash on several occasions.

IN THE SPIRIT OF ROBINSON CRUSOE You will feel like a great explorer stranded on a beautiful deserted island if you visit Sandy Island or Prickley Pear for the day. Except for the fact that both offshore cays feature bar-restaurants, you will feel that you have discovered one of the world's best-kept secrets.

Shoal Bay East, above and main picture

Little Bay is a small cove in Crocus Bay

PHOTO: CHRIS MASON

Limestone Bay, main picture, and Savannah Bay, below

PHOTO: CHRIS MASON

The beach at Blowing Point, above, and Rendezvous Bay, below

PHOTO: IVOR HODGE

PHOTO: IVOR HODGE

A TO Z OF WHAT TO DO IN ANGUILLA

You will never find yourself at a loss of things to do in Anguilla if you take in all or even just a few of the fun, educational or cultural activities listed below.

ARRANGE to take one of the island's organized tours. The Anguilla Archaeological and Historical Society (AAHS) takes visitors back in time with a tour of some of Anguilla's wonderful historic buildings in the **Wallblake and Lower Valley Tour**; or learn about Anguilla's once proud tradition as one of the world's top salt producers on the **Sandy Ground Tour**. For more information contact the AAHS at 497-2263 or 497-2711. For interesting insights into the island's Amerindian culture take in the Anguilla National Trust's (497-5297) **Big Spring Tour**.

BRUSH up on, or learn new cooking skills at CuisinArt Resort & Spa's regularly scheduled **cooking classes**. You will learn the fine art of gourmet cooking from some of the world's top chefs. Classes are open to everyone. A fee is charged for outside guests. For more information call CuisinArt Resort & Spa at 498-2000.

CURL up with a good book. Several of Anguilla's shops and boutiques carry a large selection of books on Anguilla's unique history and culture.

DIVE into Anguilla's crystal clear waters and discover the beauties of our island's aquascape. A number of Anguilla's water sports operators and boat skippers would be happy to arrange a day or half-day of **snorkelling** or **scuba diving** for you.

EAT, drink and be merry for tomorrow you can rest! With more than **100 restaurants** on the island, your challenge is to sample them all!

FIRE up the grill and experience a traditional **Anguilla Fish Fry**. For a taste of true authenticity seek the help of a local fisherman who will show you how it is done.

GRAB your binoculars and head down to one of Anguilla's 13 salt ponds to enjoy an afternoon of **bird watching**. The best areas to see a large selection of migratory and indigenous birds are Road Bay Salt Pond, Cauls Pond, East End Pond and West End Salt Pond. And be sure to pick up a copy of 'A Field Guide to Anguilla's Wetlands', published by the Anguilla National Trust (497-5297).

HAVE you ever dreamed of **horseback riding on the beach**? Call Cliffside Stables (497-3667) or El Rancho del Blues (497-61644) and live the dream.

INTERESTED in finding out more about Anguilla's history? Learn fascinating facts during your visit to the **Heritage Museum**.

JUMP up and jam to Anguilla's pulsating soca, calypso and reggae music during **Summer Festival** (August) and **Moonsplash** (March) celebrations or all year long at some of our local hot spots.

KICK back and enjoy the smooth, mellow sounds of jazz on the beach during Anguilla's annual **Tranquillity Jazz Festival** held in November.

LISTEN to a cricket match broadcast on one of Anguilla's local radio stations. Or better yet, take in a match at Ronald Webster Park and learn more about one of the oldest team sports in the Western Hemisphere.

MAKE arrangements with one of Anguilla's many experienced boat captains for a daytrip to one of Anguilla's **spectacular offshore cays**.

NEED a cure-all for whatever ails you? Head into the bush for some "worry-wine", lime tree leaves, lemon grass, bayberry leaves, sour sop or "horse rub down" and steep them in water to make some genuine **Anguilla bush tea**.

ONE, two, three, four! Take in the annual **Anguilla Day** (May 30) and **Queen's Birthday** (June) parades in The Valley.

PURCHASE an original painting or sculpture from one of Anguilla's many talented local or resident artists. A wide selection of local and Caribbean artwork can be found at any one of the island's excellent **art galleries**.

QUICK! Make sure you make it down to the beach to try and catch of glimpse of the elusive **Green Flash** as the sun sets gloriously in the West.

RENEW your spirit and relax your body while you enjoy an unforgettable **spa treatment** or **massage** at one of Anguilla's world-class spas or wellness centres.

SWIM with the **dolphins** at Anguilla's Dolphin Fantaseas. Call 497-7946.

TENNIS anyone? Get in a game at Anguilla's floodlit public courts located in The Valley. Call the Sports Officer at 497-5214 for more information.

UNLOCK the secrets of the past during a visit to the **dive wreck site** of the El Buen Consejo. Call Shoal Bay Scuba and Watersports at 497-4371.

VENTURE into The Valley on Saturdays to sample some of **Mabel's famous Corn Soup**. Or drop by the **People's Market** to buy fresh local produce.

WALK through the state-of-the-art plant at Anguilla Rums during their **Rum Factory Tours** and learn some of the secrets behind their award-winning master blends. Call 497-5006.

(X) EXAMINE the wonders of nature as magnificent **sea turtles** swim onto Anguilla's shores between April and November to nest their eggs on the beach.

YELL "Hard-lee!" as you take in Anguilla's National Sport, **boat racing**, on Easter Monday, Anguilla Day or during the Summer Festival celebrations.

ZZZZZ! Catch a few zees under a palm tree after a long wonderful day of exploring and discovering the many sides of Anguilla.

THE LAST VOYAGE

By Tara Douglas, age 15
First Place, Secondary School Competition, 1984

It was still dark outside when we left, but the low-hanging moon, glowed brightly in the sky. We patted our dog, Opiyelwaobirari (named after the Arawak Indian god of the underworld), good-bye and drove down to the harbour.

The whole world slept undisturbed in the silence that closed in around me. The slender shape of the 'Warspite' could be seen in the bay, proudly awaiting her last departure for awhile. Despite her age, she was a beautiful boat. She had been built by Anguillans out of wood in 1905 and had survived many threatening seas. She had been a symbol of Anguilla carrying its people to St Domingo and other islands for a long time. But today was to be her last journey to Sombrero Island to carry supplies to the lighthouse.

The sailors hoisted her battered, cream-coloured sails, but because there was not enough wind, the motor was used as well. I knew we were really on our way when we left the sheltered protection of the bay. For three hours we headed north-west, the humming of the motor causing the boat to vibrate as we crossed the thirty-six mile stretch of sea.

Dawn began to spread through the sky but it wasn't until we passed the two Prickley Pear Cays that the sun rose and swiftly climbed into the limitless sky and the full moon drifted out of sight. The sea grew rougher and the seventy-eight foot boat had to struggle through the rolling swells. In the far distance a huge, flat, grey rock sprung out of the sea. "Sombrero," I thought to myself.

We docked at 9 a.m. The 'Warspite' was tied to a ring in the rock and we clambered ashore. I had never seen such a remote, bleak place before. Indeed, it was just as I'd always imagined the very end of the world to be like. Sharp, treacherous, grey rock stretched as far as I could see, but that was all. White waves flung themselves at the island in desperation (I was told that barracudas, whales and sharks enjoyed an undisturbed existence in the sea), and the wind swept across the bare rock. Seagulls circled overhead scouring the three quarter mile long island for the crabs that scuttled across

the rock, their only companions being the fat lizards basking in the sun.

Four men, living in a white barrack-like building maintain the new lighthouse whose light travels nineteen miles from 6:00 p.m. until 6:00 a.m. to warn passing ships of the reefs awaiting them. The rest of the time they have free, however, to spend as they like, whether it's fishing, playing games, watching television, reading or just thinking. They work in six week shifts, returning home to the Anguilla that has melted away into the horizon.

There is no doubt that life on Sombrero is a struggle for survival; survival against the elements that have the whole island at their mercy. When hurricane 'Donna' visited in 1960, she left the old iron lighthouse in ruins; a skeleton to crumble away gradually. In such storms, waves flood the island, for there are no reefs to protect it.

Memories of phosphate mining that took place in the past are carved into the rock. Huge pits and caves are found throughout the island, but are silent and deserted. In some, saltwater has collected, eventually to evaporate, leaving salt crystals behind. We left at noon. The journey back was a smooth one and as we sailed into the harbour, the sinking sun turned the sea into liquid gold.

On arriving home again we were grief-stricken. Our dog, the very same dog that had been so full of energy only hours before, lay dead in front of our house, his chain twisted around a shrub. He had obviously died of heat stroke. Sorrowfully, we buried him. He had loved us as much as we had loved him and his life had ended so suddenly, so prematurely. He just wasn't ready to die.

The Warspite sat in the harbour for a couple of months waiting to be hauled out. But, unfortunately, she did not survive long enough. Hurricane "Klaus" passed by leaving a trail of destruction behind him. A modern freight ship smashed the Warspite's mooring chain and she was cast upon the beach, where she lies today - a pile of rubble. Both the Warspite and our dog had been victims of the elements.

Art in Anguilla

Courtney Devonish

Anguilla, with its luminous blue green waters and powder silk sands, is a Mecca for artists of all kinds. Galleries, artists' workshops and craft studios abound. An ever increasing number of galleries and studios (13 at last count) feature original paintings and prints, pottery, sculpture, quilts, dolls and lace work representing the creative work of scores of local, regional and international artists. A biennial arts festival, 'The Anguilla International Arts Festival', held every two years, also brings scores of international artists to the island. Others come to paint, draw and photograph Anguilla, its people and its serene waters and beaches. Additional artists come for workshops in painting and pottery regularly scheduled on the island.

Anguilla's beaches are among the most beautiful in the Caribbean, and the friendlessness of its people make it a welcoming and inspirational place for artists. Traditional chattel houses, sea grape and palm trees, local residents and aquamarine waters have all inspired painters, sculptors and potters alike. It is not rare to see visiting artists with pad in hand exploring the byways of the island.

The first artists in Anguilla were the Arawaks whose drawings are visible in local caves. Shards of their pottery have also been found throughout the island and are treasured by collectors.

Local artists, including Irenee Edwards, work in a delicate process called Hardanger as well as a few painters and wood carvers, who followed these

ABOVE: Cheddie's Carving Studio
LEFT: The Savannah Gallery is located in one of Anguilla's older wooden houses
BELOW: Beach-walkers become 'artists'

PHOTOS THIS PAGE: CHRIS MASON

PHOTO: CAROL LEE

traditions in later years. In addition, boat-making inspired the crafting of small boats skilfully produced to model the large and indigenous wooden sailing boats for which Anguilla is famous. These small wooden boat replicas are popular among the tourists looking for a piece of locally made craft.

Galleries and artist studios are located in every part of the island. Beginning in the West End, there is a complex of three galleries offering a range of art, sculpture, jewellery, paintings and prints, furniture and antiques. These include Anguilla's longest-established gallery, the Devonish Art Gallery. It is the showcase of internationally known sculptor and potter, Courtney Devonish. The gallery also features the work of Carrolle Devonish who creates one-of-kind bead jewellery, and local pottery, antique maps and paintings and prints. Collectors hold local artist, Cheddie Richardson's carvings in high esteem. His Driftwood Gallery features works in driftwood, wood and bronze as well as local art and furniture. The newly opened West End location of the World Art and Antiques Gallery houses art, furnishings and antiques from the Far East and Africa. Also within the West End circle is the workshop of fabric artist Beth Barry who produces cotton creations using fabrics from Senegal.

Heading east on the Main Road you will find Le Petite Gallerie in South Hill. The gallery features the colourful Caribbean themes in the artwork of Susan Graff. At the Rendezvous Bay Hotel, you will find a small gallery featuring local and Caribbean artists. On Back Street you will find 'Tiger Art', the workshop of Susan Croft, whose work is available in several locations throughout the island. At the Sandy Ground roundabout, you will find Bartlett's Collection, a shop featuring local arts, crafts and pottery. Going down the Sandy Ground hill you will find the studio of Lydia Semeria, a long-time artist on the island. Her art speaks of the island, the Caribbean region, its people and its

PHOTO: CAROL LEE

COURTNEY DEVONISH (Above)

Barbadian-born Courtney Devonish is well known internationally for his wood sculptures and his ceramics. He has exhibited throughout the Caribbean, the United States and Europe. In 1987, an assignment by the Canadian Training Awards enabled him to travel throughout the Caribbean training artists in clay. He settled in Anguilla and has the longest established art gallery on the island. He developed the Anguilla International Arts Festival and has worked to promote Anguilla as an arts destination.

Highly respected in the community, he continues to pursue his studio work while training apprentices, teaching and operating the Devonish Art Gallery with his wife, Carrolle, a bead artist. He was recently featured in the magazine AMERCAN STYLE in an article promoting the arts in Anguilla. Devonish aims to "create a thing of beauty" using simple and bold semi-abstract forms including the female form, birds and fish as sources of inspiration.

colours. Nearby, is the Pineapple Gallery featuring Haitian art, garden furniture, antiques and Caribbean art. On North Hill there are two art studios; L'Atelier Art Studio, featuring the oil and pastel paintings and prints of French artist Michele Lavalette, and The Palm Garden Art Studio, which houses the watercolour and acrylic paintings of local artist Michele Owen-Vasilis.

On George Hill, the new studio of Lynne Bernbaum offers original oil and water colour paintings and prints. She is especially known for her sepia tone paintings and prints. World Art & Antiques Gallery has a second home in The Valley. It also features art and antiques from the Far East and Africa.

If you follow the Crocus Hill Road, you will come to Rose Cottage, which houses the Loblolly Gallery. It represents the paintings and prints of local artists, pottery including tiles and hand crafted jewellery. In the neighbouring cottage, the Savannah Gallery features an extensive Haitian art collection, crafts as well as art from other Caribbean island artists.

At the top of Crocus Hill, you will find the Estate Hope Art Studio featuring the work of Quilter Carol Richardson. Richardson's quilts, pillow covers and wall hangings represent the culture of community-based quilt making in its traditional form. Her unique and creative quilting materials represent the cultural traditions of the Caribbean, Africa and the world. On the Sea Rocks, artist and writer Joanne Mason works in computer generated art. She has produced two popular Caribbean storybooks with art for children that have been popular with visitors.

The tranquil qualities of life in Anguilla have encouraged the growth and development of an artist community, which continues to grow. Anguilla features a peacefulness, which encourages art possibilities. The island has become a welcoming environment for artists in all mediums.

Paintings from Paradise

The spectrum of art in Anguilla is broad to the extent that it would be impossible to mention all who contribute in the many fields and media. However, paintings remain forever popular, capturing one moment in time, to treasure as a reminder of a visit, decorating a wall in a far off place or just existing as a visually pleasing work of the familiar. From highly professional to primitive, from expansive canvasses to small sketches there is a world of choice.

Lynn Birnbaum, a professional artist offers well thought-out, stylised, Caribbean scenes and topics including livestock. Local views and landscapes are favoured by Louise Brooks in a naively honest, colourful expression as with Melsadis Fleming, who also likes to represent traditional houses in her vibrant productions. Corine Connor, folk artist, holds the eye with his dedicated observance of native detail, each picture telling a story. Aileen Lamond, a professional painter in oils focuses on large scale portraiture and historic Architecture and Michelle Lavalette, also a professional painter, introduces a French impressionistic influence to her Caribbean scenes. Iris Lewis, a professional designer, lends her own particular slant to painting island subjects, often concentrating on details. Marge Morani, a pallet knife painter in acrylics, represents local scenes often including people in the composition. Paula Waldon is an experimental painter with a wide range of subject and media and Lydia Semeria paints with economy of design in her imaginative and vibrant content.

Other art work is found throughout Anguilla in galleries, small shops, and restaurants. It would be difficult not to find a piece to precisely suit individual taste. The choice is endless. The search totally absorbing.

Paintings by Louise Brooks, above and bottom right, and by Melsadis Fleming, below

Architecture in Anguilla

Iain K N Smith

Architecture in Anguilla can be compartmentalised into a few easily recognisable eras. Little if nothing remains of the prehistorical Arawak architectural era, apart from a couple interesting wooden models of a long house and a round house, giving us an idea of how they built and lived.

The first really recognisable era then becomes the early historical one. Interest in Anguilla began as early as 1609 but very little, if anything, remains of the earlier settlements. The most important of the remaining historical monuments form the basis of our knowledge of the architecture of that time. The majority of these buildings were constructed between the late 18th and early 19th centuries, and range from the small domestic dwelling to the imposing Wallblake House.

The designers and builders of the most humble to the most noble of these buildings took into consideration nearly all of the most significant storm protection ingredients. A properly structured and constructed timber building is one of the best types of buildings for both hurricane and earthquake zones. Anguilla is in both. The structure moves and flexes and when the wind abates the structure moves back into its original place. All of the older buildings, built from 1800, were constructed in this way and by using the strongest of hardwoods, such as lignum vitae and greenheart, with wallaby roof shingles from Guyana on the correct pitch of roof - forty degrees - ensured that these buildings remain for our visual enlightenment and all without the benefit of architects.

One of the most inspiring of these old contemporaries is Wallblake House. In a recent, significant restoration of Wallblake House much of the existing wooden structure was replaced and repainted in the original wall and shutter colours. But perhaps the most important aspect of the Wallblake development and its historical appeal, is not just the main house but the overall grouping of the buildings and their settings which form the complete development. The stables, the kitchen with its wonderful brick cooking place and internal

Unique religious architecture at St Gerard's Roman Catholic Church

An 'Aruban style' house

Rose Cottage, is a good example of a traditional Anguillian house

'Cerulean', an attractive private development, is popular with tourists

courtyard cistern catching all the rain water without down pipes. All of this exists exactly as it did when it was initially conceived and is what makes Wallblake so very important not just for Anguilla but for the whole region.

Some of the grandest architectural statements stem from religion playing a significant role in Anguillian society. Although it is not in the same time frame or era as previously mentioned, one of the most interesting and unusual examples of Anguillian religious architecture is St Gerard's, the little Roman Catholic church that stands in the grounds of Wallblake House.

There are a number of late 19th and early 20th century, splendid, robustly delicate examples of domestic architecture of these times throughout the island, among them, the "White House", owned by Sir Emile Gumbs, in Sandy Ground; the Koal Keel, previously known as the "Wardens Place" in Lower Valley; and across the road, Miss Marjorie Hodge's complex of two small houses of different times linked together with bread ovens and the old barrel vaulted cistern.

Two structures which cover the commercial and industrial buildings were a great influence on the Anguilla of the early period. At the north end of Sandy Ground, between the road and the salt pond stands a group of four buildings dating back to the early 1900s. This was the hub of the salt industry, an economic mainstay of the time.

The factory building, situated across from Wallblake House, was once the busiest centre of trade and commerce. It is not the most imposing of buildings but its place in the evolution of Anguillian society entitles it to a mention in architectural history. It was a general store, it sold postage stamps, it was the cotton ginnery, where the limited supply of cotton was weighed, seeds removed and shipped to England.

From the end of the plantation era to the beginning of tourism development, the island seems to have been in architectural limbo with little commercial, social or domestic progress.

In about 1945 droves of Anguillians, who had worked abroad, came home, bringing with them the architectural influences predominating in places where they had worked. A new kind of house began to dot the landscape, built of poured concrete walls and frequently gable ended with

'Koal Keel' is one of Anguilla's earlier houses

'The Factory' is scheduled for restoration and change of use

The White House

Typical old timber houses will be restored and repositioned

galvanised roofs. These became known as the "St Thomas house". It was not, however, for another ten years that the concrete block was introduced into Anguilla and in another style, the "Aruba House".

After tourism became a major economic influence in the 1980s, Anguilla became rapidly known as an up-market destination. Since then, the island has seen a continual increase of, not only elegant hotels but also of unique homes.

This development has, naturally, taken place on the coastline, with its views of the neighbouring islands. Finally, as the island progressed, local, commercial development took place. This can be seen in the expansion of the two indigenous banks, Caribbean Commercial Bank and the National Bank of Anguilla being two of the most prestigious buildings in The Valley.

It is natural that this pattern of development will continue in all fields of domestic, commercial and tourism expansion and it is hoped, to the same high standard, mostly seen today. This will ensure Anguilla continues to rank among the best places to live, work and relax.

National Bank of Anguilla

Historic Wallblake House

Built in 1787, Wallblake House is the oldest and only surviving plantation house in Anguilla. It is one of the few plantation houses in the Caribbean where the entire complex of buildings, including the kitchen, stable and workers' quarters, have survived virtually intact.

The exquisite home, built by William Blake, formed part of the ninety-seven acre sugar, and later cotton, plantation, which also included the Old Cotton Gin (now housing Ranny & Joe's Ice Cream Shop) and the area now used by Wallblake Airport. Many of the records of the plantation were kept in St Kitts and were, sadly, destroyed. So, the history of Wallblake House was recaptured mainly through word of mouth and sketchy details.

The house was left to the Catholic Church by Marie Rey Lake in 1959. No restoration efforts were undertaken until The

Wallblake Trust was established to lead the fundraising drive. Wallblake House, originally built by hand, was also painstakingly restored, detail by detail, by hand, as close as possible to what is known to be the original design and colour scheme. The original wood that formed the upper portion of the main house and the roofs was hardwood from Guyana (formerly British Guiana), and the restoration effort also used this material in replicating the design. The intricate patterns in the decorative wooden features throughout the main house are exquisite and great pains were taken to maintain the original beauty.

After seven years of labour-intensive craftsmanship amidst dedicated fundraising drives, Wallblake House now stands beautifully restored and available for community appreciation and use.

Village and Museum Project

In the previous chapter, the historic architecture of Anguilla was examined which includes a section describing the period of wood construction dating from the 19th century until the introduction of the concrete block to the island.

Unfortunately, this part of architectural history is disappearing at an alarming rate. Some of the larger and grander examples of this period remain well kept by families who have inhabited them for generations and who cherish their heritage, but sadly and for the greater part, the more humble dwellings, being too small and inadequate for modern lifestyles are falling into disrepair through neglect or hurricane damage.

However, they too reflect a way of life and are proud examples of local craftsmanship, their structure exhibiting unique and individual features such as decorative door and window frames, intricate fretwork (gingerbread) on balcony and roof trims and similar features on interior (ceilings) and as room divisions above door height allowing free flow of air from room to room.

Having been painfully aware of this ever-continuing loss, the Anguilla Archaeological and Historical Society has, over the past ten years, encouraged conservation of these properties in situ where possible. However, in the event of a house being torn down to be replaced by a modern building, and in an effort of recreate a living museum, the society has managed to save and store important architectural features and, in one case, the entire house itself was rescued - uplifted just as the builders had begun demolition.

At a site on Crocus Hill, the highest point on Anguilla, commanding a magnificent view, stands the ruin of the Old Court House. Permission was successfully sought by the Society from the Planning Board to erect a 'Historic Village' there, in which approximately nine examples of those houses, either rescued intact or reconstructed from saved

The Old Court House as it was

parts, would be situated on the land adjacent and across from the ruin. At a later date, it was proposed to endeavour to reconstruct the Old Court house ruins and incorporate it into the project as a 'national' museum instead of leaving it in its present decaying condition.

The ground floor of the Old Court House, which is constructed of thick stone walls, once contained the prison where prisoners of war from the French invasion of 1796 were massacred. These supported the walls of the upper floor, made of timber construction which housed the courts and was the main seat of administration up to the late 1950s.

The completion of this ambitious project has a long way to go, but with co-operation, guidance and careful monitoring, there is no reason why Anguilla should not record its own distinctive past in a visible and educationally interesting form. The Anguilla Archaeological and Historical Society is dedicated to this end with the support of the Anguilla National Trust, the Anguilla Tourist Board, the Anguilla Hotel and Tourism Department and Anguilla Maritime Research. **Aileen Smith and Ken Banks**

The ruins of the Old Court House / Iain K N Smith

Sport in Anguilla

Omari Banks

Whaldama 'Ras B' Brooks

While boat racing is perhaps the most widely enjoyed sport on the island, Anguillians also participate and support a diverse range other sports throughout the year.

CRICKET

As one of the smallest cricketing nations in the world, there is very little documentation on the sport locally, but as an island which has proudly waved the British flag for hundreds of years, cricket has long been a sporting activity here. The game has frequently been played in backyards, roadways, schoolyards and pastures. Although it was not until the late 1970s that Anguilla was formally integrated into the sub-regional fraternity of the Leeward Islands circuit, there had long been the trappings of organised cricket.

The exploits of the late pioneers Teacher Wenham, Teacher Uriel, Teacher Calvin, Collin Bynoe, Ashley Carty, Kenneth 'Richie Godfather' Richardson, along with more recent and current administrators and partners in the 'king of sports' - Alkins Rogers, Rodney Rey, Wycliffe Richardson, Ralph Hodge, Tommy Astaphan and Valentine Banks among others have lent in great measure to the survival of the sport in Anguilla.

Anguilla has turned out a number of first class cricketers over the years in the Caribbean and England. Such names as Eustace Proctor, Cardigan Connor, Lanville Harrigan, Alex Adams, Omari Banks and Chaka Hodge are among the international brotherhood of first class cricketers.

Allrounder Eustace Proctor distinguished himself as being the first Anguillian to play for the sub-regional side. That outing was Leewards under the captaincy of the great Viv Richards against Guyana at Bourda in the mid 1980s. Fast medium bowler Cardigan Connor's professional career was in England and Australia, and his company at Hampshire on the English County circuit included the celebrated likes of the late Malcolm Marshall, the fast bowling legend, and Gordon Greenidge, both of whom were integral to the glory days of the West Indies in the 1980s and early 1990s in particular. Lanville Harrigan will likely go down as one of the best opening batsmen not to have played international cricket for the West Indies. In his element, he has demonstrated in no uncertain terms that his explosive qualities could take any bowler to task. Alex Adams has proven himself as a consistent allrounder for the Leeward Islands, acquitting himself creditably with the bat in the opening position, being more than useful with his offspin, and a safe pair of hands anywhere in the field.

Anguilla's most recent first class players have been allrounders Omari

Chaka Hodge

Banks and Chaka Hodge, who are products of Cardigan Connor's nursery. Hodge toured England with a West Indies Under 15s squad at a world competition, and Banks was an integral part of the success of the West Indies Under Nineteens in their tour of England in 2001.

The island produced its first international cricketer in Omari Banks in 2003, turning out for the West Indies against the World Champions Australia for his first Test Match at the Kensington Oval (Barbados), dubbed the Mecca of Caribbean cricket. At the tender of age of twenty, Omari wasted no time showing the world he has the qualities that potentially great cricketers are made of - admirable temperament, sound technique, confidence, and composure. In only his second Test Match, Omari played pivotal roles with bat and ball in a world record West Indies performance against Australia at the ARG in Antigua. Set an improbable 418 in the fourth innings of the Fourth and Final Test, Omari, batting at number 8, scored a crucial 47 not out as he featured in decisive partnerships with Shivnarine Chanderpaul and Vasbert Drakes and immediately became the cricket darling of the Caribbean. His rise to a West Indies test player is a tremendous inspiration to the island's youngsters, and re-ignited local zeal for the sport.

Omari has made a profound impression on a number of regional and international observers with his forward looking attitude and serious work ethic. The 21-year-old is being widely viewed as a potentially world class allrounder. He has shown his worth in his still 'green' international career with his cool head and positive approach, and a prevailing consensus locally, regionally and internationally is that Omari appears to have a long and meaningful future in West Indies cricket.

Lanville Harrigan

ATHLETICS

Athletics has been gaining in prominence in Anguilla in recent years. Trevor Davis aka Ras Bucket carried the island's colours all over the world, pitting his skills against the very best in the world at global meetings in Europe, the United States, the Caribbean, and at home. Since his retirement, the discipline is being closely followed with some of the successful performers from the annual Primary Schools Athletics Competition and the Albena Lake-Hodge Comprehensive going on to participate in collegiate athletics in the United States, while simultaneously pursuing tertiary education. The likes of sprinter Timothy Brooks, Khalid Brooks, a multi-event athlete, middle distance runner Shyrone Hughes, and sprinter Desiree Cocks have all been beneficiaries of that programme.

FOOTBALL

Football as an organised sport in Anguilla can trace its roots, in part, to the British military invasion of the island in 1969. It was by simply watching the British soldiers and engineers play the sport that the then youngsters of Valentine Banks, Leslie Richardson, Freeman Gumbs, Ralph Hodge, and Roland Hodge, among others, quickly learned the sport.

In subsequent years, the Anguilla Football Association was formed, facilitating the island's entry into the sport's regional and international fraternity. Anguilla holds membership in the Caribbean Football Union, CONCACAF and the world's football governing body, FIFA. Local officials are aiming to take the sport to another level by upgrading infrastructure and technical assistance, thanks to facilities made available by FIFA.

Trevor Davis is Anguilla's leading athlete and represented his country at the 1997 World Athletics Championships in Greece

ABOVE: Cyclists from Anguilla and other Caribbean nations line up for the start of the 2003 John T. Memorial Cycle Race

CYCLING

Apart from being part of the traditional VSS/ALHCS annual Sports Day, cycling was predominantly restricted to a mode of transport and pastime. But the sport took off in the early 1970s following the efforts of the sports administration pioneer, the late Colin Bynoe. The sport gained further momentum in the early 1980s when sporting enthusiast, the late John Thomas, initiated competitions between local riders and those from St Maarten. Now, the Anguilla Amateur Cycling Association stages an annual showpiece event - the John T Memorial Cycle Race – which attracts participants from all over the Caribbean. Brothers Ronnie and Charles Bryan and Kris Pradell are the current local stars. They have also represented the island at the 2002 Commonwealth Games in Manchester, England. Cycling has, however, been sustained by such veterans as Evan Gumbs, Eldridge Richardson and Phillip Richardson.

VOLLEYBALL

Volleyball has surged in profile since the mid-1980s when organized male and female competitions were instituted. Names of such clubs and individuals as Hooters, Tornadoes, Gannynippers, Guerrillas, Potentials, Society Crush and Freebirds, and Orris Oroctor, Kenn Banks, Claudius Connor, Cameron Lloyd, Kathleen Rogers, Wilma Proctor, Khalida Banks, Valerie Hodge and Paulina Proctor, have rung bells in the ears of the sport's lovers. In recent years, the island's players have obtained more exposure by participating in the OECS Men's and Women's Volleyball Competitions.

BASKETBALL

Basketball generates a great deal of interest among Anguilla's youngsters, who see it as a lucrative career option. This feeling has been helped following the success of Tim Duncan, the US Virgin Islander of Anguillian parentage who currently plays with the United States NBA champions, San Antonio Spurs.

The local government, with assistance funds from the island's Social Security Board, has constructed courts in the various districts to facilitate and enhance the youngsters' interest. The general interest is apparently paying off as in the past two years, three Anguillians have won scholarships to play college basketball in the US and pursue a tertiary education degree. The three young beneficiaries are Randy Javois, Jason Hodge and Javille Brooks, all of whom were spotted by scouts from the Clinton Community College in Iowa.

The development of basketball in Anguilla owes a great deal to 'elder statesman' Emmanuel Webster, who has virtually fathered the sport and its players here.

GOLF

Golf is generally associated with upmarket tourism destinations such as Anguilla. However, it is only recently that the country has pursued the development of a state of the art facility. The construction of a well designed, 18-hole golf course will enhance the sport's profile and could represent a diversification of the sporting base and economy.

SWIMMING

Anguilla boasts some of the very finest beaches in the world with crystal clear waters, but no public swimming pools. Swimming is not yet an organized sport,

ABOVE: As in most of the other Caribbean nations, dominoes is a popular and keenly contested pastime
BELOW: National senior football club champions for 2003, Roaring Lions

ABOVE: Women's football has been growing in popularity
FROM TOP RIGHT: National football clubs 2003; The Attackers, Cool Runnings, Spartans International and Island Harbour

but remains a widespread pastime for the majority of the island's people. Gone are the days of the traditional St Maarten to Anguilla Race which attracted a wide following from both islands and beyond.

'SIT-DOWN' SPORTS

Dominoes is the most popular 'sit-down' sport in Anguilla, as it is throughout the Caribbean. It has long been a part of the goings-on at some of the bars and restaurants, as well as residential yards. But in recent years, organized competitions have been taking place locally, and two leading clubs - The Studio and Warriors - have been in the vanguard of such initiatives. In the case of The Studio, they have gone a step further by being regular participants in an international contest staged in Jamaica. Whist has become a popular card game, more so among older Anguillians, but the country has been represented in sub-regional and regional competitions.

PHOTOS THIS PAGE: CHRIS MASON

ABOVE: The eagerness to win is no less fierce in a game of draughts
LEFT: Softball is a relatively new sport in Anguilla

A NATIONAL HERO AND ICON

Nazma Muller

Question: Which cricketer's debut Test series was attended by almost half the people from his country, including those who took a ferry, specially run for the occasion, at 2am on a Sunday morning, arriving in Antigua just in time for the match; who then got back on the ferry after the match, to arrive home just in time to get ready for work?

Answer: Omari Banks. And, yes, what seemed like almost half of Anguilla flew or took the ferry to Antigua to see him play. And they didn't regret it, because two days later, Tuesday, May 13, the whole of the West Indies experienced an explosion of pure, unadulterated joy. By 11 o'clock that morning, throughout the Caribbean - from Anguilla to Guyana - eyes were peeled to TVs, ears cocked to radios, as their flannelled knights performed a miracle.

Chasing a fourth innings total of 418, the West Indies were 372-7, with the last of the middle-order batsmen out. It was left to veteran Vaspert Drakes and the 20-year-old Anguillian to carry on fighting. The prize: world record history.

Intrigued by the cool confidence of the unknown youth from the tiny island, I took a flight to Anguilla to meet him.

Bankie Banx is lounging on a striped couch, his grey dreadlocks framed against St Maarten's mountains, just five miles away. A Rasta king in his castle, Bankie, father of the princely Omari, is holding court on the deck of the Dune Preserve, a whimsical, sprawling beach bar he designed and built himself out of boats, timber and driftwood – and rebuilt three times. Each time the Dune's has been hit by a hurricane, Bankie gathered what was left and rebuilt it.

We're standing on the main deck, looking across the white sand and gently rippling waves, when a Marleyesque voice comes on, the melody an engaging mix of reggae and country western. It's Bankie's. It turns out he has nine albums to his name. Back in the late '70s and '80s, he was hailed as the Black Bob Dylan in indie circles, his lyrics a potent combination of Black Power, spiritualism and humour.

Eleven years ago, after touring and living in Europe and the United States, Bankie returned to Anguilla to build the Dune Preserve in memory of his mother. From its decks, you can see the whole of Rendezvous Bay, the turquoise waters of the Caribbean Sea rolling gently over Anguilla's double reef system and onto the softest, whitest, most brochure-perfect sand. This is Omari's stomping ground. Some nights, he can be found here, jamming on his electric guitar with Bankie and his 14-year-old sister, Tahirah, who plays the keyboards and drums.

I've found the dreamer side of Omari Banks. His father has been living his dream since he made his own guitar from plywood and copper wire at the age of nine. The youngest of Marjorie Banks's six children, Bankie is the rebel. His brother, Val, Omari's mentor and first cricket coach, is now the CEO of the National Bank of Anguilla, and vice president of the West Indies Cricket Board. Another brother, Victor, is the Minister of Finance. His sister, Linda, is a clinical psychologist.

"I grew up in the Anguilla Revolution," Bankie says, by way of explanation for his alternative career path. "I grew up with all the good stuff in the Caribbean: Walter Rodney, Rasta, Bob Marley, Jimmy Cliff, Che Guevara, Fidel Castro, Malcolm X, all that good stuff … rock 'n' roll, Jimi Hendrix, Bob Dylan."

He heard it all, from the radio station on the British frigate that had invaded the island in 1969 after the revolution. But, unlike other Caribbean bands at the time, he soon tired of playing calypso, reggae and soul, and started his own band, Roots and Herbs. These were the days of Rasta persecution, when the dreadlocked were targeted for their ganja smoking.

Thirty years later, Bankie's still got the aura of the outcast about him. But he's happy; he's back home, in his paradise in the sun. When I ask Omari how he keeps so cool in the crease, he replies: "My dad says it's a combination of confidence in yourself and just wanting to be the best that you can be, and cricket was the original truth." The original

Omari's father, Bankie Banks / Photo: Ivor Hodge

Omari's mother, Donna Banks

truth? What an intriguing expression. It makes sense though, when I meet Donna, his mother.

A tall, attractive woman with a shoe fetish and an evangelical fervour, she trundles around in a jeep, from the Chief Minister's office, where she is Special Assistant for Tourism, to classes in the evening where she teaches accounting with the University of the West Indies (UWI) Distance Learning programme. After that, she begins the hunt for Tahirah, who, like Omari, is close to her 21-odd cousins. "It was always my challenge to find which cousin's house he was at, and then go and get him."

Donna has been in the business of tourism for 22 years - from 1981 to 1992 she was director at the Anguilla Tourist Board. After majoring in accounting at the Cave Hill campus of UWI, she did a Masters in travel administration and tourism in Washington DC.

This is the pragmatic powerhouse behind Omari, an anchor of Christian beliefs who gave him a name that means "the highest", and a second, Ahmed, which means praiseworthy. And she made sure he took time off from his cricket obsession to go to church on Sundays. "A lot of that has to do with the demeanour that is displayed on the field," she says, "because he really understands who God is and what God does for you and what he can do for you."

This tiny island had the foresight to carve a niche in upmarket tourism in the 1980s. "Quality tourism", they call it. They didn't want hundreds of backpackers trampling the reefs and putting pressure on their hard-pressed water system.

Everyone I talk to is helpful and friendly, and they each have their own Omari story. From the elderly taxi driver to the waitress at the Anguilla Great House, to teacher Daphne, his music teacher, they all say the same thing: "the boy was driven".

Cardigan Connor, a former professional cricketer, coached Omari throughout his teens. "At the age of nine, he wanted to play for the West Indies," Connor recalls, "and it wasn't just a pipe dream. Most kids might say they want to be a doctor or a lawyer, but they don't really know what it

means. With Omari, he didn't just say it, he wanted it. And he worked at it."

For Anguillians, Omari's fulfilment of his dream to play for the West Indies is both validation and inspiration: the world now knows about their island because of him, and, if the dozens of little boys (and Tahirah) practising in The Park in the afternoons are anything to go by, he won't be the last Anguillian to play for the West Indies.

Passion on the High Seas

David Carty

Cricket is the national sport of the English-speaking Caribbean. Anguilla is an English-speaking Caribbean island, yet boat racing is Anguilla's national sport. This may seem contradictory and of minor importance to our subject, but it is a telling pointer not only to Anguilla's uniqueness but also to the fact that this national obsession is an expression of a tiny culture's roots in a particularly important maritime past.

Prior to 1967, Anguilla was a backwater in Caribbean society. Because of its geography and topography the frequency of drought, aridity of its soil and the social and economic destruction caused by colonial wars in the eighteenth century, Anguillians could barely eke out a living from meagre plantations. In most other Caribbean societies plantations were the foundation of social and economic life. This was not the case in Anguilla. Because of this and the truism that "necessity is the mother of invention" Anguillians became mariners by force of circumstance.

Ships and the sea were the only ways in which a tiny society could survive. The small salt industry and the fortuitous association with Nova Scotian schooner fleets which came to the island during the late nineteenth and earlier twentieth centuries in order to buy salt for the salt fish industry, enabled Anguillians to learn and hone their skills in all the arts of ship building and boat building. Schooners, sloops and small craft of all shapes and sizes slid off the azure beaches during the heyday of the age of sail and gave the island a reputation for excellence in all the maritime arts. These vessels traded up and down the length of the Eastern Caribbean carrying anything from salt, livestock, dry goods, and whatever else needed to be transported from island to island. They also carried migrating labourers westward to the cane fields of the Dominican Republic and even to Cuba.

The schooner 'Warspite' was one of the finest examples of Anguillian craftsmanship at that time. Sleek, fast and legendary in the lore of sailing voyages across the Caribbean Sea, the 'Warspite' has been documented by American naval architects as having achieved hull speeds to rival the famous Nova Scotian schooner 'Blue Nose' considered to have been one of the fastest schooners ever built. Tragically, the 'Warspite' was lost in 1985 during Hurricane Klaus. The frequency of Anguillian vessels travelling in convoy to the Dominican Republic and the resultant competition between them were to become the seeds of the sport of boat racing which blossomed from 1940 to the present day (For more information on this, read the book "Nuttin Baffling").

In addition and in tandem with the schooner trade, Anguillians built small craft ranging in size from 18 to 27 feet. These boats, rigged with a simple Bermuda rig were used primarily during daylight hours for fishing. But because

PHOTO: CHRIS MASON

PHOTO: DEAN BARNES

PHOTO: DEAN BARNES

of an erroneous tax on alcohol and spirits imposed by the colonial government during the 1930s, these fishing vessels became smuggling boats at night. Smuggling became a rampant trade with St Maarten and St Barths which had no such tariffs on spirits, and these small craft became the immediate ancestors of the Anguilla racing boats.

Today, Anguillian boat racing is a living expression of Anguilla's maritime culture and tradition. The boat and the race are unique in every way. True to their historic design, which goes back to the 17th century, the boats carry no decks. All ballast is internal meaning that it is not fixed to the hull but is placed into the hull in the form of lead ingots, iron bars and sand. With this type of ballast and with no decks the racing boat has little buoyancy insurance and can be sunk in a flash if captains and crews are not constantly careful and alert. Unlike most modern yacht races and grounded in the schooner trade to the Dominican Republic the race is always a two point race.

All boats run off the wind from a starting point which is usually on the beach, then round a buoy placed at a fixed point downwind and then beat back to a buoy at the beach of departure. During the up wind leg of the race, boats that converge on each other when on opposing tacks have no right of way. To avert an inevitable collision both crews must shout, "Hard lee, hard lee" at each other and tack away before they become the object of salvage, driftwood and flotsam. Boats can carry crews of between ten and 18 men, most of whom serve as moveable ballast, moving from side to side according to which tack the boats are on.

Although modern materials and some technological advances have been introduced, the Anguilla racing boat still remains basically true to its historic tradition. It is an uncomfortable, dangerous and difficult boat to sail. But despite all this, it remains the object of keen competition between villages and fans and the beloved and hilarious talking (or arguing) point between boat racing enthusiasts. In many respects it is genuine expression of Anguilla's island culture. The first week in August is the highpoint of the boat racing season with five races held at different points on the island. Other important boat race days are Easter Monday and Anguilla Day which falls on the 30 of May.

PHOTO: CHRIS MASON

PHOTO: DEAN BARNES

PHOTO: CHRIS MASON

ANGUILLA – TRANQUILLITY WRAPPED IN BLUE

ANGUILLA – TRANQUILLITY WRAPPED IN BLUE

ANGUILLA – TRANQUILLITY WRAPPED IN BLUE

Everyone for Tennis

Brenda Carty

In 1995, a young Anguillian, Mitchelle Lake, started a Tennis Camp for children during the summer holidays. He had a tennis scholarship and was a student at Gardner-Webb University in the United States where he studied mathematics. His aim was to encourage other Anguillians to enjoy the game of tennis and have similar opportunities to study through tennis. He has continued each year and expanded and formed the Anguilla Tennis Academy (ATA) that now includes up to twelve coaches from the US and more than 150 children.

The ATA has grown so much that a state-of -the-art facility is now being built at Blowing Point. There will be six floodlit tennis courts and a stadium court to seat one thousand spectators. This will enable Anguilla to host regional matches and attract international tennis stars for exhibition matches. The facility has a main building with a conference room, pro tennis shop, showers, lounge and other facilities. It has been designed by Myron Goldfinger of New York, and funding is through donations from businesses in Anguilla and overseas. Individual donations through the purchase of inscribed bricks are being used to pave the entrance to the facility and will serve as a reminder to the children of the people who helped pave the way for their future development.

Mitchelle Lake says that after completion the project will provide opportunities for young children through the sport of tennis while strengthening the sense of community, knowledge and health, and at the same time promoting sport tourism. He said that there will be regular tennis lessons for children and adults, and coaches from the US will be employed. Further information can be obtained from www.tennis.ai

Participants of the annual summer Tennis Academy

Proposed design for the Anguilla Tennis Academy

The public signing of the Memorandum of Agreement for the six acres of land given by the Anguilla Government for the Tennis Academy. Pictured, from left to right, are the Hon. Victor Banks, Minister of Finance, Mitch Lake, Hon Eric Reid, Minister of Sport, Academy Board Members Leslie Richardson and Brent Davis, and Mark Capes, Deputy Governor of Anguilla.

An Under-Sea World of Beauty and Adventure

Michel Faligant

Anguilla is already well known for its mile long white sandy beaches, the unforgettable friendliness of its people and its tranquillity. It is also known as the wreck capital of the Caribbean.

Nine wrecks were intentionally sunk from 1982 to 1993 by the Anguilla Government in order to create artificial reefs for the enjoyment of scuba divers. These wrecks, which comprise of freighters from 110 to 230 feet long, resting at depths ranging from 40 to 100 feet, are habitats for a wide variety of coral. Even after relatively few years, these artificial reefs have an abundance of marine life including many schools of fish, barracuda, margate, snapper, grunt, angelfish, turtle, lobster, rays and shark.

Anguilla benefits from a double reef system; one system is situated along its littoral and the second one ranges from the east of the island (Island Harbour) to Prickly Pear and Dog Island. The first reef is rich in soft corals such as gorgonians, with their bouquets reaching 15 to 20 feet; sea fans and sea wipes that create an underwater ballet of spectacular colours. The outer reef is covered with a wide variety of hard corals such as giant brain, pencil, flower, elkhorn, starkhorn and plaque.

Sea currents at the various dive sites range from minimal to none at all. The sites are considered to be shallow dives, with the deepest site at The Steps off Scrub Island which reaches a depth of 120 feet. These types of site make Anguilla a safe place to dive, to discover or learn to scuba dive. Three dive operators provide everything for the experienced diver as well as for beginners.

ANGUILLA – TRANQUILLITY WRAPPED IN BLUE

BIODIVERSITY WRAPPED IN BLUE

Karim Hodge

Located at the junction of the north-eastern corner of the Caribbean Sea, where it merges with the Atlantic Ocean, Anguilla is a low-lying, small, limestone island in the Eastern Caribbean. It is shrouded in dry woodland scrub forest and surrounded by several offshore cays. The biodiversity of the island itself and some of the cays is unique and is fragile as well as complex.

The structure of the environment and ecological communities on Anguilla is seldom simple. The island's topography is unique when compared with most other Antillean islands. It is low-lying and dry, with a maximum elevation of about 65 metres. The porous karstic limestone (weathered coral) structure allows water to seep through rather than accumulate on the surface. All surface waters are invariably saline. Freshwater is found in a narrow layer of subterranean water and floats on the deeper salt water, which continuously permeates the island's core. This combination of surface features is responsible for the arid environment to which the native vegetation has adapted.

Remnants of the native drought resistant forest still exist in Katouche Valley, in areas of Brimigen and the proposed Fountain Cavern National Park near Shoal Bay East. The forests are hardy and able to withstand the long dry season and harsh ravages of intense hurricane activity. However, Anguilla has a rather unique problem: goats! These introduced herbivores consume anything green within their reach, consequently most of the island is covered in scrub-like forest. Despite this 'hostile' environment, Anguilla boasts an extraordinary list of over 500 plants.

Maps produced in the fifteenth century, warned unwary visitors of unusual forests and strange creatures that inhabited these islands. They wrote of the remarkable marine life in the 'New World', the abundance of giant lizards (*Iguanas*) with their whip-like tails and sharp claws, and of "ancient mariners" (sea turtles). These documents encouraged the colonisation of the West Indies and fostered a distinctive group of sea-hardened people whose nautical skills became known throughout the world. The archipelago boasts a list of twenty-one species of reptiles and amphibians, which includes critically endangered species of sea turtles and two species of ground lizard.

Anguilla has one of the most important unbroken coral reef chains in the north-eastern Caribbean. And its coastal and marine biodiversity is the island's most important natural asset. During the past seven years, a ban has been enforced on turtle fishing, and conservation programmes have been introduced to ensure the survival of the local sea turtle population. Five areas of the island's marine environment have been set aside for special protection as Marine Parks. These areas represent important varieties of marine ecosystems, from sea grass beds to coral reefs. Many varieties of parrotfish inhabit these reefs and the sight of 'ancient mariners' never fails to impress local fishermen and scuba divers. Anguilla's many sunken wrecks also serve as a home for all types of marine life. Today, the native marine and terrestrial species are vital to the development and sustainability of the island's ecosystems. This variety of terrestrial and aquatic species reflect the evolutionary history of the archipelago and provide some insights into the formation of the island itself, the ecosystems that existed before humans arrived, and the unique and complex ecological communities existing today.

On land, Anguilla is home to 136 species of birds, a large percentage of which migrate from as far north as Hudson Bay in Canada. They follow routes that have been travelled for thousands of years to feed in Anguilla's rich wetlands at East End, Cauls and Sandy Ground Pond. It is not uncommon to see young white-cheeked pintail ducks with their broods of ducklings on the pond, young black-necked stilts covered in fur, coots, moorhens, snowy egrets, varieties of heron such as green, tri-coloured, great blue and the black and yellow crowned night herons, and on the off-shore locations of Dog Island, Prickly Pear Island, Scrub Island and Sombrero Island, to see the mass breeding and nesting grounds of the magnificent frigate birds and the masked and brown booby colonies.

The myriad of life forms depend on each other. For example, most plants depend on birds and iguanas for seed dispersal while insects contribute to pollination. The natural environment of the island is also a rich national heritage which carries great responsibility. In order to conserve and protect this unique tropical landscape, policies of sustainable development are being actively pursued while Anguilla engages fully in regional and international co-operation on environmental protection. The key to continued conservation is through education, both at home and abroad, through development programmes, and the further encouragement of eco-tourism.

Anguilla in Bloom

Brenda Carty

ABOVE: Dill flower
BELOW: Mangoes
OPPOSITE: Bougainvillea

PHOTOS: CHRIS MASON

Anguilla's natural landscape is low scrubland but there are some attractive tropical trees, shrubs and flowers that have been planted over the years.

One of the most prolific shrubs is the oleander which grows to about five feet or more if it is not pruned. The flowers which can be seen all the year round are various shades of pink, peach and white and grow in clusters at the end of the branches. It flourishes in many gardens and borders because it is poisonous to goats and it adapts well to dry conditions. There is a dwarf variety that is seen in the landscaping at several businesses and hotels.

The bougainvillea grows very well too and is one of the most colourful ornamental vines. It flowers throughout the year and has pink, red, white or orange flowers. It climbs on walls and fences with its sharp thorns attaching to the wall easily. It can also be trimmed to form interesting shapes.

The hibiscus is another shrub that grows well in the island. It is used to form hedges and there is an attractive one at Wallblake Airport. There are several hybrid varieties of hibiscus but the common red one is mostly seen here.
The most common indigenous trees on the island are the cedar and the loblolly. The cedar grows along many of the roadsides and in April/May has delicate pink or white flowers. It reaches heights of fifteen to twenty feet and can be pruned to fit in with the landscaping of gardens.

The flamboyant or poinciana is very striking when in flower with bright red flowers and feathery leaves. There are long brown pods containing the seeds that stay on the tree for a long time and can be seen easily when the leaves fall off in the dry weather.

The frangipani is a small tree that grows wild in the eastern end of the island, these bear white flowers although the cultivated ones have red flowers.

The tall mahogany trees that border the Coronation Avenue were planted to commemorate the coronation of George VI in 1937. They make a splendid avenue and at Christmas time the trunks are decorated with thousands of tiny lights. Another tall tree is the tamarind tree that grows up to 70 feet in height. It bears pods that have seeds inside with a sticky brown pulp that is not very sweet but still enjoyed by many. The pulp can be removed and mixed with sugar to make tamarind balls or can be made into a drink.

The ficus Benjamina tree grows well in Anguilla as can be seen on the Queen Elizabeth Avenue. The neem tree was introduced here in the 1950s because it is drought resistant and grows quickly. It grows up to thirty feet and has light green leaves divided into many leaflets. The white flowers have a pleasant scent.

The sea grape grows well along the coastal areas but some also thrive inland. It provides shade on some of the beaches and produces bunches of

ANGUILLA – TRANQUILLITY WRAPPED IN BLUE

PHOTO: JACQUELINE CESTERO

PHOTOS THIS PAGE UNLESS OTHERWISE STATED: CHRIS MASON

MAIN PICTURE: Turpentine tree
ABOVE FROM TOP: Bull; Pope cactus/
Turks head cactus?; Seed pod of the
locally-known 'Headache bush'

grapes that turn purple when ripe. They are much sought after by children who enjoy picking and eating them.

Because of the lack of plentiful rain, fruit trees are not as prolific as in other Caribbean islands. The pawpaw (papaya) tree grows very well, especially in sandy soil. Citrus trees, especially lime, are also grown and some gardens have banana or mango. The "mango garden" near to Sandy Hill has many mango trees that produce a small sweet mango. Local fruits such as genip, sugar apple, soursop, sapodilla and pommeserette are indigenous to Anguilla and produce popular fruits though there are not many to be found unless there is rain.

Anguilla's wildlife is limited to birds, iguanas, lizards, frogs, tortoises and snakes. The visitor will see many roaming goats and sheep but these belong to people who let them roam in order to get food.

Reportedly, some fifty years ago there were many iguanas on the island but recently, because of the habitat being destroyed, they are far less in number. There are two species that can still be seen in Anguilla - the Lesser Antillean Iguana, which is found in the north coast area between Little Bay and Brimigen, and the Green Iguana which is found in West End and in the area between Island Harbour and East End.

ANGUILLA – TRANQUILLITY WRAPPED IN BLUE

Ground lizards are common throughout the island and some grow to about six or eight inches in length. In the months from January to March when the days are shorter they mostly stay in their holes, otherwise they are visible during the daytime. There is a ground lizard that is only found at Little Scrub and another species that is only found at Sombrero. There are also tree lizards that live in trees, fences, walls and shrubs. The gecko or woodslave is found mostly in homes and buildings where they climb on walls, especially where there are lights, and catch insects.

Two types of frogs can be seen on the island - the whistling frog and the Cuban tree frog. They like well-watered areas and hide in trees and plants. The Cuban tree frog became a problem a few years ago when they became more prolific and started to get into cisterns. However, people have wired the down-pipes to the cisterns to keep them out.

Wild tortoises can sometimes be seen in the scrubland and they may wander out to homes. They grow to about 18 inches in length. The Anguilla bank racer is a non-poisonous snake that is fairly common in the bush land but not often seen around homes. There are centipedes and scorpions but visitors will hardly see these unless walking in remote areas.

ABOVE: Pride of Barbados
BELOW: Anole lizard

Rose berry tree

ANGUILLA – TRANQUILLITY WRAPPED IN BLUE

PHOTO: CHRIS MASON

Mango tree and, below, the only remaining donkey in Anguilla

CLIMATE AND WEATHER

Anguilla's climate can be described as almost perfect, it is a tropical climate with average temperatures between 80 and 85 degrees (27-30C) in the day and a little lower at night, with the north-east trade winds providing a cool breeze for most of the year. The hottest months are August, September and October but even at that time there is usually a breeze. The average rainfall over the past ten years is 36 inches per year and there is no rainy season although the months of May, November and December often have more rain.

The hurricane season is officially from June to November, however, August, September and October are the months when hurricanes more often occur. For thirty five years from 1960 until 1995 there were no hurricanes on the island. Hurricane Luis in 1995 caused severe damage to homes, boats, communications and agriculture. In 1999, for the first time, Anguilla suffered flooding, especially in The Valley and East End as a result of 19 inches of rain from Hurricane Lenny.

Residents are now very aware of the need for protection, they listen to the weather channel for details of approaching storms, and homes, businesses and hotels all have hurricane shutters that can be erected reasonably quickly. **Brenda Carty**

Cedar flower

Bougainvillea

Pink cedar

Pride of Barbados

Pink hibiscus

Red Chinese hibiscus

Wild bush flower

Oleander

Desert rose

Purslane

Oleander flower

Periwinkle

ANGUILLA – TRANQUILLITY WRAPPED IN BLUE

Pomegranate blossom

Bougainvillea

Lantana flower

Sea bean blossom

Oleander

Oleander

Anguilla island orchid

Wild bush flower

Amaryllis

Orchid

Oleander

Dendribium

Flamboyant flower

Wild flower

Dwarf poinciana

Night lily

Tamarind tree blossom

Passion fruit flower

Cordia

Mauby bush

Spider lily

Worry wine flowers

'Headache bush' blossom

Frangipani flower

Birds of Anguilla

Sir Emile Gumbs

Anguilla, with its out islands of Sombrero, Dog Island, Scrub Island, Prickly Pear and Anguillita is only 35 square miles. Yet even to the casual observer it has a wide variety of bird life. The sandy bays, low cliffs, rocky shoreline and a score of salt ponds make this coral island a natural habitat for marine and aquatic birds. The absence of mongooses and monkeys is a boon to the arboreal and terrestrial birds.

The most common bird on Anguilla is the zenaida or turtle dove. Formerly hunted as a delicacy, it is now protected since voted the National Bird of Anguilla in 1993. This brown bird with the red legs of the pigeon family, with white on wing and fringe of tail, can now be seen all over the island in open spaces, on road sides, telephone wires and recently in back yards. The resonant cooing is a beautiful sound. The smaller ground dove is similar but much less common.

The very small Antillean bullfinch, with black males and green females, are berry and seed eaters, as is the related tiny black-faced grassquit commonly seen in garden and grassy areas, or scrounging scraps from veranda tables.

The black and yellow breasted bananaquit, and the two indigenous hummingbirds - the tiny emerald crested, with sharp straight bill, and the larger green-throated Carib, with the long decurved bill - because of their dependency on nectar, are commonly seen in gardens and woodland areas probing flowers with their long tongues.

The bold pearly-eyed thrasher, drab brown with whitish markings on the breast and white circle around the eye, has a most remarkable number of voice variations including querulous whistles, squawks and a growl like that of a cat which has caught a mouse - hence its local name "catbird". It is almost omnivorous, eating anything from fruit and berries, table scraps, lizards, baby birds, and eggs, to insects including centipedes.

The grey kingbird, or chinchary, can be seen perched on telephone wires. They are white below with grey upper parts and wings, and black pointed bills. They are very aggressive and territorial when nesting, and will attack any living creature venturing too near to their nests, including cats, dogs and even a passing peregrine falcon. The only other native flycatcher is the tiny shy olive green Caribbean elaenia, or 'weave', which also eats small berries and soft seeds.

Several other members of the hawk/falcon family winter here, but no nesting has ever been recorded. The most frequent visitor is the peregrine falcon or "duck hawk" which roosts on rocky cliffs or very tall trees. Often seen flying over Road Pond, the sight of this large falcon appearing out of the western sky, like a jet aeroplane, to strike down a duck in full flight and returning in a tight circle to grasp its prey is a never-to-be-forgotten experience. Much to the delight of bird watchers, the courtship ritual of these birds is quite a display

PHOTOS THIS PAGE: CHRIS MASON

FROM TOP: The shy and elusive night heron; Turtle dove, Anguilla's national bird; The Caribbean coot

of aerial acrobatics. The slate-coloured Merlin and broad-winged red-tailed hawk are the most common of the other visitors. The only other native member of the hawk family is the American kestrel, or "killy killy", a small reddish but multi-coloured falcon. With extremely good eyesight, they hover while searching for food - mostly lizards, mice and insects.

Hundreds of lesser yellowlegs winter here, together with many other waders, including plovers, sandpipers, snipes, willets, dowitchers, wimbrels and ruddy turnstones. Some nest here and stay year-round. Two night herons are resident, and they are easily identified by their stocky bodies, large heads and long heavy bills which enable them to feed on the largest of crabs on Anguilla. They also lurk around buildings searching for insects, including cockroaches and centipedes. They are nocturnal but are sometimes visible on dark rainy days.

The great blue heron and great white egret now visit in increasing numbers in the winter. Mangrove cuckoos also visit and sometimes nest. After a flood in November 1974, Anguilla experienced a plague of brown caterpillars that threatened all the leaves of the flamboyant trees until thousands of mangrove cuckoos arrived, gobbled up all the caterpillars and then disappeared about two weeks later. White cattle egrets arrived in Anguilla in the late 1960s and can now be seen all over the island, mainly among cattle and in open grassy areas.

With its varied coastline and outlying islands, Anguilla is home to an amazing number of birds roaming the seas. Some return at night while laughing gulls often sleep closely bunched together on the surface of the sea. Laughing gulls congregate in Road Pond between May and June for their annual mating ritual, their raucous laughter sounding as though they are telling dirty jokes all night. The black magnificent frigate, or "man-o-war', and the boobies are unique in that they are the only known seabirds that nest all year round - mainly on Dog Island and Sombrero. The female frigate is easily recognizable by a large white breast patch while the male is all black except for a red pouch, which is only visible during courtship. Also unusual is that the female is the provider, while the male sits on the eggs. This also protects the bare-skinned hatchlings from the sun until they are feathered. These birds are the pirates of the sea, robbing other seabirds of their catch, following large fish in the hope of picking up scraps from their kill or circling over areas where fishermen clean their catch. With their seven-foot wing span they cannot lift off from the water so they have to capture all their food on the wing. The brown and blue-faced boobies feed on flying fish and squid, often taking them on the wing, or power-diving into the sea, surfacing up to 30 feet away.

Its large size-foot wingspan and its foot-long bill easily identifies the brown pelican. They dive for baitfish from a height; on impact the lower flexible mandible

PHOTOS THIS PAGE: CHRIS MASON

CLOCKWISE FROM ABOVE: White-cheeked pintail teal; great egret; black-necked stilt; mangrove cuckoo; snowy egret

ANGUILLA – TRANQUILLITY WRAPPED IN BLUE

PHOTO: CHRIS MASON

opens to trap its catch inside the large pouch. Upon surfacing, the head is drawn up to drain the water from the pouch. Sometimes the very light laughing gull will alight on the pelican's head, attempting to steal some of its catch. Pelicans nest in the trees near to Little Bay and Crocus Bay, but mainly on Dog Island.

Many species of terns roam the ocean around Anguilla some roosting nightly on the outlying islands, but in May and June they descend in thousands upon the out islands to nest. It is an incredible sight and many years ago, when collecting eggs, it was advisable to wear very wide-brimmed straw hats to protect ones head and shoulders from droppings. Terns, including the royal, bridled, common roseate, least tern and sandwich tern are mostly white with black on the wing tips and head. Exceptions are the brown noddy, which is very dark brown with a white cap, and sooty tern with white crown, black upper parts all the way from neck to tail and white under parts.

PHOTO: CHRIS MASON

The ponds in Anguilla are home to a wide variety of birds that are more visible than ever, since they are no longer hunted. One can now drive around the Road, East End and West End Ponds and observe the white-cheek pintail teal, easily identified from afar by the gleaming white cheeks, the black gallinaceous moorhen, with the bright red frontal shield, the red-legged or black-necked stilt with its incredibly red legs, immaculate white under parts and black upper parts and wings and the pure white snowy egret with its black legs and bright yellow toes. Some yellow warblers are native and nest here, including the cape may warbler. Other warblers are only spring visitors.

Undoubtedly, Anguilla's most beautiful bird is the red-billed tropicbird, with its immaculate white under parts, jet black eye stripe and wing tips, barred black and white upper parts and wings, two very long white tail feathers and a post office red bill. They nest in holes in cliffs and rocks on Anguilla and all of the out islands.

PHOTO: PENNY SLINGER

MAIN PICTURE: The brown pelican
ABOVE: Laughing gulls on Scilly Cay; and brown boobies on Dog Island

Experience of a Lifetime

Amber Olson-Pape

Most people come to Anguilla to explore its dazzling beaches and escape the everyday hustle. Meads Bay is known for its outstanding white sand beach, ideal for sunbathing and swimming. This beach is also home to Dolphin Fantaseas, one of Anguilla's most exciting activities. Dolphin Fantaseas offers guests the rare experience of interacting with dolphins, giving people the opportunity to gain an understanding of these fascinating mammals while inspiring individuals to obtain an appreciation for marine life and the environment in which they live.

At Dolphin Fantaseas guests experience a marine paradise and discover the thrill of up close and personal playtime with dolphins and stingrays. If you have ever dreamt of swimming with dolphins, this will be your chance to bring your dream to life by enjoying an experience that is exciting, unique and amazing.

Dolphin Fantaseas has a variety of activities, ranging from feeding one of the many stingrays in the stingray pool, talking with the resident parrots, and, of course, swimming with the dolphins. A key part of a visit to Dolphin Fantaseas is educating guests about the importance of preserving and protecting the oceanic life, which is accomplished through the interactive programs as well as the staff educating guests during their encounter.

PHOTO: CAROL LEE

THE TALE OF THE ANGUILLA LONG DOG

What in the world is an Anguilla Long Dog? All over Anguilla, especially in the eastern end of the island, these unusual dogs can be spotted in many backyards. A variety of colours, even spotted, some with long hair, some with short and some with a combination of both but they all have one thing in common . . . they are long! Ask around and you will get many tales as to how this particular dog came to be on a Caribbean island, but Anguillians like this one the best.

Long ago, on a clear blue Caribbean Sea, a lone ship sailed the warm waters in search of treasure and plunder. Its crew was a raucous bunch of Irish sailors with a handsome, arrogant captain at the helm. All through the islands they cruised hoping to find their fortune on the high seas or at the tropical locations where they docked.

The captain was a big, bold man much feared and respected by his crew. He ruled his ship with an iron hand but was fair in his dealing with his mates. Normal in most respects, this captain had one exception. Instead of the usual parrot often seen on the shoulders of the head man, this captain's favourite pet was a small dog that was always by his side. The dog was unusual, to be sure, almost twice as long as he was tall with thick stubby legs and a short crooked tail. He was sandy brown in colour with a tuft of hair on his shoulders like a lion's mane and a huge pile of wavy fur flowing off his hind quarters. Strutting around on the deck with his captain he was quite a sight to see. And he was not just for show; this dog had his duty to the ship as well. Everyday he would sit on the bow staring at the sea in search of ships to plunder, or ships from which to run. He was so keen that he could spot a ship before it was actually visible on the horizon. Then the barking would start. He would kick up such a fuss that the men on the ship would go for their spy glasses in search of the approaching vessel. More than once he saved them from certain capture.

Often he would spot a ship loaded with goods on its way back to the old country. Quick as a wink the sailors would fire their guns, halting the unlucky ship to rob it. The crew and captain would quickly board the vessel and take anything of value before releasing it and its captain back to the sea. The crew was good at its job and their hold was quickly filling with the riches they plundered.

This led to a problem. The boat was so full of goods that the captain realized they would not be able to outrun a Navy ship if one decided to pursue them. It was a long way back to Ireland and the Caribbean Sea held many dangers. He decided it was time to head for home before the storm season approached and while they were having this run of good luck. The captain took a course north avoiding the small islands along the way hoping also to avoid being seen by other ships. These pirates were so successful that they were getting a reputation along the island chain. If spotted from village forts, they would immediately be pursued by whatever ship was guarding the harbour.

Luck was with them, however, and everyone was starting to relax as they reached the last few islands in the chain before

heading into the Atlantic and home. Then their luck changed. An early storm blew up and not even the captain's dog saw it coming. The crew struggled to hold the ship on course through the raging winds and dashing waves. It was a good ship and strong but with its hold full of heavy plunder it was no match for the weather.

The ship pitched about in the dark sea, off course and with no way of stopping. The sails were beginning to tear and the masts were in danger of falling. The captain and crew had no idea where the boat was going since the sky was black as night and the rain hit them in blinding sheets. Suddenly there was a rocking jolt and a loud crack as the boat hit something solid. The reefs around these islands were dangerous even when the weather was good. The crew feared the worst since they had no idea how far they were from shore. As the boat started to take on water the captain yelled to his crew to abandon ship. Life boats were lowered and the soaked and frightened men began a hasty retreat from the doomed vessel, leaving behind all their ill-gotten gains. Waiting for the last boat, the captain jumped from his listing ship with his trusted dog close behind. The small boats pitched about in the rough sea but fortunately for the crew the land was just a short distance away. They reached a tiny protected bay with a curve of white sand thankful to be alive. As the storm raged on the exhausted crew pulled their boats onto the shore and collapsed on the soft sand under a stand of swaying palm trees.

Morning came and the crew was awakened by the stares and muttering of a small group of island folk. They were the East End fishermen of Anguilla arriving to check the condition of their fishing boats after the storm. Not realizing these half-drowned men were a band of pirates, the fisherman welcomed them and offered food and lodging. The pirates immediately accepted and since their boat was lost forever, decided to stay on the island and make a new start.

The pirates were a strong bunch and in no time had built houses and small boats for fishing. The captain, still the leader of the group, decided to call their new village Ireland Harbour after their beloved Ireland. He married a local woman and set up house, soon forgetting his life at sea. The captain's dog also found companionship among the local dogs of Anguilla and it was not long before short long dogs with a noble spirit and a fierce bark were spotted all over the island. Ireland Harbour eventually became Island Harbour and you can still see evidence of the Irish blood in the people of the village. And that is how the Anguilla long dog came to be …or at least this is one story.

The typical long dog is of medium height, slim by nature with a long tail, pointed ears and short hair. They are well able to take the heat and will eat just about anything. Great watch dogs, they are always on the alert for anyone passing by their yard which they defend with vigour. These dogs are so loyal and lovable that in recent times visitors to Anguilla have been adopting them - and once again, the Anguilla long dog has become a traveller. **Joanne Mason**

National Progress and Development

Aidan Harrigan and Marcel Fahie

PHOTOS: IVOR HODGE

Anguilla's economic development really began in earnest in 1980 following its formal secession from the Associated State of St Kitts-Nevis-Anguilla. The resolution of Anguilla's status in 1980 signalled the beginning of a concerted partnership between successive UK and Anguilla governments to foster the development of Anguilla and its people. It also paved the way for significant foreign direct investment on the island, as investors signalled their confidence in Anguilla's new political dispensation. Economic activity became centred around tourism, and the industry continues to dominate economic output. Since development really began in 1980, Anguilla can be said to have undergone two "development decades" (the 1980s and 1990s) and is approaching the halfway point of its third development decade. Anguilla has made significant strides during this period. An important milestone along the way during this time was the cessation of United Kingdom Government recurrent budgetary assistance or grant-in-aid in 1985. Since then Anguilla has met its own recurrent budgetary needs and an increasing share of its capital investment needs as well.

The growth of the Anguillian economy has mirrored the growth in the tourism industry. Starting from a base of 8,172 visitor arrivals in 1980, Anguilla has averaged over 100,000 visitors annually since 1991. Gross Domestic Product (GDP) has more than tripled to EC$240 (US$90) million over the last 15 years and median household and per capita incomes are currently around EC$47,000 (US$17,700) and EC$14,000 (US$5,300) respectively. As a direct result the population has increased by over 70 percent since 1982 from 6,680 to 11,561 in 2001 compared to an increase of barely 1,000 in the preceding twenty years. A large part of this increase has been due to in-migration, mainly from other Caribbean countries. Non-Anguillians now make up 28 percent of the population.

The fruits of the expanded economic development can be seen in the provision of free education and heavily subsidised healthcare. There is virtually 100 percent enrolment at both primary and secondary levels. On the health side, infectious and waterborne diseases have been virtually eliminated. In consequence, infant mortality is low (around 6 per 1000) and life expectancy is high (74 years). Housing on the island is generally solidly built (hurricane-proof), provided with safe water, electricity and good sanitation; overcrowding affects under 10 percent of households. Ownership of many modern consumer goods is high: vehicles (74 percent), telephone (84 percent), TV (90 percent), washing machines (79 percent) and refrigerators (95 percent). However, despite progress made Anguilla, like other small island developing states (known in the literature as SIDS), remains a highly vulnerable economy susceptible to external economic shocks and natural disasters such as hurricanes so that gains made can quickly be reversed.

PHYSICAL DESCRIPTION

Anguilla is the northernmost island of the Leeward Islands in the Eastern Caribbean. The nearest island is St Maarten, which lies about eleven miles to the south. Anguilla is long and thin being about 16 miles long but only about three miles wide at the widest place. The total land area is about 35 square miles. Anguilla is low-lying with an undulating rocky terrain. The highest point is Crocus Hill at an elevation of about 210 ft. There is little agriculture and most of the undeveloped land is covered by low scrub vegetation. There are numerous sandy beaches around the coast, which provide a considerable tourist attraction. Elsewhere the coast is rocky, rising into low cliffs on parts of the north coast. Anguilla has no known reserves of commercially exploitable minerals. However, with a 200-mile extended fisheries zone to the north it has significant potential for fisheries development.

ECONOMIC ACTIVITY AND ECONOMIC GROWTH

Economic output is dominated by tourism. In 2002, output as measured by gross domestic product totalled EC$240 (US$90) million. Hotel and restaurants, the main indicator of tourism activity, accounted for greatest share of economic output, 27.8 percent. Other tertiary sector activities are also important with

Anguilla's capital, The Valley, as seen from Roaches Hill

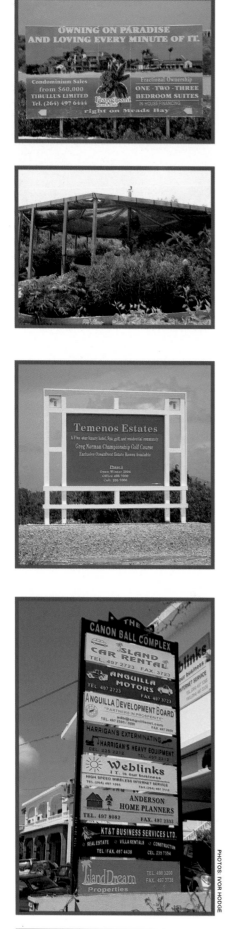

government services, banking and insurance and communications accounting for 18.2 percent, 14.5 percent and 9.4 percent of GDP, respectively. Primary activities (agriculture and fishing and mining and quarrying) are relatively unimportant in terms of GDP. Manufacturing is also relatively insignificant, accounting for only 1.5 percent of GDP.

Overall, when the inter-sectoral linkages are taken into account tourism accounts for close to 60 percent of Anguilla's gross domestic product as in addition to hotels and restaurants, it also cuts across banking, communications, transport and other sectors.

In terms of economic performance, Anguilla enjoyed quite robust growth rates during the 1980s driven largely by construction activity in the tourism industry as foreign investors embarked upon the first round of major investment in hotel plant on the island. The average annual rate of growth during the period 1983 to 1992 was 9.9 percent. Economic performance since then has been fitful and uneven and has been affected by several external shocks and natural disasters. For example, Anguilla was impacted by hurricanes on an almost annual basis during the period 1995 to 1999, including major ones in August 1995 and November 1999. These hurricanes, Luis and Lenny, were estimated by the United Nations Economic Commission for Latin America and the Caribbean to have cost US$55 million and US$75 million worth of damage, respectively. The average annual rate of economic growth during the period 1993 to 2002 was 3.6 percent. The contrast in fortunes in the 1980s and 1990s serves to highlight the vulnerability of the Anguillian economy, as is the case with small island developing states in general, so that gains made can quickly be reversed.

TRADE

Anguilla is a highly open economy with an import trade quotient of close to 80 percent of GDP. The United States (including Puerto Rico) is Anguilla's main trading partner and accounts for 59 percent of all imports to Anguilla. Anguilla is an associate member of the Organization of Eastern Caribbean States (OECS) and the Caribbean Community and Common Market (CARICOM), and trade with member territories account for most of its remaining imports, including oil, which is imported from Trinidad and Tobago. Total imports to Anguilla during 2002 were EC$188.7 (US$69.9) million.

Anguilla's merchandise exports are negligible, amounting to EC$1.7 (US$0.6) million in 2002. The major export item is concrete blocks to neighbouring islands such as St Maarten, St Barthelemy and St Eustatius. Given the situation with imports and exports, Anguilla recorded a deficit of EC$187.0 (US$69.3) million on its merchandise trade balance. This deficit, however, was largely offset by the export of tourism services with visitor expenditure estimated at EC$149.3 (US$55.3) million in 2002.

GOVERNMENT FINANCES

Since economic growth is a natural revenue multiplier it is not surprising that the trend in government finances during the 1990s has mirrored the uneven economic performance as a whole. After registering a small surplus of EC$0.4 (US$0.1) million in 1998, government's fiscal balance decline over the next few years was such that a deficit of EC$14.8 (US$5.5) million was recorded in 2001. This performance can be explained as follows. In 1999, Anguilla was struck by Hurricane Lenny, a major hurricane. The damage to hotel plant meant that most hotels were closed during the peak of the 1999/2000 tourism season (i.e. November 1999 to March 2000). Since tourism accounts for about 70 percent of government revenue collections when all the levels of impact (direct, indirect and induced) are taken into account, this impacted negatively on revenue collections. At the same time, the Government of Anguilla was required to make significant expenditures relating to the hurricane reconstruction effort. The situation was compounded in 2000 by the downturn in global economic activity as the long run of economic expansion in the US came to an end. As the main source of visitor arrivals (65 percent), tourism activity in Anguilla is inextricably linked to demand conditions in the US. The cyclical and seasonal variations in tourism demand in 2001 were exacerbated by the events of September 11, which served to further curtail travel.

Another important reason for the trend towards budget deficits over the period 1999 to 2001 include unplanned expenditures to meet international standards in areas such as civil aviation and the provision of fire services. This underscores the high per capita cost of public administration in small countries such as Anguilla, especially in the current international climate with its emphasis on "good governance", safety and security.

In response to these developments, in March 2002 the Government of Anguilla began the implementation of a Fiscal Stabilization Plan to cover the period 2002 - 2005. On the expenditure side, the central element of the plan was to reduce overall expenditure in 2002 by 7 percent from the amount budgeted. This was to be accomplished by: (a) implementing a partial freeze on hiring new public servants; (b) tightening controls on Government's purchase of goods and services; (c) implementing cost saving measures to reduce Government's operating costs; (d) restricting capital expenditure to when capital revenue became available to fund projects; (e) converting the accumulated overdraft to a long-term loan to reduce debt service costs; and (f) transformation of the operations of loss-making Government Departments to facilitate their operation on a cost minimization or revenue maximization basis. On the revenue side, emphasis was placed on improving revenue collections by reducing arrears to Government, increasing the rate of some taxes, introducing new taxes and stimulating economic activity by concluding agreements with private developers for multi-million dollar investments in tourism projects.

The Government of Anguilla's Fiscal Stabilization Plan has had a marked impact to date. In 2002, there was a significant turn around in the government's finances so that a surplus of EC$1.0 (US$0.4) million was recorded at the end of the year. A crucial part of this was the tight rein, which was imposed on expenditure. The Government intends to continue to impose a similar sense of fiscal discipline in 2003 and over the medium term. The budget estimates established for 2003 are as follows: recurrent revenue – EC$92.1 (US$34.1) million, capital revenue – EC$15.2 (US$5.6) million, total revenue – EC$107.3 (US$39.7) million, recurrent expenditure – EC$90.0 (US$33.3) million, capital expenditure – EC$14.0 (US$5.2) million, total expenditure – EC$104.0 (US$38.5) million, projected surplus – EC$3.3 (US$1.2) million.

The Government of Anguilla adheres to best practices in the management of its finances, and its accounts are audited on an annual basis by the UK Government's National Audit Office.

INWARD INVESTMENT OPPORTUNITIES

The Government of Anguilla will be seeking to facilitate increased economic activity so that average annual growth rates of GDP in the region of 10 percent can be recorded over the medium term. Economic growth is a natural revenue

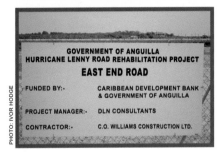

PHOTOS: IVOR HODGE

multiplier in that it contributes to increased government revenue collections. The GOA will be looking to foreign direct investment (FDI) to play a major role in the growth and development of Anguilla. For this reason the Government of Anguilla takes pride in successfully concluding negotiations in 2002 with a group of investors for a golf tourism project at Rendezvous. This project, which started in January of 2003, is expected to involve a minimum investment of EC\$337.5 (US\$125.0) million over ten years. The Government of Anguilla is proud of the achievement not only for the amount of investment that the project will bring to Anguilla but also for the manner in which the discussions and negotiations with the developers were undertaken. It represented the first case where the investment appraisal and approval process was co-ordinated by a central task force. This multi-disciplinary task force has now been reconstituted as the "Tourism Investment Committee" and mandated by Executive Council to appraise all major tourism-related investment proposals for Anguilla. The goal for the Tourism Investment Committee is that it be the forerunner of a statutory Investment Promotion Agency (IPA) to facilitate foreign investment in all sectors of the Anguillian economy using the concept of 'investor targeting'. At the present time the Tourism Investment Committee is co-ordinating efforts to develop a mega-yacht marina and duty free shopping complex at Sandy Ground, two major tourism projects for the Eastern (undeveloped) end of the island, an offshore medical school/health tourism project and the Anguilla Tennis Academy, a sports tourism project for Blowing Point.

The attractiveness or appeal of a country to FDI is dependent on a number of factors including the fiscal regime and the physical and social capital infrastructure provided in support of investment. Anguilla as a low tax jurisdiction is very attractive to foreign direct investment. There are no personal or corporate income taxes, capital gains taxes, withholding taxes, or restrictions on the repatriation of profits. The Government is also committed to providing the required physical and social capital infrastructure. In this vein it has embarked on a EC\$54 (US\$20) million expansion of Wallblake Airport to include, inter alia, the following: the extension of the runway from its current length of 3600ft to 6000 ft; upgrade and extension of the terminal facilities; refuelling facilities; and, a fixed based operation to accommodate private jets. Planning for the project which has been on-going for the past two years was intensified in December 2002 and work is expected to commence on the runway extension in September 2003 and be completed by May 2004. The expanded and improved air transport facilities and services will facilitate increased visitor arrivals and allow the GOA to generate greater surpluses from tourism, which it can in turn invest in new growth poles such as international business and financial services, e-commerce, transhipment and fisheries and in doing so diversify economic activity.

LOCAL BUSINESS DEVELOPMENT

While the GOA will actively be courting foreign direct investment it will just as diligently be working to facilitate the local Anguillian investor class. This will be done by supporting individual businesses or developers as well as collectively through vehicles such as a national investment company. The role of national investment companies or national development companies, as they are sometimes known, in the development of economic success stories such as Singapore is well documented.

As a European Union Overseas Country and Territory (OCT), the GOA

will also be aggressively pursuing with the European Investment Bank (EIB) access to its Global Loans (GL) facility. This facility involves providing funds to OCT development and commercial banks that in turn "on-lend" these funds to small and medium sized enterprises. It is therefore an ideal vehicle for the Anguilla Development Board and the two indigenous commercial banks (the National Bank of Anguilla and the Caribbean Commercial Bank) to facilitate the development of the small business sector in Anguilla.

The new OCT Decision also provides for loans from the EIB's own resources (EIB-OR) and the OCT Investment Fund (IF). The IF is specifically geared towards private sector companies active in the OCTs. At the present time there are a number of qualified entrepreneurs in Anguilla who operate viable and growing businesses and who are in need of expansion funds. Accessing the facilities mentioned above would assist greatly in promoting the development of small scale, high value, high quality manufacturing for export and for domestic consumption. Anguilla's custom luxury and leisure boat building company, Rebel Marine, is a prime example of such a small scale manufacturing enterprise which has developed a sterling reputation regionally and internationally for the quality of its products.

The Government of Anguilla through its membership of the Eastern Caribbean Currency Union (ECCU) will also be encouraging Anguillian private and institutional investors and businesses to take advantage of the investment facilities provided by the ECCU, namely: the Eastern Caribbean Securities Exchange (ECSE), the Eastern Caribbean Home Mortgage Company (ECHMC), the Eastern Caribbean Enterprise Fund (ECEF) and the Eastern Caribbean Venture Capital Fund (ECVCF). Such facilities expand financial intermediation to the regional level thereby providing scope and scale economies and a greater pool of funds for investment in Anguilla.

Road Bay deep water port

Keeping Anguilla in Touch and on the Move

Ken Banks

In keeping with its reputation as an up-scale tourist destination, the Government of Anguilla is committed to the continued upgrading to the state-of-the-art telecommunications services presently available and the creation of computing and information infrastructure as national policy. Telecommunications Liberalisation is seen as a key aspect to achieving this. The government has begun the process of liberalisation of the telecommunications sector, which is expected to be completed by mid-June 2004.

At present, telecommunications penetration in Anguilla, both for fixed lines and cellular is at developed world levels, with over nine thousand fixed lines and six thousand mobile connections. Mobile services can be post or prepaid. Visitors to Anguilla can have a mobile service available immediately and a new fixed lines service can be installed within a week. At present, Cable and Wireless is the only telephone service provider. However, the Government is currently preparing for the issue of at least two additional mobile licences by the end of 2003.

Anguilla has one of the highest per capita penetrations of Internet Technology in the world. This includes dial-up, cable modems, ADSL and WiFi services. These are available at most hotels and are provided by Cable & Wireless and Weblinks, a locally-owned company. The commitment of the Government of Anguilla to information technology is exemplified by the launch of the Anguilla Commercial Online Registration Network (ACORN), the first twenty-four hour online registry in the world, and other recent e-government initiatives. In early 2004, visitors to Anguilla will be processed using a computerised immigration system.

The Government of Anguilla has recognised the need to diversify the domestic economy in order that the island might achieve a degree of economic self-sufficiency in the medium term with resultant benefits. It has determined that e-commerce and related databased activities represent an opportunity to introduce a clean, non-invasive industry, which will complement the existing high-end tourism and financial services sectors. Already, there are a number of notable private sector e-commerce initiatives in Anguilla carrying out business worldwide. A number of web businesses have now chosen Anguilla as their initial base of operations and there is the growth of a community of online programmers and other computer technicians on the island.

Electricity services in Anguilla are based on the North American Standards (120v 60c/s). The Anguilla Electricity Company Limited (Anglec) is the sole provider of electricity. The service is available to all the residential areas. However, at present there is no universal service obligation, hence new homes or developments in new areas are required to pay the cost of extending

PHOTOS: IVOR HODGE

the distribution system. This cost can be recovered as new customers are added to the extended network.

Anglec was created in 1991 and was solely owned by the Government until recently when it divested 51 percent of the shares in the company in a public offering to Anguillians and residents of Anguilla. The company generates electricity using fossil fuels and has an installed capacity of 14MW and delivers a peak load of 8MW to its four thousand customers.

While most private homes in Anguilla collect rainwater from the roof as the main water supply, there is a Government-owned piped supply serving 2800 customers mainly as a backup service. The water supply is produced by the desalination of seawater by reverse osmosis (RO), a service provided by contract to the Government by Ionics Aqua-Design, a US-based company, which supplies approximately 650,000 imperial gallons per day.

Several hotels have also installed their own RO plants to treat saltwater for their own use. The location of extraction wells and the discharge of wastewater is monitored by Government and a royalty charge is payable for all water extracted.

There are 48 kilometres (30 miles) of paved roads network in Anguilla and a further 60 km of unsurfaced road. There is a main arterial road running the length of the island and spurs taken off this lead to the coastal villages and beaches. Government is currently investing heavily in the upgrading and extending the road network.

Tourist maps of the road network are available free of charge from the

AIRPORT EXPANSION PROJECT

The main components of the Wallblake Airport Expansion Project (WAEP) are:

- Extension to the runway to from 3600 ft to 6000ft, and aircraft parking apron and associated navigational aids;

- Upgrading of the existing terminal building;

- The construction and operation of a commercial Fix ('Fixed', surely?) Base Operation (FBO)Terminal Building;

- Estimated cost US$ 20 million

The runway extension and associated works, and the terminal upgrade, are to be funded by the Government of Anguilla. Sources of funding include loan finance, grant aid from the European Development Fund (EDF) and a contribution from the Government budget.

The Fix (See above) Base Operation is to be undertaken by a private company as a concession. The firm to be chosen would be selected through a tendering process.

Work has already commenced on the construction of replacement homes for the residences that are affected by the project.

All the work for the project is to be completed by the end of August 2004.

PHOTOS: IVOR HODGE

Tourist Board office, hotels and other business establishments. For the more serious minded visitor and developer, Ordnance Survey maps of various scales are available from the Lands and Surveys Department for a small fee.

Arriving by air, visitors enter Wallblake Airport which in the Valley. It is within walking distance of the main Government Offices and about one kilometre from the main banking and business centre. A taxi service is available from the airport.

Visitors to Anguilla from Europe and North America can connect to scheduled flights at international hub airports in San Juan, Puerto Rico, St Maarten or Antigua. These services are provided by American Eagle, LIAT Caribbean Star and Winair. Charter flights are also available from Wallblake to the hub airports and other destinations.

The Government of Anguilla is soon embarking on the expansion of Wallblake Airport to facilitate the arrival of larger regional aircraft and private jets. It is also planning to let a concession for the creation of a flight service operation (FSO) to provide services for private jet passengers at a level consistent with Anguilla's up-market tourist reputation.

Most passengers coming to Anguilla by sea enter at the port at Blowing Point. Here there is a half-hourly ferry service to Marigot, St Maarten. Some passengers also arrive by private yacht at Road Bay, which also caters for the occasional small cruise ship during the winter months. The Government is currently reviewing its policy on cruise ship tourism.

Road Bay is the main cargo port and handles container lines from the US and inter-island freighters. Some cargo - mainly from St Maarten - also enters the port at Blowing Point.

Bulk fuel supplies are imported at Coritot Bay. Here, Shell Antilles and Delta Petroleum have located their fuel depots with storage facilities for petrol, diesel oil and liquefied petroleum products. A recent port development study commissioned by the Government has identified Coritot as the preferred location for port expansion.

Blowing Point Harbour

Cable & Wireless and, below, All Island Cable Television

PHOTOS: IVOR HODGE

CABLE & WIRELESS ANGUILLA

Prior to Cable & Wireless taking over telecommunications services in Anguilla in 1971, the island had no telecommunications infrastructure for many years following the devastation caused by Hurricane Janet in 1950. In 1971, the British government and the government of Anguilla invited Cable & Wireless to provide telecommunications services to Anguilla.

Up until April 2003, Cable & Wireless (WI) Ltd was the sole domestic and international telecommunications service provider in Anguilla. In 1973, the company was granted a formal External Operating License to provide Anguilla's international telecommunications services and a separate license to provide national telecommunications facilities. These expired in 1988 and were replaced by a single 30-year license.

Cable & Wireless upgraded to a fully digital network in November 1986. The provision of data and Internet services, telephone, mobile, voicemail, paging, Internet access, facsimile, leased circuit and toll free services are available from Cable & Wireless, as well as Cable & Wireless Caribbean phone cards, PBX and other equipment. Public card and coin phones are also located throughout the island.

In April 2003, Cable & Wireless and the Government of Anguilla signed a Memorandum of Understanding (MOU) which marked a significant milestone in the company's history. At this stage Cable & Wireless relinquished its legal right to the remaining 15 years of the monopoly licence. As a result of the signing of this MOU, for the first time in the company's existence in Anguilla, competing telecommunications service providers could operate in the newly-liberalised telecommunications market.

Cable & Wireless continues to demonstrate its commitment to providing sophisticated, superior telecommunication services in an increasingly efficient and cost-effective manner.

Customers will continue to receive the latest in technological advances and infrastructural upgrades in the industry, as Cable & Wireless strives to deliver quality, price competitive and efficient solutions to its customers in the liberalised telecommunications environment.

A Model Utility Built on Teamwork

The Anguilla Electricity Company Limited (Anglec) was inaugurated on the 1st April 1991. It supplies electrical power to the entire island and takes pride in the service it provides to its 6000 customers. The power station is located in Corito just south of the capital, The Valley.

The company operates as a private company with the Government of Anguilla as the sole shareholder. Prior to 1991, the Electric Utility was a department of the Government and between 1991 and 1998, the entity was managed by the Commonwealth Development Corporation but this arrangement came to an end in 1998 when the Government appointed a Board of Directors to oversee the Company.

Although affected by a number of hurricanes in the past eight years, the resilience of the people of Anguilla is manifested in the employees at Anglec who resolutely rebuild the various electrical systems to ensure that the domestic and commercial customers receive the service to which they are entitled.

The management approaches the task of managing the utility using teamwork and excellent customer service as its principal operational guidelines. The company is determined to make Anglec a model utility that will attract the attention not only of other regional utilities but also of small utilities throughout the world.

FROM BUSH LAWYERS TO QUEEN'S COUNSEL

Josephine Gumbs-Connor

Anguillians still maintain the image in the Caribbean as a law-abiding people. Some may say that this is on account of the small size of the island, but Anguillians would reckon that having to eke out an existence from the combination of an unyielding land and an unevenly matched relationship with St Kitts, made Anguilla a ripe environment for a well-placed sense of justice.

Until the 1960s, the legal system in Anguilla was loosely structured; law and order were maintained in two streams – the Doctor as Magistrate dealt mainly with criminal matters, but most civil matters were dealt with by a community Court held under a nut tree. Indeed, there was infrastructure in the shape of a court-house and police station (the remains of which are still visible) but little else suggested a formal legal environment.

Anguilla's colourful history in the law dates back to the 1920s. In that period, medical doctors, who were appointed to the island, became doctors/surgeons and were also the magistrates and as such actively received cases and dispensed justice while also handling administrative matters - all without one whit of formal legal training. A Magistrate would be assisted by the constabulary consisting of one sergeant and corporal and one private who were the law enforcement for the entire island and who themselves had little training. Naturally, decisions of this rudimentary system were not always accepted. On these occasions, the Governor of the Colony in Antigua would be contacted in order to seek a review. Such appeals would be heard by an itinerant judge who would visit Anguilla once or twice a year to hear civil and criminal cases in the High Court jurisdiction.

A more formal structure began with the appointment of Wardens who acted as Magistrates and were responsible for the administration of the island. However, with the expulsion of overseas Wardens during the Revolution, Anguillians proceeded to appoint their own. Magistrates such as Peter Adams and Rev. Raphael Lake, both of whom had no formal legal training,

Caribbean Juris Chambers

dispensed justice using morality as a yardstick.

Following the Revolution and having had the benefit of secondary education, Anguillians were sensitised to the need of formal legal training. Anguilla saw its first lawyer in the name of Miss Bernice Lake QC who practiced toe-to-toe with her male Kittitian colleagues, Dr William V Herbert, Fred Kelsick and Dennis Byron, now the Chief Justice of the Eastern Caribbean Supreme Court, and later Don Mitchell, now a Judge of the Supreme Court, all of whom had legal Chambers in Anguilla. Miss Lake would go on to have a most distinguished career which includes her being recognized as the first female Queens Counsel appointed in the Eastern Caribbean jurisdiction and the creator of Anguilla's first written Constitution (1976).

In this climate, Anguilla gained its own Magistrates; the first was Mrs Lolita Davis-Ifill and now Mr Homer Richardson. And added to these is Miss Elneth Kentish, a Judge practicing in Barbados. Today, even though the population is approximately 12,000, Anguilla can boast of having 18 local legal practitioners many of whom have their own Chambers, and a complement of local practitioners at the Public Bar.

Law firm Keighley Lake & Associates

Law firm Wigley & Associates

DOING BUSINESS IN ANGUILLA

John Benjamin

INTRODUCTION

This page is designed to assist businesses and individuals to Anguilla who have no knowledge of the business community in Anguilla.

OVERSEAS TERRITORY

Anguilla is a British Overseas Territory. Britain is responsible for all of the island's matters of foreign affairs and for the defence of the island. The local Legislative Council is responsible for internal matters. The Queen appoints a Governor and Deputy Governor to oversee the island.

LEGISLATIVE COUNCIL

The Chief Minister heads the Legislative Council. He is selected from the political party that wins the majority of the Council seats at a General Election.

The elections are held every five years. There are presently seven constituencies in Anguilla, each represented by one elected member.

POPULATION

The population of Anguilla is approximately 12,000 with a working population of about 4,000. The rate of unemployment is possibly the lowest in the world.

OFFICIAL LANGUAGE

The official language in Anguilla is English.

TELECOMMUNICATIONS

Anguilla has a modern telephone system, which is fully digital, and an Internet Service, both currently operated by Cable & Wireless (W.I.) Ltd. The area code is 264. The Government of Anguilla has signed

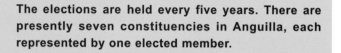

ANGUILLA – TRANQUILLITY WRAPPED IN BLUE

ANGUILLA – TRANQUILLITY WRAPPED IN BLUE

a liberalization agreement with Cable & Wireless (W.I.) Ltd. which opens the door for other providers in the field of telecommunications.

LEGAL SYSTEM: COMMON LAW SYSTEM

The legal system of Anguilla is based on the Anguilla Constitution order 1982, statutes and British common law system. English precedents and those of other British Commonwealth countries are persuasive in court. Anguilla law is based on the principles and practice of the common law of England which is still applicable where the local statutes are silent. Most local statutes are based on pre-1940s English law. The final appeal still lies in the Privy Council.

EASTERN CARIBBEAN SUPREME COURT

The island's judiciary falls under the umbrella of the Eastern Caribbean Supreme Court. The islands covered by the Eastern Caribbean Supreme Court are: Anguilla, Antigua and Barbuda, British Virgin Islands, Dominica, St. Lucia, St. Kitts, Nevis, St.

ANGUILLA CHAMBER OF COMMERCE AND INDUSTRY

Over the years, the Anguilla Chamber of Commerce and Industry has grown from acting locally to making connections with other Chambers of Commerce and Organizations far beyond the Anguillian borders.

In the late 1970s, under guidance of a few innovative Anguillian entrepreneurs, the Anguilla Chamber of Commerce was established to serve the business community of the nation. It was not until after the revolution in 1967 and defragmentation of the constitutional links with St Kitts that Anguilla became independently active in trade and commerce. Sectors such as agriculture, fishing, and livestock breeding formed the main components of the island's GDP. Most Anguillian's travelled to other countries for their economic well-being.

The rise of tourism and offshore industry opened up new venues for economic growth on the island. The Government's vision to emphasize an up-market tourism policy, led to a period of rapid construction, new hotels, rental villas and condominiums, which substantially expanded the island's private sector.

Several major infrastructure projects contributed to the construction boom, which helped to put Anguilla on the map as a prime destination for leisure travel, but also created a necessity to establish organizations such as the Chamber of Commerce and Industry, Anguilla Tourist Board and the Anguilla Hotel & Tourism Association.

Evolving changes in the global market, such as the movement of free trade and other commodities, will affect the way business is conducted locally. The Anguilla Chamber of Commerce has positioned itself to encourage diversification of local products and services. Industries such as fish processing and other light manufacturing companies would be a welcome asset to the island.

With the establishment of a Business Communication Centre, where members of the business community can gather to discuss common matters of concern, the Chamber of Commerce aims to open venues to enhance intra-regional as well as international trade-related matters. Included among the primary objectives is training and transfer of technology. Part of their curriculum is to offer workshops, seminars, business education sessions and customer satisfaction programs in conjunction with reputable consulting agencies.

The Chamber of Commerce has also embarked on an ambitious campaign to provide administrative support in particular to micro businesses, which will inevitably contribute to the level of the current standards. Vacationers, investors and business associates are welcome to visit the office to acquire information on business arrangements, referrals and other amenities.

ANGUILLA – TRANQUILLITY WRAPPED IN BLUE

Vincent and the Grenadines, Grenada and Montserrat. The island is served by a Puisne Judge who presently resides on Anguilla. The judge serves the Islands of Montserrat and Anguilla. The High Court of Anguilla sits in its civil and criminal jurisdiction at least three times per year: January/February; June/July and October/November.

CIVIL AND CRIMINAL JURISDICTION IN ANGUILLA

The High Court deals with the most serious offences and all civil matters involving property valued at EC $15,000 (US $5,800) and above. The Magistrate Court deals with minor offences (misdemeanours). There is a resident magistrate on Anguilla. The Magistrate Court sits all year round.

SIX REASONS WHY YOU SHOULD DO BUSINESS IN ANGUILLA

1. No Income Tax

2. No Corporate Tax

3. No Inheritance Tax

4. No Foreign Exchange Control Regulations

5. Statutory Protection of Assets and Confidentiality

6. Affordable and Professional Personnel

TAX SHELTER

Anguilla is a tax shelter, similar in many ways to other British tax shelters. The British Virgin Islands, Bermuda, The Bahamas, Barbados, Antigua, St. Kitts, Nevis and the Cayman Islands also offer similar facilities and services.

TAXES

There is no personal income tax or company tax on the island. The government taxes are derived from stamp duty on the transfer of property, duty on the importation of goods to the island, hotel accommodation taxes, and stamp duty on the Alien Land Holding License.

Rebel Marine

Rebel Marine is a small quality conscious custom boat building company situated in the village of North Hill near Road Bay. If Anguilla is a travel secret, Rebel Marine is a secret wrapped within a secret. Building on the tradition of centuries of boat building this small company turns out quality custom boats for selective clients throughout the United States and the Caribbean. Locally owned and staffed, Rebel Marine is almost an anomaly. It manufactures a sophisticated high value product on an island which otherwise has no manufacturing.

The company specializes in building custom cold moulded boats ranging in size from 28 to 43 feet. Styles usually fall in the category of express sport fishermen, high performance boats, runabouts, and picnic boats. Rebel offers a variety of in-house designs and has the ability to build to specific designs supplied by prospective clients. Three US boat builders have regularly sub-contracted their work to Rebel, a clear recognition of Rebel's capacity to build and deliver a quality product at very competitive prices. Indeed, Rebel has a definite ambition to be one of the very first boat builders in the Caribbean region to export high quality custom boats to the United States and beyond and is well on the way to

making this dream a reality. Many clients from the United States take advantage of the fun of travelling to a unique tropical island, enjoying its getaway barefoot luxury while watching the progress of their dreamboat taking shape before their eyes. Many visitors to the island who frolic across Anguilla's turquoise seas in modern state of the art boats are stunned to learn that the boats are all built right here on Anguilla.

A large measure of Rebel's success is due to its conscious policy to build on the strong traditions of Anguilla's maritime past while utilizing modern materials and technology. Quality epoxy resins and fibreglass fabrics are used in conjunction with state of the art coreings and marine grade plywoods to produce strong, lightweight boats capable of superior performance and fuel efficiency. In collaboration with its sister company Anguilla Techni Sales, boats can be outfitted with the latest electronic gadgetry and equipment. Customized stainless steel and aluminium railings, tee tops and fixtures are all built locally to an impeccable finish.

If Anguilla is considered as a destination with unique qualities, Rebel Marine adds a touch of class to that uniqueness.

A LEADER IN TECHNOLOGY AND OPEN FOR BUSINESS

In 1995, the Government of Anguilla took the decision to develop the financial services sector as a means of strengthening and diversifying the overall economic base and to provide another employment source for Anguillians, many of whom were obtaining university educations. The island already possessed most of the characteristics which are essential to an international financial services centre. These have assisted financial planners to put together legitimate structures requiring a zero tax jurisdiction.

The British and Anguilla Governments jointly embarked on a progressive programme to launch Anguilla as an upmarket, well-regulated and exclusive financial services centre.

The significant growth in government revenues earned from the financial services sector over the last few years is a testament to the success of the policies to date. There are ambitious plans for the future and within the past few years Anguilla has made significant strides in its efforts to position itself as a major player in the international financial services arena.

Anguilla Commercial Online Registration Network (ACORN) is the world's first completely electronic online company registry system. It was developed in Anguilla with financial assistance from the British Government and technical assistance from Companies House in the UK, an Executive Agency of The Department of Trade and Industry.

ACORN allows for the instant electronic incorporation and registration of Anguilla Ordinary Companies, International Business Companies, Limited Liability Companies, and Limited Partnerships. The Companies Registry Ordinance, enacted in 1998, provides the practical legal framework for ACORN's operation by enabling the filing of documents in electronic form and the recognition of electronic signatures.

Since 1998, ACORN has been a true demonstration of technology at its best. It has effectively done away with paper, in that it allows authorized users to file company documents electronically from anywhere in the world, across time zones, 365 days a year, 24 hours a day. The time it takes to complete these filings through ACORN is phenomenal. Incorporation takes a mere three minutes to complete, with the agent receiving instantly an emailed copy of the certificate and articles of incorporation (original documents are collected and forwarded by the local registered agent).

Anguilla is one of Britain's Overseas Territories in the Caribbean. Although essentially self-governing, the Governor appointed by Her Majesty's Government is responsible under the present constitution for foreign affairs, defence, internal security and international financial services. Day to day operations of the financial services sector are in the purview of the Minister for Finance, Economic Development, Investment and Commerce and administered by the Financial Services Department.

In carrying out its functions and in considering applications by organisations wishing to establish businesses within the sector, the Department adopts a firm but flexible regulatory approach. This is reflected in the establishment of the Money Laundering Reporting Authority (MLRA), an inter-governmental committee responsible for monitoring and reporting suspicious activities such as terrorism financing and money laundering.

It is of paramount concern to the Government that Anguilla's reputation is not tainted by the use of the jurisdiction for money laundering, terrorism financing or other illegal purposes. For this reason, all licensed institutions are expected to carry out proper due diligence and "know your customer" checks so that they are satisfied as to the identity of their clients and legitimate origin of their clients' funds.

Although commercial confidentiality is ensured by legislation, the authorities in Anguilla cooperate fully with law enforcement agencies and regulators in other jurisdictions. In common with other reputable jurisdictions, the Financial Services Department is subject to safeguards to protect legitimate business, and is able to share regulatory information with overseas regulatory authorities.

When options for upgrading Anguilla's financial services legislation were being considered, the decision was made to replace, rather than amend, the existing legislation with a wide range of specially developed Acts. Since 1995, Anguilla has had the benefit of a comprehensive, well integrated and cohesive package of financial services legislation.

The legislation is designed to afford flexibility to practitioners and contains many innovative provisions. For example, the Trusts Ordinance abolishes the Rule against Perpetuities and permits accumulation of income throughout the entire term of the trust. In line with modern developments in trust law, purpose trusts are permitted and the concept of a protector has been introduced. Asset protection trusts and forced heirship are also catered for in the legislation.

The need to develop legislation is well understood. Government and the private sector co-operate through an active joint legislation committee which monitors legislative developments internationally, examines new financial products and provides a focus for proposals to amend existing legislation. As a result, the legislation has already been developed further and improved in both 1998 and 2000.

In October 2003, the Government of Anguilla will enact the Financial Services Commission Act which provides for the establishment of an independent Financial Services Commission to regulate the financial services sector. The Commission will be independently staffed and resourced as recommended by the KPMG Review of Regulatory Standards in 2000. The Companies Registry will remain under the Ministry of Finance thus enabling the Registry to engage full time in promoting and marketing.

Constantly upgrading and enhancing to meet the needs of the offshore

industry, in 2002 ACORN was given the ability to incorporate electronically companies with Chinese characters symbolizing the name. These companies, as is the case with all foreign named companies, also provide an English equivalent of the Chinese symbols, which is recorded on the Certificate of Incorporation. This facility also allows agents to incorporate Chinese named companies instantly without the need for additional verification of the English equivalent of the Chinese symbols.

Incorporations with Chinese character names are reviewed at the Registry and both the Chinese and the English name equivalent are recorded on the register to ensure no duplication of name in either language. Anguilla now boasts the ability to register companies in six languages, namely English, French, Spanish, Russian, German and Chinese. While this approach to registering Chinese companies is quite novel, the avoidance of duplicate English equivalent names on these type of

companies provides Anguilla with an enhanced regulatory oversight of these companies.

To facilitate the banking community, a company status search and a name availability search portal has been placed on our public website (www.axafsc.com) this again demonstrates Anguilla's commitment to maintaining a well-regulated jurisdiction while remaining at the forefront of technological advancement.

The Hon Victor F. Banks oversees the development of Anguilla's growing financial services sector, a sector that has a growth rate of 25-30% each year. In a recent address he noted: "As a growing financial centre, Anguilla has two primary objectives, namely, to attract legitimate business and to provide quality service. We will achieve this by embracing technology to facilitate efficiency and accountability in the new global economy. The liberalisation of the telecommunications system, zero tax-status, multi-year work permits and incentive programmes to encourage the youth of Anguilla to pursue studies and careers in the financial services sector are all part of our development strategy to reach our potential."

Mr Banks, further stated, "as an offshore financial service jurisdiction, Anguilla offers a level of service which is second to none. Anguilla offers red carpet service, not red tape. The Government of Anguilla is committed to the perpetuation of this quote while maintaining our reputation as a well-regulated jurisdiction". As a testimony to the fulfilment of this quote the Government has committed to the establishment of an Independent Financial Services Commission.

"We invite you to our fountain to savour Anguilla's waters as it is an opportunity to do business in an extremely pleasurable environment. Anguilla is definitely open for business and with its ability to adapt to new technology, enterprising and the highly qualified work force, Anguilla is the jurisdiction of choice for the 21st Century."

ANGUILLA'S INDUSTRIAL PAST

While tourism and offshore finance underpin the island's modern economic development, before those industries there were sugar, tobacco, indigo, cotton, phosphate, sisal and salt. 'A Handbook History of Anguilla' by Colville Petty shares some of the following interesting titbits about those industries that kept the island's economy afloat leaving only salt to survive as an industry from historical times to the dawn of the modern era.

TOBACCO The earliest English settlers (1650) found that the island's soil was good for growing tobacco, which was one of the crops grown by the indigenous people of Malliouhana. According to one report from the period, a few English families had settled around the Cauls Pond and cultivated cotton as a means of livelihood.

COTTON Sea-island cotton had initially replaced tobacco as one of the leading crops of the earliest English settlers and Anguilla's cotton was said to be of fine quality. As early as 1658, it was reported that Anguilla's cotton was "widely prized by experts in the trade". Initially, the poor returns from cotton led to the decision to turn to sugar but over a century later, cotton exports were valued at over £9,000 but were surpassed by indigo, the export of which was valued at almost £10,000. One 1843 report indicated that the former slaves were reaping large crops with corn and cotton named as those under significant acreage and twenty years later production had increased to 500 acres. The revival of cotton to become an important export crop by the turn of the twentieth century led the Governor to report for 1906, that it was cotton that had made the island's revenue exceed expenditure for the first time in years, "thus lessening its financial dependence on St Kitts.

By 1907-1908, the Governor could report that the increase in cotton production was due primarily to the acquisition of two petroleum cotton ginneries that were housed at what became known as The Factory. By 1913, cotton exports were declining because of reduced demand during World War I and to a severe infestation of the boll weevil that wiped out the industry shortly

The old cotton press at The Factory / Nik Douglas

after. The remains of the cotton gin can be viewed at the ice cream parlour across the road from the Roman Catholic Church in The Valley, and small clusters of cotton plants can still be found in Island Harbour, Rey Hill, North Side and other areas where the plant once grew in abundance.

SUGAR Export statistics for the year 1787-88 show sugar trailing far behind those for indigo and cotton indicating even then that Anguilla was not a profitable colony as far as sugar production was concerned. By the time of emancipation in 1838, it was clear that sugar had not been king for a long time and the cultivation of sugar canes had "virtually disappeared" by 1842.

PHOSPHATE Phosphate of lime was discovered in large quantities during an 1810 geological survey of Sombrero, an offshore cay best known for its lighthouse, which guides international shipping through the Anegada Passage. With strong American interest in providing this phosphate as a fertilizer for its agricultural belt, the ownership of Sombrero soon became a matter of dispute but once British control was established the American-owned Sombrero Phosphate Company was leased for the sum of £1000 per annum. During the twenty-year period of phosphate mining on Sombrero, the remains of the "giant rat" Amblyrhiza inundata were found in a shipment of phosphate exported from Crocus Bay to Philadelphia. This is thought to indicate that the Caribbean islands were once part of the South American mainland. The effects of the great famine of 1890 were exacerbated by the loss of employment for the men of the island once the mining of phosphate on Sombrero ceased.

SISAL the sisal plant is found mainly in the western end of the island. In 1894, in response to the abject poverty of the island, the sum of £1,000 was spent to establish a fibre industry on the island but this was to be added to the list of those industries tried and failed.

SALT Historical records indicate that salt was produced for local consumption by the early 18th century. In 1822, the European inhabitants of the island requested that Anguilla become a Freeport to encourage American ships to buy Anguillian salt, production of which ranged from 50,000 barrels and peaked at 100,000 barrels. At its peak, the industry shipped four hundred tons of salt monthly to Trinidad as well as to other Caribbean islands including Guadeloupe, Martinique, Barbados and Grenada.

Salt picking in Sandy Ground / Penny Slinger

In an era of no refrigeration, salt was an extremely important commodity used to "corn" various meats and fish, preserving them for later use. Today there are a few initiatives to package and market small portions of salt as souvenirs and for the natural health markets. Remains of the salt works can be seen at the Pump House Bar and Restaurant which has become a popular nightspot in Sandy Ground. **Ijahnya Christian**

MEETING THE NATION'S EDUCATIONAL NEEDS

The Government of Anguilla recognises that education plays a fundamental role in helping to determine the character of the Anguillian society, This is reflected in its mission statement: "The Government of Anguilla is committed to providing quality education services, through highly motivated and competent educators, to produce loyal, knowledgeable and skilled citizens of sound character, empowered to function effectively in a rapidly changing technological society."

The task for education in Anguilla is to enable its people to meet the challenges of a modern economy and society. Though extremely small, it must compete in the global market place in order to provide opportunities for the people to enjoy a decent standard of living in a peaceful society and in a healthy and safe environment.

Underpinning Government's mandate for education is the belief that all human beings have a right to education; one that will help them to be productive members of society, and also be able to enjoy the benefits of the society (Anguilla Education Policy, July 2002).

The Five Year Education Development Plan puts into action the seven policy areas encapsulated in the beliefs highlighted in the Education Policy. These seven policy areas are embodied in the following goals of the education sector.

- To improve access to education
- To improve the efficiency and effectiveness of the delivery of education
- To provide a more flexible and relevant Curriculum targeted to the needs of society and the demands of the labour market.
- To have a well-qualified cadre of education personnel operating the education system.
- To establish and maintain positive modalities of co-operation with the community.
- To support the development of the well being of all students.
- To increase resources available to meet the needs of the education system.

Education in Anguilla is compulsory for students between the ages of five and 17 years and is free in all public educational institutions. Anguilla, hence, has enjoyed universal primary and, since 1986, universal secondary education.

THE FORMAL EDUCATION SYSTEM

On Anguilla, formal education is delivered through a structured education system from pre-primary to post-secondary levels. The management and co-ordination of the system are delegated to the Department of Education, which is managed by the Chief Education Officer and a team of Education Officers. The Department of Education falls under the administration of the Ministry of Social Development and Lands.

PRE- PRIMARY EDUCATION

There are eleven private pre-schools on Anguilla. Ten of these schools are subsidised by Government to facilitate access to them. Children between the ages of three and five years attend these schools. Present enrolment stands at 437.

PRIMARY EDUCATION

Children between the ages of five and twelve attend primary school. There are six public primary schools, one private assisted primary school and one private school. Special Education services are provided at two Special Education Centres attached to two of the larger primary schools. Education and support for students with special needs are provided at these centres.

Primary schools encompass Grade K (Kindergarten) through to Grade 6. There are 1462 students currently enrolled at primary schools in Anguilla. Test of Standards, in four core areas, is administered to all students in Grades 3, 5 and 6 of the primary schools. Among other uses of the Test of Standards, the Grade 6 test results are used for placement into bands at secondary school.

SECONDARY EDUCATION

Secondary education in Anguilla is provided at the two campuses (Campus A and Campus B) of the only secondary educational institution in Anguilla - the Albena Lake-Hodge Comprehensive School. As the name suggests, this public institution provides educational experiences for students in a wide range of abilities. Its diverse curriculum caters to the academic and technical and vocational subject areas while addressing the needs of a changing society. Secondary education in Anguilla encompasses Lower Secondary Education (Forms 1-3), Upper Secondary Education (Forms 4 and 5) and Post Secondary, Non-Tertiary Education (Lower and Upper 6 Forms). There are some 1145 students presently enrolled at the school.

TERTIARY EDUCATION

The Adult and Continuing Education Unit of the Department of Education, and the University of the West Indies Distance Education Centre (UWIDEC), provide Tertiary Education in Anguilla. Adult and continuing education offers primary and secondary teacher training programmes. The UWI extension campus in Anguilla offers a range of distance education programmes to students in Anguilla.

Guardians of the Nation's Health

Foster Rogers

The government health services in Anguilla comprise primary and secondary health care systems with a referral mechanism in place to transfer clients from the clinics to the hospital. The Primary Health Care Department was instituted in 1996 as a health care delivery approach to ensure that appropriate, affordable and accessible services are delivered to the people of Anguilla in a timely manner. Additionally, it was envisaged that the Primary Health Care approach would decrease barriers to health care experienced by all levels of society. It comprises Environmental Health, Community Nursing, Dental Health, School Health, Nutrition, Community Mental Health and Health Promotion Units.

Ministerial responsibility for health is vested in the Minister of Health & Social Development, who is advised by the Permanent Secretary, the Health Planner and the Director of Health Services (CMO). The Director of Health Services, assisted by three senior managers, is responsible for the delivery of health services and management of the system.

The Primary Health Care Department is divided into five health districts, namely: Island Harbour, East End, Valley, South Hill and West End.

The estimated population for Anguilla is 12,000. The proportion of the population that resides in each health district varies considerably, however, the present deployment of staff (population to staff ratio) is better than internationally accepted standards.

The Primary Health Care system is designed primarily as the first point of contact between the people of Anguilla and the health services. Services provided include preventive programmes such as immunization, family health, nutrition and health promotion initiatives, medical sessions with physicians either daily or weekly, special clinics for hypertension and diabetes, family planning and dental clinics.

Environmental Health and the National Water Laboratory are extremely important parts of the Primary Health Care system. These sectors regulate and implement programmes for all activities on the island with regard to food safety, solid and liquid waste management, water quality, port health, occupational safety and health and vector control. In short, the highly trained and skilled personnel that work in these sectors protect the health of the locals and visitors alike, ensuring a high standard of services.

The construction of a modem polyclinic in the Island Harbour Health District is the beginning of a new model of primary health care delivery to the population. Various services, such as dental, medical, nursing, minor surgery, mental health, family health and community health, will be delivered from this venue. This will bring more traditional hospital-oriented services to the community thereby reducing the patient load at the PAH and improving access.

Princess Alexandra Hospital

The Princess Alexandra Hospital (PAH), a 36-bed facility, comprises the secondary health care system. It is currently the only hospital on the island that caters for patients that need overnight and long term care. The PAH concentrates on a core set of nursing and medical services. The five specialties available at the PAH are General Surgery, Anaesthesiology, Paediatrics, Internal Medicine and Obstetrics/Gynaecology. Additionally, a modem state of the art dialysis centre has been operational at the hospital for over a year. This allows locals and visitors a like to access dialysis care on a timely and cost-effective basis.

All surgical, medical, or emergency cases that need tertiary level care are referred to hospitals or centres overseas. The PAH accounts for the bulk of the expenditure in the health services (65 percent), and the Government of Anguilla is anticipating that a new and modern way of managing and operating health services will place further gains made in the health system over the last decade.

The Anguilla Health Authority, a corporately managed system, will be introduced in January of 2004. The Government is convinced that the health services would be better managed and operated under a statutory corporation. The devolution programme is therefore a priority for the Ministry of Health over the next year.

The people and Government of Anguilla have had positive experiences with autonomous organizations over the last twenty years: Anguilla Social Security Board, Anguilla Electricity Company, Anguilla Development Board and the Anguilla Tourist Board. In essence, the legal framework that enables parastatal institutions is well entrenched and constitutionally sound. These organizations have proven to be viable and productive and have impacted positively on the development of Anguilla.

HUGHES MEDICAL CENTRE (above)

Since its completion in 2001, the Hughes Medical Centre has been delivering care in family medicine, obstetrics and gynaecology, rheumatology, gastro-enterology, radiology, laboratory medicine, adult and paediatric cardiology, and in its core specialty: general, reconstructive and cosmetic surgery. It is equipped with the most modern medical devices and instrumentation, two operating theatres, and monitored recovery units and luxurious overnight suites. For the convenience of patients, there is also a prescription and over-the-counter pharmacy conveniently located in the centre for easy access following examinations or procedures.

Although offering many general medical services, the centre's raison d'etre is to provide a private facility for surgical care, especially in the specialties of Cosmetic and Reconstructive Surgery and Gynaecological Surgery. The centre's founder, board certified Plastic & Reconstructive Surgeon, Dr Lowell Hughes, specializes in providing natural-looking results with personalized, unhurried care. At Hughes Medical Centre, a full spectrum of cosmetic enhancements is offered as well as reconstructive services for the most intricate, major reconstructive cases one might imagine. The centre's consultant gynaecologists offer the most up-to-date surgical care in a caring, private environment.

The private health sector in Anguilla is vibrant, efficient and of high quality. There are numerous private physicians who have practices that are well established. These centres are distributed throughout the country, and improve the access of Anguillians to private health facilities.

Of particular note, and those that represent high quality are the Hughes Medical Centre, Hotel de Health and the Hodge Medical Centre.

The Hughes Medical Centre is regional centre of excellence for plastic and reconstructive surgery. Additionally, visiting specialists, including cardiology, provide services that are not normally available on the island.

The private sector physicians not only compliment and work with the government health system, but in so doing improve the tourism product on the island. Facilities are therefore available to meet varying demands.

The Miriam Gumbs Senior Citizen's Home, attached to the Princess Alexandra Hospital, provides services to the elderly population. The facility offers inpatient care to a maximum of sixteen clients and represents the values of the Anguillian society that our elderly population must be protected and treasured.

It is therefore evident that health system in Anguilla offers a wide range of services that cater to every segment and demographic of society. There are limits to what can be offered in a community of this size, however arrangements with reputable institutions regionally and internationally serve to provide access to care that is not available on island.

The above, in addition to government's continued efforts to improve the quality of the health system through continually updating and reforming the health sector, augur well for the future development of Anguilla. For this, a healthy population is essential.

ALTERNATIVE HEALING

Phyllis Fleming-Banks

The development of tourism in Anguilla has coincided with the western world's renewed interest in traditional/alternative healing. This has meant that those who not too long ago might have scoffed at herbal/bush remedies, are today seeking out the various forms of natural and less chemically dependent health care. It is therefore quite likely that the "tranquillity wrapped in blue" experience in Anguilla might also include a steeping in a potpourri of local and/or imported herbs, sea salt or sea weed blended with the Asian/Oriental healing arts of massage, acupuncture, aromatherapy or reflexology.

While almost everyone's grandmother or great aunt can still "doctor" you up with some good local bush medicine, including a little bit of worry wine (blue vervain) for stress and some aloes (aloe vera) for burns or cleansing, the acknowledged expert in herbal healing on the island is John E. Edwards. "Thunder" or "Dr John" has been concocting and dispensing herbal remedies for most of his life. His title, 'doctor' is not derived from any formal institution - Thunder acquired his vast array of knowledge and insights into herbs from his grandmother. He has the gift of instinctively knowing what herbs to prescribe for various diseases and ailments. For more than 40 years, this low-key, unassuming boat-builder, sailor, fisherman, artist, musician, storyteller and painter quietly and freely diagnosed and cured the ills of family, friends, neighbours, acquaintances and strangers, while employed in "regular jobs".

In the mid-1990s, however, with the increasing interest in herbal healing and hundreds of testimonials from those who had benefited from his healing expertise, Edwards earned national, regional and international recognition, and Thunder became "Dr John". Notable among the tributes were those from people who claimed that they had been cured from cancers and were managing HIV/AIDS using his treatments. Even though there is no formal recognition of alternative medicine on the island, he was granted a government building (a former public health clinic) to open his 'practice'. From Nature's Gift in South Hill, Dr John began devoting his time to developing his herbal practice.

Today, Edwards has expanded his practice to St Maarten and the surrounding islands. While international researchers continue to probe him about his "cure" for HIV/AIDS, medical doctors on these islands are verifying that patients who had displayed symptoms of full blown AIDS have gone into remission after stopping anti-retrovirals and antibiotics and starting Edwards' herbal treatments. Some practitioners have contacted the Harvard AIDS Institute, requesting assistance in further testing of patients to see if these "persons who were in the late stages of full-blown AIDS and now displayed no visible signs" of the disease had "developed neutralising antibodies against the virus" as they clinically looked better". The head of a medical centre credited Edwards with being "one of the most knowledgeable herbalists in the Eastern Caribbean", while another doctor has declared that Edwards holds the "possible breakthrough in the management of HIV/AIDS".

Edwards, himself, says that he has treated about eighteen people with full blown AIDS since 1994. While the skirmish surrounding patents and accreditation goes on, he continues to receive accolades from those suffering from all kinds of ailments including diabetes, sickle cell, lupus, infertility and menopause.

Keeping stride with the global trend, Anguilla's upscale resorts offer a variety of spa and wellness programmes to pamper, heal and rejuvenate their guests. CuisinArt's ten-day interactive retreat programme, which includes "nutrition, exercise, body pampering and therapeutic and medical guidance", is geared towards stress and weight reduction. Their spa and wellness programme also offers a variety of hydrotherapy treatments in addition to traditional massage, aromatherapy and reflexology.

Malliouhana's new spa boasts a large menu of traditional and contemporary treatments. Yoga, meditation, deep tissue and sports massage treatments are complemented by stone therapy, lymphatic drainage, restorative thermo massage and therapeutic "ultra baths".

Cap Juluca's Spa Services include a holistic programme to rejuvenate and regenerate the mind, body and spirit. Their unique menu, which is marketed as "an opportunity to experience healing and personal growth" brings together the "powerful synergy of diverse spiritual therapeutics by a team of skilled healing art practitioners". Their list of signature treatments includes yoga, shamanic healing, astrology and transpersonal work as well as "life in movement" energetics sessions which combine martial arts and tai-chi. The resort also provides two evolutionary healing processes that combine "massage, bioenergetic work, aromatherapy and shamanistic awareness of the body to alleviate stress, anxiety and depression, remove chakric and cellular block and promote and enhance life force. Cap Juluca's spa menu also includes Jamu massages and Balinese Javenes spa rituals.

A number of wellness centres have also emerged to meet the needs of the increasing number of visitors and locals who are looking for alternative healing. Operated by internationally certified therapists, facilities like Taino Wellness Centre, Skin Plus, Anguilla Alternative Wellness Service, Herbal Limited, Ossia Esthetics and Louis Price and Associates provide a wide range of treatments, from acupuncture to reflexology. Complementing these alternative healing services, are a few health food stores like Simply Natural, Herbal Limited and the Health Nook.

As alternative/natural healing becomes more internationally accepted, medical doctors in Anguilla are also beginning to incorporate the methods and services of the alternative practitioners.

With its reputation as a peaceful, relaxing hideaway, this growing range of herbal/alternative healing options undoubtedly serves to enhance Anguilla's "tranquillity wrapped in blue" image.

Beware of the Sun

Dr Louis Bardfield

Unlike most of the nearby Caribbean islands, Anguilla is unique. Some of the finest white sand beaches in the world are found here in Anguilla and we seem to be blessed with a lot more sunshine than any of our neighbouring islands.

Because of the island's narrow shape, the sun's direct rays combine with additional rays that are reflected off the surrounding mirrored waters, white sandy flat shorelines and clouds, making Anguilla a sort of focal point for higher quality sunshine. However, along with this abundance sunshine, unsuspecting tourists, as well as native Anguillians, should be aware of the possible dangers of excess ultra-violet (UV) exposure.

Recently, the problem UV exposure has taken on a greater intensity due to the degradation of the ozone layer, which filters the harmful effects of ultra-violet radiation (UVR). Depletion of the ozone layer has caused an increase in the amount of short wave UV levels that reach the earth, and this type of UV tends to cause the most damage.

In additional to the typical 'sunburn' dangers, continued exposure to certain UV radiation (320-400nm) can result in photo-chemical damage to the human eye. Cumulative exposure can cause premature cataracts, pterygium formation, corneal and retinal irregularities and dry eye.

If you are exposed, or unprotected to excessive amount of UV radiation over a short period of time, you are likely to experience an effect called photokeratitis. Like a 'sunburn of the eye' it may be painful and you may have symptoms including red eyes, a foreign body sensation of gritty feeling in the eyes, extreme sensitivity to light and excessive tearing. Fortunately, this is usually temporary and rarely causes permanent damage to the eyes.

Long term exposure to UV radiation can be more serious. A number of scientific studies and research have shown that exposure to small amounts of UV-B radiation over a period of many years may increase your chance of developing a cataract and can cause damage to the retina, the nerve-rich lining of your eye that is used for seeing. Damage to the retina is usually not reversible.

The effects of UV radiation are cumulative, meaning that the longer your eyes are exposed, the greater risks. Therefore, you should wear quality sunglasses that offer good protection and a hat or cap with a wide brim whenever you are working or playing in the sun.

Fortunately, eye protection from UV radiation is readily available. Standard prescription sunglasses can be prescribed with special UV blockers that specifically filter out harmful UV rays.

A good pair of non-prescription sunglasses should block out most of the UV radiation harmful to the human eyes. But not all sunglasses provide adequate protection, and one should seek professional advice.

The Media in Anguilla

Nat Hodge

One of the results of the Anguilla Revolution of May 30, 1967, was the establishment of the media on the small Caribbean island. Up until the 1960s, Anguilla had no radio stations, television stations nor newspapers.

In September 1967, Anguilla launched its first newspaper *The Beacon*. It was produced on a Gestetner machine owned by St Mary's Anglican Church Rectory. The Editor was Atlin Harrigan, who had migrated to England, then to the US Virgin Islands and had finally settled back home. He wrote frequent letters in *The St Kitts Democrat*, complaining about the poor conditions of life in Anguilla. He eventually became one of the foremost leaders of the Anguilla Revolution. He began publishing *The Beacon* while serving as a member of the Anguilla Council. In his editorial he wrote: "For the first time in the history of Anguilla, we have found it possible to publish a newspaper... whereby the people of Anguilla and the world outside ... can learn what is happening on the island and...voice their opinions.

"I have chosen the name *The Beacon*, because all the big ships passing to the north of Anguilla are grateful to Anguilla for her beacon at Sombrero [Lighthouse] to guide them to their destination..."

The paper received much support from Anguillians and friends in the United States and the United Kingdom. The donation of a table size off-set press enabled the paper to substantially increase its size and circulation. It began with 300 copies and eventually reached a circulation of 3,000.

On March 19, 1969, British troops landed on Anguilla to maintain law and order. At the beginning of April, Anguillians were surprised to hear a broadcasting station which identified itself as "Radio Anguilla". The broadcasts came from the British ship HMS Minera which was anchored off Road Bay. It was one of the ships that had brought part of the occupation force to the island. The 500-watt radio station was set up both for the British forces and the Anguillians. The equipment was later brought ashore and installed in a section of the Agricultural Building. In welcoming the station, the newspaper Editor wrote: "The Beacon welcomes the radio station as a valuable sister

> "For the first time in the history of Anguilla, we have found it possible to publish a newspaper . . . whereby the people of Anguilla and the world outside . . . can learn what is happening on the island and . . . voice their opinions."

medium of communication on the island. It should play a very important part in keeping the island really informed… Anguillians in the nearby islands will now be able to get the latest happenings on the island first hand."

With the establishment of Radio Anguilla the people became more a listening public than a reading public. Moreover, *The Beacon* later encountered differences of opinion between the political leadership. At one point its printing press was taken away. The paper eventually folded in April 1971. Another small weekly newspaper, *The Observer*, published by the late Atkin Rogers, appeared on the scene for a short time.

In September 1975, *The Times*, a weekly paper, came on the scene. However in April 1976, it reported that the shareholders had decided to publish a monthly journal instead. The reason given "was the very poor response of the merchants of Anguilla to advertise." The paper eventually folded.

Also in April 1976, the British Government handed over Radio Anguilla to the local Government. It became the Department of Information and Broadcasting. In 1980, a 1,000-watt transmitter, for use by the station, was donated to the Government by the Caribbean Beacon. In 1989, the station was relocated on the top floor of the Customs Department. The Caribbean Beacon began its religious programming in 1981. It was previously owned by American broadcaster, William Kitchen. In 1992, it was purchased by Dr Gene Scott of Wescott Christian Center in California and substantially expanded. It is licensed to broadcast on 690 AM with 100 kilowatts; 1610 AM with 100 kilowatts; on SW with 100 kilowatts and FM on 35 kilowatts.

In 1988, yet another weekly newspaper, *Vantage*, began publishing. It was owned by a number of local shareholders and was edited by James Fleming, an Anguillian economist. It ceased publishing in 1990.

At present, Anguilla is served by two weekly newspapers and a few other publications. One of the newspapers is *The Light*, published by George Hodge, who taught for many years in Canada. He began publishing the paper in April 1993. He also publishes *What We Do In Anguilla*, a monthly tourism tabloid started in 1987. His other publication for a number of years is the annual tourism magazine also called *What We do In Anguilla*.

The other weekly newspaper is *The Anguillian* published by Nathaniel Hodge who retired from the public service post of Director of Information and Broadcasting in September 1998. He started the paper in December that year. Another publication is *Anguilla Life Magazine*. It is published quarterly by East Caribbean Publishing Company. The Publisher and Editor-in-Chief is Claire Devener, an American travel writer residing on Anguilla.

Several newspapers and periodicals from the Caribbean, the United States and the United Kingdom are regularly available at supermarkets and other outlets on the island.

Cable Television was started in Anguilla in 1984 by Cuthwin Webster and other shareholders. It had two 'head-ends', one at Island Harbour and the other in The Valley, providing residents with eight channels. In 1988, it was purchased by Caribbean Cable Television Holdings Ltd. The two head-ends were combined at one location and the channels were increased to twelve. By 2003, over 55 channels were available to customers. The parent company operates All Island Cable Television which also offers internet services. DIRECTV is the most recent company granted a licence to operate on the island. The other media include Heartbeat Radio FM 107.5; Kool FM 103.3; Voice of Creation 106.7 and New Beginning Radio 99.3. Anguilla has emerged from an island where communication services were non-existent to one where there has been tremendous growth in the sector.

AN EVOLUTION IN RADIO

Radio Anguilla was born out of political expediency. For years prior to the 1967 revolution, those Anguillians who possessed receiving radios listened to far away broadcasting stations like the BBC and the Voice of America, and nearby stations like WIVI in St Thomas and WVV in Vieques. In the early 1960s, St Kitts, to which Anguilla was then constitutionally and politically linked, acquired ZIZ but it was essentially a broadcasting service for that island and its people.

The political upheaval in 1967 found Anguilla without its own radio communications. This inability to communicate by radio with the people of the island was an awkward situation in a time of revolution. At times, announcements had to be broadcast in St Thomas in the hope that Anguillians back home would hear the information. Public meetings had to be the order of the day. The coming of the then one-sheet weekly *Beacon* newspaper was a godsend to many as it kept them informed about general matters.

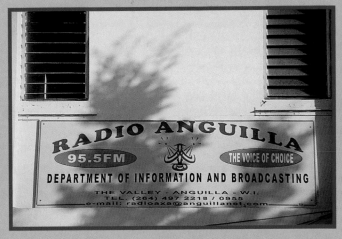

The British invasion of Anguilla in March 1969 was to add a new dimension to communications. On April 3, 1969, Anguillians were surprised to pick up the transmission of a nearby radio station and were alarmed when the station identification was made, "This is Radio Anguilla ...". The broadcast came from the British frigate HMS Minerva anchored off Road Bay, using some extra radio communications equipment it carried. But the broadcast service was not meant for Anguillians, but rather the British paratroopers and other personnel who were occupying the island. The radio was essentially to entertain them with the British pop music they had missed as well as to re-broadcast the BBC News and British programmes.

The British frigate could not, however, remain indefinitely in Anguillian waters and so the decision was taken to set up the radio equipment on the island. Within days it was installed in the storeroom of the old Agricultural Department in The Valley (now demolished) and two transmitter towers were hastily erected. On April 9, 1969, Radio Anguilla began broadcasting from its new location, but still for the British occupation on the island.

However, the need to communicate with Anguillians eventually led to a gradual shift in the focus of Radio Anguilla which was able to refute misinformation and to begin a well-needed service to the island.

Over a period of time, the station emerged as a community radio station seeking to inform, educate and entertain the people of the island. In April 1976, the station was handed over to the Government of Anguilla and became known as the Department of Information and Broadcasting.

The station was first managed by Roy Dunlop from the United Kingdom during the period September 1969 to August 1974. He was replaced by Menes Hodge, MBE, who served during the period 1975 – 1992, followed by Nathaniel Hodge, MBE, 1992 – 1998, and Kenneth Hodge from January 2000.

After much delay, the British Development Division in Barbados provided funds for the construction of new studios and offices for the Department of Information and Broadcasting (upstairs in the Customs Department at the Secretariat Compound). The building was completed by the end of 1988 and was occupied from February 1989 following installation of the equipment.

In 2000, the British Good Government Fund provided new equipment to modernise the station's operations. This included a new state of the art 1000 Watt FM transmitter, a broadcast jeep which allowed better mobility in broadcasting events across the island as well as computers and other studio equipment.

On April 9, 2002, the station automated most of its operations allowing for the more efficient and effective delivery of programmes and services. The station went online in 2003 which allows Anguillians in the region, the United States, the United Kingdom and the world over to tune in via the Internet for important events in Anguilla such as Carnival and broadcasts from the House of Assembly as well as to keep in touch with family and relatives back home.

The station, which celebrated its 34th anniversary this year, now holds membership in several regional and international agencies and organizations including the Caribbean Media Corporation (Caribbean News Agency and the Caribbean Broadcasting Union), GIS Online and the OECS Newslink.

The broadcasting landscape has significantly changed over the years. The station has gone from enjoying an unchallenged monopoly in the early years to one where it now has to exist alongside other media entities. There are, to date, five other local stations of which three are religious-based. This has served to widen the listening choices for the island's more than 12,000 inhabitants.

Despite these competing forces, the station still remains the choice of many with its wide range of programming designed to cater for every taste and age group.

GOVERNMENT DIRECTORY

GOVERNOR

H.E. The Governor
Governor's Office, Old Ta
Tel: 264-497-2621
Email: govthouse@anguillanet.com

MINISTERS OF GOVERNMENT

Honourable Osbourne Fleming
Chief Minister
Tel: 264-497-2518

Honourable Victor Banks
Minister of Finance
Tel: 264-497-2451

Honourable Eric Reid
Minister of Social Services
Tel: 264-497-2451

Honourable Kenneth Harrigan
Minister of Infrastructure &
Communication & Utilities
Tel: 264-497-2651

Honourable Hubert Hughes
Leader of the Opposition
Member for Road South
Tel: 264-497-6848

Honourable Albert Hughes
Member for West End
Tel: 264-497-6400

Honourable Edison Baird
Member for Road North
Tel: 264-497-5321

MINISTRIES OF GOVERNMENT

**Ministry of Tourism &
Home Affairs**
Tel: 264-497-2518
Tel: 264-497-5494 (South Hill)
Email: chief-minister@gov.ai

**Ministry of Finance & Economic
Planning & Development**
Tel: 264-497-2547
Email: mosgoa@anguillanet.com

Ministry of Social Development
Tel: 264-497-3930
Email: socialdhealth@gov.ai
　　　socialeducation@gov.ai

**Ministry of Infrastructure &
Communications and Utilities**
Tel: 264-497-2442
Email: banksmicu@anguillanet.com

POLITICAL PARTIES

Anguilla United Front (AUF)
Tel: 264-497-4783

Anguilla United Movement (AUM)
Tel: 264-497-6848

ACCOUNTANTS

Audain & Associates
Landsome Road
Tel: 264-497-5620
Fax: 264-497-5220

KPMG
Herbert's Commercial Centre
Tel: 264-497-5500
Email: cvromney@kpmg.com

AIRLINES

Air Anguilla
Wallblake Airport
The Valley
Tel: 264-497-6426

American Airlines/American Eagle
Wallblake Airport
The Valley
Tel: 264-497-3501
Fax: 264-497-3502
Email: eagleaa@anguillanet.com
Website: www.aa.com

Caribbean Star Airlines/Starpac
Wallblake Airport
The Valley
Tel: 264-497-8690
Fax: 264-497-8689
Website: www.flycaribbeanstar.com

LIAT (1974) Ltd
Wallblake Airport
The Valley
Tel: 264-497-5000
Fax: 264-497-5576
Email: liataxa@hotmail.com
Website: www.fly-liat.com

Winair
Wallblake Airport
The Valley
Tel: 264-497-2748

Trans Anguilla
Wallblake Airport
The Valley
Tel: 264-497-8690
Fax: 264-497-8689

APARTMENTS, CONDOMINIUMS & VILLAS

Carimar Beach Club
Meads Bay
Tel: 264-497-6881
Email: carimar@anguillanet.com

Harbor Lights
Island Harbour
Tel: 264-497-4435
Email: harborlights@anguillanet.com

Madeariman Beach Club
Shoal Bay East
Tel:264- 497-3833
Email: info@madeariman.com

Maria's Beach Apartments
Sandy Ground
Tel: 264-497-2427
Email: shermah@anguillanet.com

Masara Resort
Katouche
Tel: 264-497-3200
Email: lambertventures@yahoo.com

Nathan's Cove
Meads Bay
Tel: 264-497-2596

Ocean Breeze
Long Path
Tel: 264- 497-2466
Fax: 264- 497-3084

Paradise Cove
The Cove
Tel : 264- 497-6603
Email: para-cove@anguillanet.com

Royal Palms
South Hill
Tel: 264-497-6484
Email: royalpalms@anguillanet.com

Roy's Beachfront Inn
Crocus Bay
Tel: 264-497-2470
Email: royboss1@anguillanet.com

Seahorse Apartments
Rendezvous Bay
Tel: 264-497-6751
Email: seahorseofanguilla@hotmail.com

Seaview
Sandy Ground
Tel: 264-497-2427
Email: shermah@anguillanet.com

Skiffles Villas
Lower South Hill
Tel: 264-497-6619

Sunshine Villas
South Hill
Tel: 264-497-6149
Fax: 264-497-6021

Sur La Plage
Meads Bay
Tel: 264-497-6598
Email: surlaplagevillas@aol.com

Temenos Villas
Long Bay
Tel: 264-222-9000
Email: reservations@temenosvillas.com

Villa Mortons
The Valley
Tel: 264-497-4749 / Fax: 264-497-4101

ART GALLERIES & MUSEUMS

Anguilla National Trust
The Valley
Tel: 264-497-5297
Fax: 264-497-5571

Bartlett's Collections
South Hill
Tel:264-497-6623
Email: bartlett@anguillanet.com

Cheddie's Carving Studio
West End Road
Tel:264-497-6027
Email: cheddie@anguillanet.com

Cuisinart Resort & Spa
Rendezvous Bay
Tel: 264-498-2000 / Fax: 264-498-2010

Devonish Art Gallery
West End Road
Tel: 264-497-2949

Echoes of the Caribbean
Meads Bay Hideaway
Tel: 264-498-5555

Estate Hope Art Studio
Crocus Hill
Tel: 264-497-8733
Email: carolann966@msn.com

Heritage Collection
East End
Tel: 264-497-4440
Fax: 264-497-4067

L'Atelier Art Studio
North Hill
Tel: 264-497-5668
Email: micheleart@anguillanet.com

Le Petite Gallery
South Hill
Tel: 264-497-6110
Fax: 264-497-6110

Loblolly Gallery
The Valley
Tel: 264-497-4229 / Fax: 264-497-3838

Lynne Bernbaum Art Studio
George Hill
Tel: 264-497-5211
Email: lynne@lynnebernbaum.com

Palm Garden Art Studio
North Hill
Tel: 264-497-5707
Email: owenvas@anguillanet.com

Pineapple Gallery
Sandy Ground
Tel: 264-497-3609
Email: manasse@anguillanet.com

Rendezvous Bay Hotel & Art Gallery
Rendezvous Bay
Tel: 264-497-6549
Fax: 264-497-6026

Savannah Gallery
The Valley
Tel: 264-497-2263
Email: savannah@anguillanet.com

World Art Antiques Gallery
Old Factory Plaza
Tel: 264-497-5950
Email: worldart1@yahoo.com

AUTOMOBILE DEALERS

Anguilla Motors Ltd
Airport Road
Tel: 264-497-2723
Email: islandcar@anguillanet.com

Apex Car Rental & Sales
The Quarter
Tel: 264-497-2642
Fax: 264-497-5032

Connor's Car Rental & Sales
South Hill
Tel: 264-497-6433 / Fax: 264-497-6410

AVIATION

Wallblake Airport
Main Office
Tel: 264-497-2384
Fax: 264-497-5928
Email: wallblakeairport@anguillanet.com

Wallblake Airport
Air Traffic Control
Tel: 264-497-2526
Email: airtrafficcontrol@anguillanet.com

Wallblake Airport
Fire Station & Security
Tel: 264-497-8395

Wallblake Airport
VIP Lounge
Tel: 264-497-3510

BANKS

Caribbean Commercial Bank
The Valley
Tel: 264-497-2571
Email: ccbaxa@anguillanet.com

Eastern Caribbean Central Bank
Fairplay Complex Building
Tel: 264-497-5050
Email: eccbaxa@anguillanet.com

First Caribbean International Bank
The Valley
Tel: 264-497-2301 / Fax: 264-497-2980

National Bank of Anguilla
The Valley
Tel: 264-497-2101
Email: nbabank@anguillanet.com

Scotia Bank Anguilla Ltd
Fairplay Complex Building
Tel: 264-497-3333

BAKERS

Amy's Bakery
Blowing Point
Tel: 264-497-6775

Chandeliers Patisserie
South Hill
Tel: 264-497-6259

Fat Cat Gourmet To Go
George Hill
Tel: 264-497-2307

Gee Wee's Bakery
Lower South Hill
Tel: 264-497-6452

Hall's Unique Bakery & Café
The Valley
Tel: 264-497-5538 / Fax: 264-497-5719

Highway Bakery
George Hill
Tel: 264-497-5512

Le Bon Pain Bakery & Pastry Shop
Island Harbour
Tel: 264-497-4090

Lynette's Bakery
Landsome Road
The Valley
Tel: 264-497-3465

Mary's Bakery
The Quarter
Tel: 264-497-2318

Nikki's Cake Stand
Sachasses
Tel: 264-235-7397

BARBERS

Clip Top Barber Shop
South Hill
Tel: 264-497-7633

Drak's Barber Shop
Herbert's Commercial Center
Tel: 264-497-3392

Original Barber Shop
South Hill
Tel: 264-497-5494

Side View Barber Shop
The Valley
Tel: 264-497-3392

Timi's Barber Shop
Island Harbour
Tel: 264-497-4346 / 264-235-4695

BIKES & SCOOTER RENTAL

A & S Scooter Rentals
Tel: 264-497-8803

Exotic Plus
The Valley
Tel: 264-497-3533

Flambayo Bicycle Shop
George Hill
Tel: 264-235-5370

BOAT RENTAL & CHARTERS

Chocolat
Sandy Ground
Tel: 264-497-3394

Gotcha, Garfield Sea Tours
North Hill
Tel: 264-497-2956
Email: gotcha@anguillanet.com

Johnno's Charters
Sandy Ground
Tel: 264-497-2728

Link Ferry
Little Harbour
Tel: 264-497-2231
Fax: 264-497-3290

NoFear Charters
Long Bay
Tel: 264-497-8704

Sandy Island Enterprises Ltd.
Sandy Ground
Tel: 264-497-5643

Sea Grape Charters
Island Harbour
Tel: 264-235-7364

BOUTIQUES

Caribbean Silk Screen
South Hill
Tel: 264-497-2272
Fax: 264-497-3148

Janvels Boutique
Blowing Point
Tel: 264-497-6221

Kimmy's Fashion Boutique
Fairplay Commercial Complex
Tel: 264-497-3876
Fax: 264-497-3303

Kish Baby World
Clarita Mason Mall
Tel: 264-497-2008

Liacias Place
George Hill
Tel: 264-497-3729

Lucy's Boutique
South Hill
Tel: 264-497-6584

Millie's Boutique
James Ronald Webster Building
Tel: 264-497-2581

Oluwakemi's Afrocentric Boutique
Landsome Road
The Valley
Tel: 264-497-5411

Shoes Plus & Images Boutique
George Hill
Tel: 264-497-5810
Fax: 264-497-5810

Something Special
Cove Road
Tel: 264-497-6655 / Fax: 264-497-2735

Three C's Boutique
Sandy Ground
Tel: 264-497-2067

BROADCASTING

Radio

Caribbean Beacon Radio
The Long Road
Tel: 264- 497-4341

Heart Beat Radio
Sugar Hill
Tel: 264-497-3354
Email: hearbeat107.5@hotmail.com

Kool FM 103.3
North Side
Tel: 479-0103/0104
Email: mekool13@hotmail.com

NBR Grace FM
Shoal Bay Road
Tel: 264-497-0977
Email: nbrgracefm@yahoo.com

Radio Anguilla
The Valley
Tel: 264-497-2218
Email: radioaxa@anguillanet.com

Voice of Creation Radio JESUS
Sachasses
Tel: 264-497-0106
Email: vocstation@hotmail.com

Television

All Island Cable TV
Tel: 264-497-3600
Email: alisland@anguillanet.com

Direct TV
Tel: 264-498-4276

KCN Television
Tel: 264-497-3519
Email: kcn@anguillanet.com

CAR RENTAL

Apex Car Rental
The Quarter
Tel: 264-497-2642
Email: avisaxa@anguillanet.com

Avis Car Rental
The Quarter
Tel: 264-497-2642
Email: avisaxa@anguillanet.com

Caribbean Rental Ltd
The Valley
Tel: 264- 497-4662
Email: d-3ent@anguillanet.com

Connor's Car Rentals
South Hill
Tel: 264- 497-6433
Email: lucy@saintmaarten.net

Highway Rent A Car
George Hill
Tel: 264-497-2183

Island Car Rental
Wallblake Road
Tel: 264- 497-2723
Email: islandcar@anguillanet.com

Junie's Car Rental
Blowing Point
Tel: 264-497-7114 / 264-235-6114

Summer Set Car Rental
George Hill
Tel:264- 497-5278
Email: summerset@anguillanet.com

Thrifty Car Rental
The Valley
Tel: 264-497-2656

Triple K Car Rental
The Forest
Tel: 264-497-2934
Email: hertztriplek@anguillanet.com

CLUBS & ASSOCIATIONS

Brownies & Cubs
Tel: 264-497-2871 / 264-235-6104

Camp Beware
Tel: 264-497-2888
Email: egelm@anguillanet.com

Football & Cricket
Tel: 264-497-6665
Tel: 264-497-8395

Girl Guide Movement
Tel: 264-497-5430 / 264-497-3456

Scouts & Guides
Tel: 264-497-5430 / 264-497-3456

CONFERENCE CENTRES

Altamer Villa
Tel: 264-498-4000
Email: reggleton@altamer.com

Anguilla Great House
Tel: 264-497-6061
Email: flemingw@anguillanet.com

Anguilla Teachers' Resource Centre
Tel: 264-497-5704
Email: ocodproj@anguillanet.com

Chandeliers Conference Centre
Tel: 264-497-2201/6259

Malliouhana Hotel & Spa
Tel: 264-497-6111
Email: malliouhana@anguillanet.com

Paradise Cove Resort
Tel: 264-497-6603
Email: para-cove@anguillanet.com

Rendezvous Bay Hotel
Tel: 264-497-6549
Email: info@rendezvousbay.com

CONSTRUCTION

Anderson Home Planners &
Construction Inc.
Wallblake Road
Tel: 264-497-8082 / Fax: 264-497-2335

Brooks Construction Co Ltd
George Hill
Tel: 264-497-8523
Fax: 264-497-8523

Carmay's Furniture & Construction
Materials
Wallblake
Tel: 264-497-2807
Fax: 264-497-3114

Hilton Construction Co Ltd
South Hill
Tel: 264-497-6586

James Construction Rental & Sales
Stoney Ground
Tel: 264-497-0853

KT & T Business Services
Airport Road
Tel: 264-497-4438
Fax: 264-497-4438

Leeward Construction Co Ltd
The Valley
Tel: 264-497-5613
Fax: 264-497-5613

Orchard Romney Beck & Associates Inc.
The Valley
Tel: 264-497-6275 / Fax: 264-497-6355

CUSTOMS

Customs Department
Main Office, The Valley
Tel: 264-497-2513
Fax: 264-497-5483
Email: customs@gov.ai

Customs Department
Blowing Point
Tel:/Fax: 264-497-6853

Customs Department
Road Bay
Tel: 264-497-2213

Customs Department
Wallblake Airport
Tel: 264-497-2514

DOCTORS

Hodge Medical Services Ltd
The Johnson Building
The Valley
Tel: 264-497-5828
Fax: 264-497-8329

Hughes Medical Centre
Lower South Hill
Tel: 264-497-3053
Fax: 264-497-3083

Hotel de Health
Palm Court
Seafeathers Bay
Tel: 264-497-4166 / Fax: 264-497-4194

Dr Arjoon Jagan's Clinic
North Valley
Tel: 264-497-2632

DENTISTS

Anguilla Dental Unit
The Valley
Tel: 264-497-2343 / Fax: 264-497-5486

Centre for Dental and Facial Aesthetics
The Anguilla Professional Complex
The Valley
Tel: 264-498-1212 / Fax: 264-497-1214

DEVELOPMENT ORGANISATIONS

Anguilla Development Board
Tel: 264-497-2595
Fax: 264-497-2959

Anguilla Mortgage Company
Tel: 264-497-5450
Fax: 264-497-3572

DRUGS

Drugs Hotline
Tel: 264-497-4000

EDUCATION

Education Department
Tel: 264-497-2874

Gloria Omolulu Institute
Tel: 264-497-5430

EMERGENCY SERVICES
AMBULANCE   911
FIRE   911
POLICE   911

FERRY SERVICES

Deluxe Ferry
Blowing Point
Tel: 264-497-6289

Early Bird Ferry
South Hill
Tel: 264-497-6967

Excellence Ferry
Long Path
Tel: 264-497-4797

Glass Bottom Tours
Shoal Bay
Tel: 264-497-4360

Joshlin Ferry
Blowing Point
Tel: 264-497-6289

Lady Maria
Rey Hill
Tel: 264-497-3128

Link Cat
Little Harbour
Tel: 264-497-2231

Niki V Ferry
Tel: 264-497-6334

Samantha Ferry
Blowing Point
Tel: 264-497-6334

Shantiwa Ferry
South Hill
Tel: 264-497-6426

Teezech Ferry
South Hill
Tel: 264-497-6426

FUNERAL HOMES

Rey's Funeral Home
George Hill
Tel: 264-497-2278
Fax: 264-497-3037

Two Sons Funeral Home
North Hill
Tel: 264-497-3249
Fax: 264-497-2903

FINANCIAL & INVESTMENT SERVICES

Anguilla Financial Services
Tel: 264-497-3881
Email: anguillafsd@anguillasfd.com

HAIR & BEAUTY SALONS

Donnette's Hair & Nail Salon
Blowing Point
Tel: 264-497-8983

Ebony & Ivory Beauty Center
Stoney Ground
Tel: 264-497-0001

Elsa's Hair Styles
Long Road
Tel: 264-497-4454
Fax: 264-497-4496

Exquisite Nails
North Hill
Tel: 264-497-8411 / 264-235-8411

Hair World & Accessories
Herbert's Commercial Center
Tel: 264-497-0052

Hazel's Beauty Salon
George Hill
Tel: 264-497-2954

Lucy's Hair Salon
South Hill
Tel: 264-497-6584

Shakhar's Hair Salon
Upper South Hill
Tel: 264-497-7412
Fax: 264-497-8004

Stephanie
The Quarter
Tel: 264-497-3076

Unique Salon
The Quarter
Tel: 264-497-3567

HIKING

Oliver Hodge
Tel: 264-497-3696

HORSEBACK RIDING

Cliff Side Stables
North Hill
Tel: 264- 497-3667
Email: gotcha@anguillanet.com

El Rancho Del Blues
Blowing Point
Tel: 264-497-6164 / Fax: 264-497-6106

HOSPITALS & MEDICAL CENTRES

Hodge Medical Services
Johnson Building, Box 146
The Valley
Tel: 264-497-5828 / Fax: 264-497-8329
Email: hodgeb@anguillanet.com

Hughes Medical Centre
West End
Tel: 264-497-3053 / Fax: 264-497-3085
Email: hughesmedical@anguillanet.com
Website: www.hughesmedical.com

Princess Alexandra Hospital
The Valley
Tel: 264-497-2551
Fax: 264-497-5745
Email: alexandrah@anguillanet.com

HOTELS & RESORTS

Anguilla Great House Beach Resort
Rendezvous Bay
Tel: 497-6061
Email: fleming@anguillanet.com

Arawak Beach Inn
Island Harbour
Tel: 497-4888
Email: relax@arawakbeach.com

Cap Juluca Hotel
Maundays Bay
Tel: 264-497-6666
Email: capjuluca@anguillanet.com

Coccoloba Resort
Barnes Bay
Tel: 264-497-8800
Email: valtur-cocoloba@anguillanet.com

CoveCastles
Shoal Bay West
Tel: 264-497-6801
Email: covecastles@anguillanet.com

Cuisinart Resort & Spa
Rendezvous Bay
Tel: 264-498-2000
Email: reservations@cuisinart.ai

Frangipani Beach Club
Meads Bay
Tel: 264-497-6442
Email: frangpani@anguillanet.com

La Sirena Hotel
Meads Bay
Tel: 264-497-6827
Email: lasirena@anguillanet.com

Malliouhana Hotel & Spa
Meads Bay
Tel: 264-497-6111
Email: malliouhana@anguillanet.com

Rendezvous Bay Hotel & Villas
Rendezvous Bay
Tel: 497-6549
Email: rendezvous@anguillanet.com

Shoal Bay Beach Hotel
Shoal Bay
Tel: 264-497-2011
Email:shoalbaybeach@anguillanet.com

Shoal Bay Villas
Shoal Bay
Tel: 264-497-2051
Email: sbv@anguillanet.com

IMMIGRATION

Immigration Department
Main Office, The Valley
Tel: 264-497-3994
Fax: 264-497-0310

Immigration Department
Blowing Point
Tel: 264-497-6665

Immigration Department
Sandy Ground
Tel: 264-497-3611

Immigration Department
Wallblake Airport
Tel: 264-497-2411

INNS & GUESTHOUSES

Allamanda Beach Club
Shoal Bay
Tel: 264-497-5217
Email: info@allamanda.ai

Ferryboat Inn
Blowing Point
Tel: 264-497-6613
Email: ferryb@anguillanet.com

Harbour Villas
Island Harbour
Tel: 264-497-4393
Email: hvillas@anguillanet.com

Inter Island Hotel
Lower South Hill
Tel: 264-497-6259

La Palma
Sandy Ground
Tel: 264-497-6620 / Fax: 264-497-5381

Lloyd's Guest House
The Valley
Tel: 264-497-2351
Email: Lloyds@web.ai

Milly's Inn
Shoal Bay
Tel: 264-497-4274

Paradise Apartments
Rey Hill
Tel: 264-497-2168 / Fax: 264-497-5591

Patsy's Seaside Villas
Blowing Point
Tel: 264-497-6279
Email: patsysseaside@hotmail.com

The Pavillion
Blowing Point
Tel: 264-497-8284
Email: pavillioninn@aol.com

Sydans Apartments
Sandy Ground
Tel: 264-497-3180 / Fax: 264-497-5381

INSURANCE COMPANIES

A-Affordable Insurance Services Inc.
Tel: 264-497-5757
Email: a-assins@anguillanet.com

British American Company
Tel: 264-497-2653
Email: britam@anguillanet.com

Caribbean Alliance Insurance Co. Ltd
Tel: 264-497-3525
Email: d-3ent@anguillanet.com

D-3 Enterprises Ltd
Tel: 264-497-3525
Email: d-3ent@anguillanet.com

Fairplay Management Services Ltd
Tel: 264-497-2976
Email: fairplayins1@anguillanet.com

Malliouhana Development Co-Operative
Tel: 264-497-2712

LEGAL

Astaphan TWR Barrister/Solicitor
Herbert's Commercial Complex
The Valley
Tel: 264-497-5555
Email: astphankelsick@axanet.com

Caribbean Associated Attorneys
Landsome Road, The Valley
Tel: 264-497-5405
Email: abelc@anguillanet.com

Caribbean Juris Chambers
Herbert's Commercial Complex
The Valley
Tel: 264-497-3571
Email: caribjur@anguillanet.com

Harney Westwood & Reigels
The Valley
Tel: 264-498-5000
Email: hwr@anguillanet.com

JAG Gumbs & Co.
Anguilla Professional Complex
The Valley
Tel: 264-497-1212
Email: jaggumbs_co@anguillanet.com

Keithley Lake & Associates
The Valley
Tel: 264-497-3142
Email: axa-offshore@anguillanet.com

Lake & Kentish Chambers
The Quarter
Tel: 264-497-2582
Email: laken@anguillanet.com

Myrna Walwyn & Associates
The Valley
Tel: 264-497-2484
Email: mrwa@anguillanet.com

Webster Dyrud Mitchell
The Quarter
Tel: 264-497-2060
Email: information@websterdyrud.com

Wigley's Chamber
The Valley
Tel: 264-497-8129
Email: wiglegJ@anguillanet.com

LIBRARY

Anguilla Public Library
The Valley
Tel: 264-497-2441 / Fax: 264-497-2434
Email: axalibry@anguillanet.com

NEWSPAPERS

The Anguillian
Tel: 264-497-3823
Email: theanguillian@anguillanet.com

The Light
Tel: 264-497-3138
Email: thelight@anguillanet.com

What To Do In Anguilla
Tel: 264-497-5641
Email: thelight@anguillanet.com

NIGHTCLUBS

Johnno's Beach Stop
Sandy Ground
Tel: 264-497-2728

Pumphouse
Sandy Ground
Tel: 264-497-5154

Rafe's
Back Street
South Hill
Tel: 264-497-3914

Red Dragon's Nightclub
South Hill
Tel: 264-497-2439

ORGANISATIONS

Anguilla National Trust
The Valley
Tel: 264-497-5297 / Fax: 264-497-5571

Boys & Girls Brigade Company
South Hill
Tel: 264-497-2612
Fax: 264-497-8460

Boys & Girls Scouts
The Valley
Tel: 264-497-2971

Freemasons
Blowing Point
Tel: 264-497-6753

Lions Club
The Valley
Tel: 264- 498-0117

Optimist Club
The Valley
Tel: 264-497-4278

Soroptimist Club
The Valley
Tel: 264-497-2711

PAINT CENTRES

Brooks & Sons Painting Co. Ltd
Old Factory Plaza
Tel: 264-497-5628
Fax: 264-497-6808

D A & A Paint Center
The Valley
Tel: 264-497-3365
Fax: 264-497-3378

Richardson's Paint Center
North Hill
Tel: 264-497-2819

PHARMACIES

Anguilla Drug Store
The Valley
Tel: 264-497-2738
Fax:264-497-5656

Paramount Pharmacy
Water Swamp
Tel: 264-497-2366 / Fax: 264-497-3866

Princess Alexandra Pharmacy
Princess Alexandra Hospital
Stoney Ground
Tel: 264-497-2551

PHOTOGRAPHERS

Andy Brown
Blowing Point
Tel: 264-235-6194
E-mail: fungkers@hotmail.com

Leroy Bryan
Cauls Bottom
Tel: 264-498-5151

Jackie Cestero
Shoal Bay
Tel: 264-497-5024

Lloyd Gumbs
North Hill
Tel: 264-235-6041

Ivor Hodge
The Farrington
Tel: 264-497-3590

Chris Mason
Island Harbour
Tel: 264-497-5670

Rocklyn Maynard
North Side
Tel: 264-235-3390
Fax: 264-497-7865

Colville Petty
East End
Tel: 264-497-4440
Fax: 264-497-4067

Rogers Photo Studio & Lab
Stoney Ground
Tel: 264-497-2832
Fax: 264-497-8342

POLICE

Royal Anguilla Police
Main Office, The Valley
Tel: 264-497-2333
Fax: 264-497-3746

Royal Anguilla Police
Blowing Point
Tel: 264-497-6533

Royal Anguilla Police
Sandy Ground
Tel: 264-497-2354

POST OFFICE

Anguilla General Post Office
Tel: 264-497-2528
Fax: 264-497-5695

PRINTERS

Anguilla Printers
Stoney Ground
Tel: 264-497-2258
Fax: 264-497-2259

Max Printing Services
Stoney Ground
Tel: 264-497-5414
Fax: 264-497-5415

Professional Services
The Valley
Tel: 264-497-3575
Fax: 264-497-3577

Rainbow Graphics
Rainbow Isle Shopping Center
Long Road
Tel: 264-497-4777
Fax: 264-498-4777

PROFESSIONAL ASSOCIATIONS

Anguilla Hotel & Tourism Association
Tel: 264-497-2944

Civil Service Association
Tel: 264-497-2451

Farmers Association
Tel: 264-497-2615

Nurses Association
Tel: 264-497-2551

Teachers Union Association
Tel: 264-497-2875

PUBLICATIONS

Anguilla Life Magazine
Tel: 264-497-2881
Email: kedivar@aol.com

Anguilla Vacation Planner
Tel: 264-497-2759
Email: atbtour@anguillanet.com

Island Dream Magazine
Tel: 264-497-2944
Email: ahta@anguillanet.com

Island Hopper Magazine
Tel: 264-497-2748

What We Do In Anguilla Magazine
Tel: 264-497-5641
Email: thelight@anguillanet.com

RELIGIOUS INSTITUTIONS

Anglican Church
The Rectory, The Quarter
Tel: 264-497-2971
Email: brookx@anguillanet.com

Apostolic Faith Church
The Valley
Tel: 264-497-2279 / 4480

Central Baptist Church
Rey Hill
Tel: 264-497-3324

Christian Fellowship Church
Blowing Point
Tel: 264-497-6681
Email: ambrich@hotmail.com

Church of God of Holiness
Queen Elizabeth Avenue
Tel: 264-497-2618
Email: checc@anguillanet.com

Church of God of Prophecy
The Quarter
Tel: 264-497-6333/2038/6703

Hill Top Baptist Church
Island Harbour
Tel: 264-497-4235

Jehovah's Witnesses
Stoney Ground
Tel: 264-497-2629

Masjid An Nur (Mosque)
Locrum , Blowing Point
Tel: 264-497-3214 / 264-235-3214

Methodist Church
South Hill Manse
Tel: 264-497-2612
Email: Methodism@anguillanet.com

Mount Fortune Seventh Day Adventist
Church Gate East End
Tel: 264-497-4218

Rastafarian - David House Solomonic
Gaathly
Blowing Point Road
Tel: 264-772-2118

St Gerard's Roman Catholic Church
Wallblake Road
Tel: 264-497-2405
Email: stgerards47@hotmail.com

Wesleyan Holiness Church
Stoney Ground
Tel: 264-497-5976

RESTAURANTS

Altamer Restaurant
Shoal Bay West
Tel: 264-498-4000
Email: reggleton@altamer.com

Arawak Café at Arawak Beach Inn
Island Harbour
Tel: 264-497-4888
Email: relax@arawakbeach.com

Ashreds A-1
Long Path
Tel: 264-497-3444

Barrel Stay
Sandy Ground
Tel: 264-497-2831

Bistro Phil's
Lower South Hill
Tel: 264-497-6810

Blanchards Restaurant
Meads Bay
Tel: 264-497-6100

The Café at Covecastles Restaurant
Shoal Bay West
Tel: 264-497-6801
Email: covecastles@anguillanet.com

Cedar Grove at Rendezvous Bay Hotel
Rendezvous Bay
Tel: 264-497-6549
Email: info@rendezvousbay.com

Coconuts at La Sirena
Meads Bay
Tel: 264-497-6827
Email: lasirena@anguillanet

Cocoplums
Meads Bay
Tel: 264-497-6072

Corals
Meads Bay Hideaway
Tel: 264-498-5555

Corner Bar Pizza
North Hill
Tel: 264-497-3937

Elodias Beach Bar & Restaurant
Shoal Bay East
Tel: 264-497-1257
Email: elodias@anguillanet.com

Elsa's Restaurant
Island Harbour
Tel: 264-497-4706

English Rose Restaurant
Landsome Plaza
Tel: 264-497-5353

E's Oven
South Hill
Tel: 264-498-8258

Fat Cat Gourmet
George Hill
Tel: 264-497-2307

Ferryboat Inn
Blowing Point
Tel: 264-497-6613
Email: ferryb@anguillanet.com

Flavours Restaurant
Back Street
South Hill
Tel: 264-497-0629
Website: www.flavoursrestaurant.com

Frangipani Restaurant
Meads Bay
Tel: 264-497-6442
Email: frangipani@anguillanet.com

Fujau
Landsome Road
Tel: 264-497-2487

Georges at Cap Juluca
Maundays Bay
Tel: 264-497-6666
Email: capjuluca@anguillanet.com

Gorgeous Scilly Cay
Island Harbour
Tel: 264-497-5123
Email: Gorgeous@anguillanet.com

Gwen's Reggae Grill
Shoal Bay
Tel: 264-497-2120

Hibernia Restaurant
Island Harbour
Tel: 264-497-2930
Email: hibernia@anguillanet.com

J & J's Pizza
South Hill
Tel: 264-497-3215
Email: j&jpizza@hotmail.com

Johnno's Beach Bar & Restaurant
Sandy Ground
Tel: 264-497-2728

Landing Strip
Clarita Mason Mall
George Hill
Tel: 264-497-2268

Le Beach Restaurant
Shoal Bay
Tel: 264-497-5598

Le Bistro at Malliouhana Hotel
Meads Bay
Tel: 264-497-6111
Email: malliouhana@anguillanet.com

Madeariman Beach Restaurant
Shoal Bay
Tel: 264-497-3833
Email: info@madeariman.com

Malliouhana Restaurant
Meads Bay
Tel: 264-497-6111
Email: malliouhana@anguillanet.com

Mangos Restaurant Ltd
Barnes Bay
Tel: 264-497-6479

Mediterraneo at Cuisinart Resort & Spa
Rendezvous Bay
Tel: 264-498-2000
Email: igiusti@cuisinart.ai

Nico's Restaurant
Herbert's Commercial Center
Tel: 264-497-2844

Oliver's Seaside Grill
Long Bay
Tel: 264-497-8780

Oriental Restaurant
The Valley
Tel: 264-497-2763

Overlook
Back Street, South Hill
Tel: 264-497-4488

Palm Grove
Junks Hole Beach
Tel: 264-497-4224

Pepperpot Restaurant
The Valley
Tel: 264-497-2328

Pimms Restaurant at Cap Juluca
Maundays Bay
Tel: 264-497-6666
Email: capjuluca@anguillanet.com

Pumphouse Bar & Restaurant
Sandy Ground
Tel: 264-497-5154
Email: pumphouse@anguillanet.com

Ripples Restaurant
Sandy Ground
Tel: 264-497-3380
Email: ruan@anguillanet.com

Roadwell Café & Art
Roadwell, Sandy Ground
Tel: 264-497-3310

Roy's Place
Crocus Bay
Tel: 264-497-2470
Email: roy@roysplace@anguillanet.com

Santorini Restaurant at Cuisinart Resort & Spa
Rendezvous Bay
Tel: 264-498-2000
Email: igiusti@cuisinart.ai

Sapphire Restaurant
Maundays Bay
Tel: 264-498-8000

Serenity Restaurant
Shoal Bay
Tel: 264-497-3328

Ships Galley
Sandy Ground
Tel: 264-497-2040

Smitty's Seaside Grill
Island Harbour
Tel: 264-497-4300

Smokey's Restaurant
The Cove
Tel: 264-497-6582
Email: info@rendezvousbay.com

Snappers
Meads Bay
Tel: 264-497-6200

Straw Hat Restaurant
The Forest
Tel: 264-497-8300
Email: peter@strawhat.com

The Old Caribe Restaurant at Anguilla
Great House Beach Resort
Rendezvous Bay
Tel: 264-497-6061
Email: fleming@anguillanet.com

The Old House Restaurant
George Hill
Tel: 264-497-2228

Trattorio Tramonto
Shoal Bay West
Tel: 264-497-8819

Tropical Sunset
Shoal Bay
Tel: 264-497-3907

Uncle Ernie's
Shoal Bay
Tel: 497-3907

Zara's Restaurant
Shoal Bay
Tel: 264-497-3229

ROADS

Communication and Utilities
Tel: 264-497-2651

SCHOOLS (COMPREHENSIVE)

Albena Lake Hodge Comprehensive
School
Campus A
Tel: 264-497-2416
Fax: 264-497-3233

Albena Lake Hodge Comprehensive
School
Campus B
Tel: 264-497-0551
Fax: 264-497-0509

SCHOOLS (PRIMARY)

Island Harbour Primary School
Tel: 264-497-4181

Morris Vanterpool Primary School
Tel: 264-497-4419

Road Primary School
Tel: 264-497-6348

Stoney Ground Primary School
Tel: 264-497-2888

Valley Primary School
Tel: 264-497-2887

West End Primary School
Tel:-264-497-6721

SCUBA DIVING & WATER SPORTS

Anguilla Dive Center
Meads Bay
Tel: 264-497-4750
Email: axadiver@anguillanet.com

Shoal Bay Scuba & Water Sports
Shoal Bay
Tel: 264- 497-4371
Email: sbscuba@anguillanet.com

SHIPPING

ABF Services
Caribbean Commercial Center
The Valley
Tel: 264-497-5646
Email: abf@anguillanet.com

Harrigan Trading & Shipping
Wallblake Road
Tel: 497-0334
Fax: 264-497-0351

Haskins Ltd
The Valley
Tel: 264-497-2428 /6031
Email: shaskins@tropical.com

Island Transport Services
The Valley
Tel: 264-497-2679
Email: transaxa@anguillanet.com

SUPERMARKETS

Albert's Market Place
Stoney Ground Road
Tel: 264-497-2240
Email: lakear@anguillanet.com

Ashley & Sons Ltd
South Valley
Tel:264-497-2641
Fax: 264-497-3084
Email: ashleys@anguillanet.com

Bennie's & Sons
Blowing Point
Tel: 264-497-2788

Bryan's & Sons Grocery
Stoney Ground
Tel: 264-497-5427
Fax: 264-497-2921

Caracasbaai Grocery & Store
Stoney Ground
Tel: 264-497-2249
Email: caracasbaai@anguillanet.com

Christine's Mini Mart
Long Bay
Tel: 264-497-6309
Fax: 264-497-8530

Fairplay Food Center
Fairplay Complex Building
The Valley
Tel: 264-497-3877
Email: fairplayinf1@hotmail.com

Foods Ninety-Five
West End
Tel: 264-497-6196 / 8892

Hideaway Grocery
Little Dix
Tel: 264-497-2654
Fax: 264-497-5089

Island Supermarket
White Hill
Tel: 264-497-4266
Fax: 264-497-4266

J & R Mini Mart
North Hill
Tel: 264-497-3546

JW Proctors
The Quarter
Tel: 264-497-2445
Email: jwproctors@anguillanet.com

Romcan Supermarket
Lower South Hill
Tel: 264-497-6265
Fax: 264-497-6145

Tropical Flower Co. Ltd
Long Path
Tel: 264-497-4315
Fax: 264-497-4787

TOURISM OFFICE

Anguilla Tourist Board
Coronation Ave, The Valley
Tel: 264-497-2759
Email: atbtour@anguillanet.com

TOURISM OFFICES (OVERSEAS)

Germany
Anguilla Tourist Board
C/O Sergat Deutschland IM Guldenen
Wingert 8c
D-64342 Seeheim
Tel: 011-49-6257-962920
Email: rmorozow@t-online.de

Monaco
Anguilla Tourist Board
Le Coronado
20 Avenue De Fontvieille MC98000
Tel: 011- 377- 97- 98- 41- 21
Email: Florence@jet-travel.com

United Kingdom
River Communications
Unit 8a, Oakwood House, 414-422
Hackney Road, London E2 7SY
Tel: 011 44 207 729 8003
Email: rivercoms@aol.com

United States
KV Tourism Marketing Communications
111 Decatur Street Doylestown, PA
18901
Tel: 267 880-3511
Email: anguillabwi@aol.com

TOURS & ATTRACTIONS

Big Springs
Island Harbour
Tel: 264-497-5297

Dolphin Fantaseas
Meads Bay
Tel: 264-497-7946
Email: anguilla@dolphinfantaseas.com

East End Conservation Area
East End
Tel: 264-497-5297

Heritage Collection
East End
Tel: 264-497-4440
Fax: 264-497-4067

Sandy Ground Salt Pond
Sandy Ground
Tel: 264-497-2711

Wallblake House
Wallblake Road
Tel: 264-497-6613

TRADE & INDUSTRY

Chamber of Commerce
Tel: 264-497-2839
Email: acoci@anguillanet.com

TRUCKING

Bess Trucking
The Copse East End
Tel: 264-235-6108

Greigs Trucking & Heavy Equipment
Services
South Hill
Tel: 264-497-6848
Fax: 264-497-6844

Island Transport Service Ltd
The Valley
Tel: 264-497-2679
Fax: 264-497-3679

Multi Trucking/Sand & Gravel
Sandy Hill
Tel 264-497-4248 / 264-235-4248

Pat's Trucking
Sandy Ground
Tel: 264-497-3528 / Fax: 264-497-5241

Pete's Trucking & Construction
Equipment
South Hill
Tel: 264-497-6296 / Fax: 264-497-0656

Universal Trucking & Heavy Equipment
Rental
South Hill
Tel: 264-497-6300

TRUST COMPANIES

First Anguilla Trust Company Ltd
Tel: 264-498-8800
Fax: 264-497-8880

HWR Services Ltd
Tel: 264-497-5000

Intertrust Anguilla Ltd
Tel: 264-497-2189

Sinel Trust Anguilla Ltd
Tel: 264-497-3311

Webster & Dyrud / Mitchell Chambers
Tel: 264-497-3096

UNIVERSITIES

University of the West Indies
UWIDEC Centre
Tel: 264-497-8156
Fax: 264-497-2355

VIDEO RENTALS

Ultimate DVD Plus
The Valley
Tel: 264-498-1123

Video Dynesty
The Quarter
Tel: 264-497-2801

VILLA AGENCIES

Anguilla Connection Ltd
Sea-Rock
Tel: 264-497-9854
Email: axaconnect@anguillanet.com

Anguilla Villas Inc.
South Hill
Tel: 264- 497-3300
Email:
overseasconnections@villasoftheworld.com

Elegant Retreats/ Prems Ltd
Tel: 264-497-2596
Email: prems@anguillanet.com

Professional Villas Services
Tel: 264-497-3575
Email: provillas@profgroup.com

Sunset Escapes
South Hill
Tel: 264-497-3666
Email: edwards@anguillanet.com

WEDDING PLANNERS

Premium Planners
The Farrington
Tel: 264-497-8068

Sunshine Lady Productions
The Valley
Tel: 264-497-2911
Fax; 264-497-3884

Weddings on the Go
The Valley
Tel: 264-497-2685
Fax: 264-497-8416

Anguilla: Une Tranquillite Envelopee de Bleu

S'étendant sur à peine 25 kilomètres de long et 5 kilomètres à son point le plus large, Anguilla se situe à 18 degrés nord de latitude et 63 degrés ouest de longitude, à 240 kilomètres à l'est de Porto Rico, dans la Mer des Caraïbes. Cette petite île unique de 90 kilomètres carrés pointe juste au-dessus du niveau de la mer – Crucis Hill, son point culminant, s'élevant à tout juste 65 mètres. Elle jouit d'un climat subtropical, avec des températures moyennes se situant entre 24 et 26 degrés l'hiver, et entre 29 et 32 degrés l'été. Du fait de son relief plat et onduleux, l'île est constamment rafraîchie par des vents alizés qui contribuent à réduire le niveau d'humidité et à maintenir une température agréable tout au long de l'année, en particulier durant les mois d'été. Les précipitations peu élevées, d'environ 89 cm par an, arrosent une végétation principalement constituée d'arbustes qui est la marque naturelle de l'île, et que viennent compléter différentes variétés de fleurs tropicales, telles que l'hibiscus, le laurier-rose et le bougainvillier, ainsi que l'incontournable cocotier.

Anguilla a une population de 12.800 habitants (selon le recensement de 1999), dont la majorité est de descendance africaine. La langue officielle est l'anglais. Les Anguillais sont réputés pour leur amiabilité, leur fierté, leur attachement à leur île et leur caractère indépendant – des qualités qui se sont développées sans doute en grande partie grâce au fait qu'ils ont toujours possédé la terre sur laquelle ils vivent et travaillent. On recense un nombre croissant de résidents expatriés venus d'Europe, des Etats-Unis et des Antilles, ayant élu domicile à Anguilla pour leur travail, leur retraite, ou un peu des deux. L'amiabilité des habitants de l'île facilite l'insertion des nouveaux arrivants, qui ont très vite le sentiment de faire partie de la communauté au sein de laquelle ils ont choisi de vivre.

Du fait de son statut de territoire d'outre-mer britannique, Anguilla possède un gouvernement à cabinet ministériel de type britannque. Le gouverneur britannique est le représentant officiel de la Reine, les affaires législatives quotidiennes de l'île étant conduites par un ministre-en-chef, assisté de son cabinet.

CHRIS MASON

HISTOIRE

Bien que découverte par Christophe Colomb en 1493, Anguilla ne fut colonisée qu'en 1650 par des immigrants originaires de Saint-Kitts. La population amérindienne d'une île voisine les exterminera cependant six ans plus tard et, pendant 150 ans, Britanniques, Français et Espagnols se disputeront la suprémacie, ravageant ainsi l'économie de l'île et sa population.

Dans le même temps, affectée par la pauvreté du sol et les pluies erratiques, la mauvaise qualité de la production de sucre et de coton conduira à la disparition du système de plantations et de l'esclavage dans l'île. Autorisés à aller chercher du travail à l'étranger, les esclaves utiliseront leur salaire pour racheter leur liberté et celle de leur famille, puis retourneront dans l'île pour reprendre possession des terres désertées par les propriétaires de plantations.

En 1825, les Britanniques, qui détiennent alors le contrôle de l'île, scindent une union politique avec les îles voisines de Saint-Kitts et Nevis. Cette alliance suscitera une grande amertume parmi les Anguillais, qui auront le sentiment d'être injustement traités sous cette nouvelle administration.

Les années qui suivirent se passeront sans incident

pour Anguilla, hormis les ravages des grandes sécheresses de 1832 et 1890, qui conduirent la Grande-Bretagne à proposer l'émigration en masse de la population toute entière, tout d'abord en Guyane Britannique, puis à Trinidad. Les Anguillais refuseront de manière catégorique, déclarant préférer manquer de nourriture chez eux que vivre dans l'abondance ailleurs ! Il y aura par ailleurs de légers troubles politiques en 1875 et en 1958 lorsque, mécontents de leur sort au sein de la fédération Saint-Kitts-Nevis-Anguilla, les Anguillais demanderont au bureau colonial britannique d'imposer l'autorité directe de la Grande-Bretagne.

La situation conduira à la crise politique en 1967, quand éclatera la révolution anguillaise, sous l'impulsion de James Ronald Webster. Ces événements aboutiront à l'expulsion de la police de Saint-Kitts le 30 mai 1967, mettant ainsi un terme à l'union politique établie entre les trois îles. La Grande-Bretagne sera contrainte d'intervenir et, tout en s'efforçant de résoudre les problèmes politiques de l'île, lancera un programme de développement social avec l'envoi sur place d'un escadron du Génie britannique. Cette initiative conduira en 1969 à la mise en place, à échelle restreinte, de réseaux d'éclairage, d'eau courante et de chaussées pavées. Le 19 décembre 1980, après de longues années de négociations et de nombreuses modifications constitutionnelles, Anguilla fut officiellement déclarée dépendance britannique séparée.

INDUSTRIE, TOURISME ET DEVELOPPEMENT

Anguilla est considérée comme un modèle de développement touristique positif par la plupart des autres îles des Antilles, qui voient se refléter dans les politiques de développement étroitement contrôlées de l'île les économies basées sur le tourisme qu'elles-mêmes possédaient jadis. Contrairement à certaines destinations qui aiment vanter ce qu'elles ont, Anguilla est fière de ce qu'elle n'a pas ! A Anguilla, il n'y a pas de grands paquebots de croisière, pas de casinos et pas de baignade naturiste. Le jet-ski est interdit, la multi-propriété telle que nous la connaissons tous n'a pas sa place dans l'île, et le shopping, bien qu'accessible à travers les boutiques et les magasins locaux, est au mieux quelque peu limité. Ce que possède l'île, par contre, est une atmosphère de paix, de tranquillité et de sérénité qui séduit et invite à se détendre, se relaxer, se ressourcer et se plonger dans une tranquillité enveloppée de bleu…

Le tourisme d'Anguilla est fondé sur les excellentes ressources naturelles de l'île, du reste limitées : des plages de sable blanc spectaculaires, baignées par des eaux cristallines d'un bleu extraordinaire ; un système de récifs protégé qui entoure l'île est en fait un excellent site de plongée et d'exploration sous-marine ; une flore et une faune superbes ; et une ressource humaine vitale, personnifiée à travers sa population chaleureuse et accueillante. Les activités touristiques puisent également dans l'histoire et la culture de l'île, symbolisés par son héritage nautique et son sport national, la course en canot. Bien que les habitants de l'île profitent de la moindre occasion pour faire courir leurs embarcations effilées, la saison des régates démarre officiellement en avril et dure jusqu'en septembre – ses points forts étant la course autour de l'île le jour de la fête nationale anguillaise, le 30 mai, et la semaine de régates organisée durant le festival d'été annuel, la première semaine d'août. Les visiteurs peuvent apprécier les compétions depuis les plages de l'île, ou suivre la course à bord d'un élégant bateau de plaisance.

Anguilla abrite une communauté d'artistes très active. Différentes formes d'art y sont représentées, dont la poterie, la sculpture, l'artisanat, la peinture et le travail sur bois. La brochure "Art Tour of Anguilla" guide le touriste à travers plus d'une quinzaine de galeries et d'ateliers, où il découvrira des artistes venus du monde entier pour poursuivre leur muse créatrice.

La cuisine anguillaise est elle-même une véritable oeuvre d'art, la fusion créatrice de différents styles culinaires venant agrémenter la saveur éclectique de la cuisine locale. Il y a plus de 85 expériences culinaires possibles dans l'île, allant des restaurants gastronomiques intimes et raffinés aux bistros de front de mer élégamment décontractés et aux rôtisseries animées et bon marché établies au bord des routes. Des cuisiniers locaux et internationaux reconnus, des menus créatifs accompagnés de vins soigneusement sélectionnés et un service efficace et courtois concourent à créer une expérience culinaire exceptionnelle, assurée d'être l'un des moments forts de votre séjour dans l'île.

Destination de premier choix, Anguilla offre une vaste gamme d'options d'hébergement – parmi lesquelles des stations balnéaires ultra-luxueuses, des villas privées élégantes, des propriétés de luxe au caractère intime, connues sous le nom d'hôtels de charme, ainsi qu'un certain nombre d'auberges et de pensions de famille. Tous ces établissements proposent des prestations de qualité à des tarifs très attrayants qui vous garantiront de passer un séjour inoubliable.

L'industrie du tourisme de l'île s'est en outre enrichie d'un certain nombre d'installations et de prestations thermales de très haute qualité dans les principales stations de l'île. Les traitements sont proposés dans des établissements modernes sophistiqués, mais peuvent être également reçus à domicile ou dans le cadre romantique d'une pagode de plage.

Les activités proposées dans l'île englobent un large éventail de sports nautiques, ainsi que l'observation des oiseaux dans leur milieu naturel, l'équitation, la marche, la

CHRIS MASON

spéléologie, la visite des galeries d'art, les excursions historiques et les promenades en bateau à fond transparent.

Ce sont aussi des expériences tout à fait uniques qui vous attendent à Anguilla. Vous aurez notamment l'occasion de nager avec des dauphins ou de patauger parmi les inoffensives raies pastenagues au parc Dolphin Fantaseas. Si vous êtes dans l'île en février ou en avril, vous pourrez apercevoir des bancs de baleines s'ébattre au large. C'est également à cette époque de l'année que l'on peut observer, sous la clarté de la lune, le curieux rituel de la ponte de la population de tortues de l'île. Prenez aussi le temps de découvrir les alignements d'Anguilla, d'explorer le riche héritage amérindien de l'île à travers la visite des Big Springs à Island Harbour, ou de partir en randonnée dans la plus petite forêt tropicale des Antilles (eh oui, une forêt tropicale sur une île où les précipitations ne sont que de 89 cm par an !) Et les amateurs de plongée sous-marine ne manqueront pas d'explorer l'extraordinaire épave de l'El Buen Consejo, un galion espagnol du XVIIe siècle qui sombra au large de la côte nord-est de l'île avec à son bord une vaste cargaison de pièces d'or, de pierres précieuses et d'objets religieux.

Anguilla est une merveilleuse destination à toute période de l'année, mais les alizés qui soufflent doucement sur le relief plat de l'île créent une brise particulièrement agréable en été. Anguilla offre de plus un excellent rapport qualité-prix pendant les mois d'été, avec des réductions allant jusqu'à 40 % sur les prix pratiqués pendant la saison hivernale. Au mois d'août se tient le festival d'été d'Anguilla,

où nous célébrons le riche héritage culturel de l'île à travers un programme de courses de canots le jour et de musique et de spectacles la nuit. Plusieurs autres festivals se tiennent durant l'année : le festival de reggae Moonsplash en avril, la course de voile d'Anguilla et le festival del Mar en mai, l'expérience culinaire nocturne d'Anguilla en juin, et le festival de jazz Tranquility en novembre.

ACCES ET TRANSPORTS

Il est facile de se rendre à Anguilla. Depuis les Etats-Unis, les principaux points de passage sont San Juan, Saint-Maarten (Saint-Martin) et Saint-Thomas, que desservent les compagnies American Eagle, LIAT et Caribbean Sun. Les voyageurs européens peuvent accéder à l'île via Antigua, Saint-Kitts ou Saint-Maarten (Saint-Martin), avec des correspondances sur Caribbean Star, LIAT ou Winair. Depuis Saint-Maarten (Saint-Martin) une traversée d'une vingtaine de minutes en ferry vous amènera jusqu'au port-ferry anguillais de Blowing Point ; sinon, l'île n'est qu'à six minutes de Saint-Maarten (Saint-Martin) par le service de navette aérienne, qui vous déposera à Anguilla en un temps record. Dès votre arrivée, la population chaleureuse et accueillante de l'île s'assurera que vous ayez tout ce qu'il vous faut pour passer un séjour inoubliable. Bien qu'il n'y ait pas de service de bus régulier, vous trouverez un service de taxis efficace, ainsi que des services de location de voitures, de jeeps, de scooters et de vélos tout autour de l'île.

Anguilla – Die Blaue Stille

Anguilla liegt auf 18° nördlicher Breite und 63° westlicher Länge 257 Kilometer östlich von Puerto Rico. Die kleine und außergewöhnliche Karibikinsel mit einer Gesamtfläche von 90 qkm (Länge 25 km, weniger als 5 km an der breitesten Stelle) liegt nur knapp über dem Meeresspiegel. Höchste Erhebung ist der Crocus Hill mit kaum 65 Metern. Anguilla hat ein subtropisches Klima mit durchschnittlichen Temperaturen zwischen 24 und 26° C im Winter und 29 bis 32° C im Sommer. Aufgrund ihres flachen und wellenförmig verlaufenden Reliefs sorgen die ständigen Passatwinde für Kühlung und eine Reduzierung der Luftfeuchtigkeit, so dass die Temperaturen das ganze Jahr über, und vor allem während der Sommermonate, angenehm sind. Die Jahresniederschlagsmenge ist mit durchschnittlich 89 Zentimetern gering und bestimmt die urprüngliche buschige Vegetation, die so typisch für die Insel ist und sich mit bunten Tropenblüten wie Hibiskus, Oleander, Bougainvillea und den beliebten Kokospalmen vermischt.

Anguilla hat 12.800 Einwohner (Volkszählung 1999), von welchen die Mehrheit afrikanischer Abstammung ist. Offizielle Landessprache ist Englisch. Die Einwohner Anguillas sind für ihre Freundlichkeit, Unabhängigkeit, die Liebe zu ihrer Insel und ihren Nationalstolz bekannt - Attribute, die wohl im Wesentlichen darauf zurückzuführen sind, dass das Land, auf dem die Anguillaner lebten und arbeiteten, diesen von jeher gehörte. Die Zahl der aus Europa, den USA und der Karibik Zugezogenen, die auf Anguilla arbeiten oder ihren Altersruhesitz haben – eventuell auch beides - wächst beständig. Die freundliche Art der Inselbewohner macht es leicht, sich zu integrieren; Neuankömmlinge fühlen sich schnell als Teil ihrer Wahlheimat.

Als Überseegebiet des Vereinigten Königreiches von Großbritannien verfügt Anguilla über eine Regierung im Stile Westminsters. Offizieller Vertreter von Königin Elisabeth II. ist ein britischer Gouverneur; legislative Funktionen im Zusammenhang mit der täglichen Verwaltung der Insel werden vom Regierungschef und seinem Kabinett ausgeübt.

GESCHICHTE

Obwohl bereits 1493 von Christoph Kolumbus entdeckt, wurde Anguilla erst im Jahre 1650 von Siedlern der Insel St. Kitts kolonisiert. Nur sechs Jahre später wurde die Siedlung jedoch von Indianern einer nahegelegenen Insel zerstört, worauf ein 150 Jahre währender Kampf zwischen Briten, Franzosen und Spaniern um die Vorherrschaft auf der Insel entbrannte, der verheerende Folgen für ihre Wirtschaft und Bewohner hatte.

Der karge Boden, unregelmäßige Regenfälle und die gleichbleibend schlechte Zucker- und Baumwollqualität führten schließlich zum Niedergang des Plantagensystems und der Sklaverei auf der Insel. Die Sklaven erhielten das Recht, sich Arbeit in Übersee zu suchen und sich und ihre Familien mit dem verdienten Lohn freizukaufen, so dass diese bei ihrer Rückkehr auf die Insel das seit Langem verlassene Land der Plantagenbesitzer in Besitz nehmen und besiedeln konnten.

1825 veranlasste Großbritannien, welches die Gebietshoheit über die Insel ausübte, eine politische Union mit den nahegelegenen Inseln St. Kitts und Nevis, die auf starke Ablehnung bei den Anguillanern stieß, da diese sich von der neuen Verwaltung ungerecht behandelt fühlten.

Ereignislose Jahre folgten, mit Ausnahme von Aufständen zur Zeit der großen Dürren 1832 und 1890, die Großbritannien dazu veranlassten, zunächst zu einer Abwanderung der gesamten Bevölkerung nach Britisch-Guyana und später nach Trinidad anzuraten. Die Anguillaner begründeten Ihre strikte Weigerung mit dem Argument, es sei besser Zuhause zu verhungern als anderswo im Überfluss zu leben! 1875 und 1958 kam es zu leichten politischen Unruhen, als die mit ihrer Behandlung als Teil der St. Kitts-Nevis-Anguilla-Föderation unzufriedenen Anguillaner das Britische Kolonialministerium ersuchten, der Britischen Hoheit direkt unterstellt zu werden.

Die politische Lage spitzte sich zu, als es 1967 unter der Führung von James Ronald Webster schließlich zur

CHRIS MASON

Revolution auf Anguilla kam. Höhepunkt der Auseinandersetzungen war die Verbannung der Polizeieinheit von St. Kitts von Anguilla am 30. Mai 1967, womit der offizielle politische Bund der drei Inseln aufgelöst war. Großbritannien sah sich zum Einschreiten gezwungen und leitete im Rahmen des Versuchs, die politischen Probleme der Insel zu lösen, ein soziales Entwicklungsprogramm ein, das mit Hilfe der Feldschwadron der „Royal Engineers" umgesetzt wurde. So gab es 1969 schließlich, wenn auch mit Einschränkungen, elektrisches Licht, fließendes Wasser und hier und da gepflasterte Strassen. Nach jahrelangen Verhandlungen und einer Reihe von Verfassungsänderungen wurde Anguilla am 19. Dezember 1980 offiziell zu einer unabhängigen Britischen Kronkolonie erklärt.

WIRTSCHAFT, TOURISMUS UND ENTWICKLUNG

Anguilla nimmt aufgrund seiner positiven Fremdenverkehrsentwicklung für viele der übrigen Karibikinseln, die in der sorgfältig organisierten Entwicklungspolitik der Insel ihre ehemals auf Tourismus basierenden Wirtschaften wiedererkennen, eine Vorbildfunktion ein. Während viele Länder sich dessen rühmen, was sie haben, sind wir auf Anguilla stolz auf das, was wir nicht haben! In und um Anguilla werden Sie weder große Kreuzfahrtschiffe, noch Kasinos, noch FFK

finden. Das Benutzen von Jet-Skis ist nicht gestattet, ein Timesharing, wie wir es heute kennen, hat keinen Platz auf der Insel und die Einkaufsmöglichkeiten sind auf ein optimales Maß begrenzt, wenngleich es eine gewisse Anzahl individueller Boutiquen und Geschäfte gibt. Was wir zu bieten haben, ist eine friedliche, ruhige und gelassene Atmosphäre, die den Besucher in ihren Bann zieht und ihn einlädt, sich zu entspannen, abzuschalten, neue Kraft zu schöpfen und so richtig in diese „blaue Stille" einzutauchen.

Anguillas Fremdenverkehr basiert auf ihren herrlichen, wenn auch begrenzten, natürlichen Ressourcen: spektakuläre und unberührte weiße Sandstrände, die vom kristallklaren, nahezu unwirklich anmutenden Blau des Wassers umspült werden; das intakte Riffsystem, das die Insel umgibt und Anguilla zu einem erstklassigen Tauch- und Schnorchelrevier macht; faszinierende Pflanzen- und Tierarten und nicht zuletzt die Bewohner der Insel mit ihrer warmherzigen und gastfreundlichen Art. Weitere touristische Highlights sind die Geschichte und Kultur der Insel, welche im nautischen Erbe und unserem einzigartigen Nationalsport, den Bootsregatten, zum Ausdruck kommen. Wenngleich die Inselbewohner keine Gelegenheit auslassen, Rennen mit ihren schnittigen Booten zu veranstalten, geht die offizielle Regattasaison von April bis September. Höhepunkte sind das Rennen um die Insel (Around-the-Island Boat Race) am 30. Mai, dem Nationalfeiertag (Anguilla Day) sowie die Regattawoche während des jährlich stattfindenden

Sommerfestivals in der ersten Augustwoche. Besucher haben die Möglichkeit, die Veranstaltungen von den Stränden aus mitzuverfolgen oder auch inmitten des Geschehens von einem der modernen Ausflugsschiffe.

Anguilla verfügt darüber hinaus über eine lebhafte Kunstszene. Zu den angewandten Techniken gehören u.a. Töpferei und Kunsthandwerk sowie Bildhauerei, Malerei und Holzschnitzerei. Die Broschüre „Art Tour of Anguilla" führt den Besucher durch mehr als 15 Galerien und Studios, in denen man Künstlern aus der ganzen Welt bei ihrer kreativen Muse zuschauen kann.

Auch die Küche Anguillas ist mit ihrer kreativen Verschmelzung kulinarischer Richtungen, die den eklektischen Gout der Inselküche ergänzen, eine wahre Kunst. Die Insel verfügt über mehr als 85 Speiselokale, die von glamourösen, exklusiven Gourmettempeln über Strandbistros von schlichter Eleganz bis hin zu den preisgünstigen geselligen Grillrestaurants an der Hauptstrasse reichen. Preisgekrönte nationale und internationale Köche, kreative Menüs, zu denen sorgfältig ausgewählte Weine gereicht werden und ein effizienter und zuvorkommender Service verbinden sich auf dieser Insel zu einem unvergleichlichen Gastronomie-Erlebnis, das mit Sicherheit zu den Höhepunkten Ihres Urlaubs gehören wird.

Als Reiseziel der Spitzenklasse verfügt Anguilla über ein breites Spektrum an Unterkunftsmöglichkeiten. So bieten hochluxuriöse Resorts, elegante Privatvillen, exklusive Luxusunterkünfte („Hotels de Charme") sowie eine Anzahl kleinerer Pensionen und Gasthäuser eine Qualität und Leistung, die Ihren Aufenthalt auf der Insel zu einem unvergesslichen Erlebnis machen.

Eine attraktive Ergänzung des Touristikangebots der Insel sind Wellness-Einrichtungen und -dienstleistungen auf Weltklasseniveau, die inzwischen in den Top-Resorts der Insel zur Verfügung stehen. Die Behandlungen können in den hochmodernen Zentren vorgenommen werden, auf Wunsch aber auch im Hotelzimmer oder sogar in einer romantischen Strandpagode.

Zum Freizeitangebot der Insel gehören neben einer Vielzahl an Wassersportmöglichkeiten das Beobachten von Vögeln, Reiten, Wandern, Höhlenexkursionen, Besuche von Kunstgalerien, historische Touren und Fahrten mit dem Glasbodenschiff.

Anguilla wartet mit einem breiten Angebot einzigartiger Attraktionen auf. Nicht entgehen lassen sollten Sie es sich, im Dolphin Fantaseas mit Delfinen zu schwimmen oder inmitten eines Schwarms zahmer Stachelrochen umherzuwaten. Sollten Sie zwischen Februar und April auf der Insel sein, sehen Sie vielleicht sogar eine sich im Meer tummelnde Schule von Walen. Zu dieser Jahreszeit ist in hellen Mondnächten auch das außergewöhnliche Nistverhalten der geschützten Meeresschildkrötenpopulation zu beobachten. Nehmen

Sie sich Zeit, das Stonehenge Anguillas zu erkunden, erforschen Sie das reiche Kulturerbe der Ureinwohner der Insel auf einem Ausflug zu den Big Springs in Island Harbour oder steigen Sie in die Wanderschuhe und unternehmen Sie einen Streifzug durch den kleinsten Regenwald der Karibik (ja, richtig, ein Regenwald auf einer Insel mit einer durchschnittlichen Niederschlagsmenge von 89 Zentimetern pro Jahr!). Das ultimative Taucherlebnis bietet das Schiffswrack der El Buen Consejo, einer spanischen Galeone aus dem 17. Jahrhundert, die mit einer vollen Ladung für die Insel bestimmter Goldmünzen, Edelsteine und religiösen Artefakten unmittelbar vor deren Nordostküste sank.

Anguilla ist zu jeder Jahreszeit ein ausgezeichnetes Ferienziel, im Sommer jedoch sorgen die sanft über die flache Landschaft der Insel streichenden Passatwinde zudem für eine angenehm kühle Brise. Außerdem bietet Anguilla in der Sommersaison ein besonders gutes Preis-Leistungs-Verhältnis – die Tarife für Unterkünfte sind um bis zu 40 % niedriger als während der Wintermonate. Im August haben Sie darüber hinaus die Möglichkeit, das Anguilla Summer Festival mitzuerleben, das unser reiches Kulturerbe zum Ausdruck bringt. Während des Tages können Sie so ein einzigartige Programm verschiedener Bootsregatten mitverfolgen und bei Nacht an den zahlreichen Musik- und historischen Festveranstaltungen teilnehmen. Zu den vielen weiteren Veranstaltungen, die über das Jahr hinweg stattfinden, gehören das Moonsplash Reggae Festival im April, die Anguilla Yacht Regatta und das Festival del Mar im Mai, die Anguilla Night Culinary Experience im Juni sowie das Tranquility Jazz Festival im November.

ANREISE UND VERKEHRSMITTEL

Die Anreise auf die Insel ist kein Problem: San Juan, St. Maarten und St. Thomas verfügen über größere Flughäfen, die aus den USA von American Eagle, LIAT und Caribbean Sun angeflogen werden; Reisende aus Europa erreichen die Insel mit Flügen der Air France (täglich) oder KLM (3 x pro Woche) nach St. Maarten. Von St. Maarten aus besteht die Möglichkeit, zum Blowing Point Ferry Terminal von Anguilla mit der Fähre überzusetzen (Fahrtzeit 20 Minuten). In Rekordzeit erreichen Sie die Insel mit dem nur 6 Minuten dauernden Shuttle-Flug. Auf Anguilla angekommen werden unsere entgegenkommenden und gastfreundlichen Inselbewohner dafür sorgen, dass es an nichts fehlt, diesen Urlaub für Sie zu einem unvergesslichen Erlebnis zu machen. Einen regelmäßigen Busverkehr gibt es auf der Insel nicht, dafür aber einen sehr effizienten Taxidienst. Darüber hinaus finden Sie auf der ganzen Insel Verleihfirmen für Autos, Jeeps, Motorroller und Fahrräder.

Anguilla: Tranquillità Avvolta Nel Blu

L'isola di Anguilla si trova a 18 gradi latitudine nord, 63 gradi longitudine ovest, a circa 240 km a est di Portorico, nel Mare dei Caraibi. Anguilla è lunga 25 km e larga solo 5. Questa piccola isola, unica nel suo genere e con una superficie di soli 90 km², sorge appena sopra il livello del mare e il suo punto più alto, Crocus Hill raggiunge a malapena i 65 metri. Il clima è sub-tropicale con temperature medie da 24 a 26° C in inverno e da 29 a 32° C in estate. Grazie al suo profilo prevalentemente pianeggiante, l'isola è rinfrescata dai venti di aliseo che riducono il livello di umidità e mantengono la temperatura a livelli piacevoli durante tutto l'anno ma soprattutto nei mesi estivi. Date le basse precipitazioni piovose medie di circa 89 cm l'anno, la flora caratteristica dell'isola consiste di una macchia tropicale di sempreverdi a cui si interpongono i brillanti spruzzi di colore dell'ibisco, oleandro e bouganville, e delle diffusissime palme da cocco.

Anguilla ha una popolazione di 12800 abitanti (censimento del 1999), la maggioranza dei quali sono di origine africana. La lingua ufficiale è l'inglese. La popolazione locale è famosa per la sua indole cordiale, l'orgoglio e l'amore che nutre per l'isola e il suo carattere indipendente, qualità che sono fiorite in quanto storicamente gli abitanti dell'isola sono da sempre proprietari del suolo su cui vivono e lavorano. L'isola ospita un numero sempre crescente di cittadini stranieri provenienti dall'Europa, gli Stati Uniti e i Caraibi, che hanno scelto di vivere ad Anguilla per motivi di lavoro o perché sono andati in pensione e, in alcuni in casi, per ambedue i motivi. La spontanea cordialità della popolazione facilita molto l'integrazione dei nuovi arrivati che si sentono immediatamente a proprio agio nella comunità in cui hanno scelto di vivere.

Anguilla è una colonia britannica ed è amministrata da un governo di stile Westminster. Il Governatore britannico è il rappresentante ufficiale della Regina mentre la vita amministrativa quotidiana dell'isola è gestita dal Capo dei Ministri e dal suo Gabinetto.

CHRIS MASON

STORIA

Scoperta da Cristoforo Colombo nel 1493, la colonizzazione di Anguilla ebbe inizio soltanto nel 1650 con l'arrivo dei primi coloni da St. Kitts. Sei anni dopo l'invasione degli amerindiani provenienti da un'isola vicina segnò la fine di questo primo insediamento. Durante i successivi 150 anni l'isola fu teatro di continue lotte tra inglesi, francesi e spagnoli che si contendevano la supremazia del territorio, con effetti disastrosi per l'economia dell'isola e la popolazione indigena.

Allo stesso tempo la sterilità del suolo, le imprevedibili precipitazioni piovose e la conseguente scarsa qualità della canna da zucchero e del cotone portarono al declino del sistema delle piantagioni e della schiavitù dell'isola. Agli schiavi fu consentito di cercare lavoro all'estero e di utilizzare il salario per riscattare la libertà propria e dei familiari con l'obiettivo finale di tornare sull'isola ed entrare in possesso e coltivare le terre abbandonate dai proprietari di piantagioni.

Nel 1825 il controllo dell'isola era nelle mani degli inglesi che dettero vita a un'unione politica con le vicine isole di St Kitts e Nevis. Questa mossa provocò un'ondata di risentimento tra la popolazione di Anguilla che si sentì trattata ingiustamente dalla nuova amministrazione.

Gli anni si susseguirono senza incidenti di rilievo ad Anguilla, con l'eccezione dei danni provocati dalle grandi siccità del 1832 e del 1890 che portarono la Gran Bretagna a proporre l'esodo dell'intera popolazione dapprima nella Guyana Britannica e in un secondo tempo a Trinidad. Gli anguillesi si rifiutarono decisamente, dichiarando che preferivano morire di fame a casa propria che vivere in abbondanza altrove! Nel 1875 e nel 1958 ci furono alcuni episodi di agitazione politica quando, insoddisfatti del modo in cui erano trattati all'interno della federazione St Kitts-Nevis-Anguilla, gli anguillesi presentarono una petizione all'Amministrazione Britannica chiedendo di essere governati direttamente dalla Gran Bretagna.

L'insoddisfazione politica raggiunse il culmine nel 1967 e sfociò nella Rivoluzione di Anguilla sotto il comando di James Ronald Webster. Il 30 maggio 1967 le Forze di Polizia di St Kitts furono espulse da Anguilla; questo episodio concluse definitivamente la formale relazione politica tra le tre isole. La Gran Bretagna fu costretta a intervenire e mentre era impegnata a risolvere i problemi politici dell'isola, si avvalse della presenza sull'isola di uno squadrone dei Royal Engineers per dare il via a un programma limitato di sviluppo urbano e sociale. Nel 1969 l'isola aveva un'illuminazione limitata, acqua corrente e alcune strade asfaltate.

Dopo molti anni di trattative e una serie di cambiamenti costituzionali a carattere incrementale, il 19 dicembre 1980 Anguilla fu dichiarata ufficialmente Territorio Britannico Dipendente separato.

INDUSTRIA, TURISMO & SVILUPPO

Anguilla è vista come un modello positivo di sviluppo turistico da molte delle altre isole caraibiche che identificano nelle politiche di sviluppo attentamente controllate dall'autorità governativa dell'isola quell'economia turistica da loro vissuta in passato. Mentre alcuni paesi amano vantarsi di ciò che hanno, ad Anguilla siamo fieri di quello che non abbiamo! Ad Anguilla non ci sono grandi navi da crociera e casinò e il nudismo è vietato. I jet ski sono banditi e, come tutti sappiamo, l'isola non ha accolto il concetto degli appartamenti-vacanza in multiproprietà; lo shopping, nelle migliori delle ipotesi e nonostante la presenza di boutique esclusive e negozi, è limitato. Quello che abbiamo è un'atmosfera di pace,

tranquillità e serenità che vi avvolge e vi invita al relax, a staccare la spina, ringiovanire, immergersi nella Tranquillità Avvolta Nel Blu...

Il turismo di Anguilla si basa sulle sue eccellenti anche se limitate risorse naturali: le bellissime, immacolate spiagge di soffice sabbia bianca lambite da un mare trasparente color acquamarina; la circostante barriera corallina incontaminata che fa di Anguilla il luogo perfetto per praticare il nuoto subacqueo; specie superbe di flora e fauna e l'indispensabile risorsa umana personificata dalla sua popolazione cordiale e ospitale. Il prodotto turistico dell'isola abbraccia altri aspetti molto importanti come la sua storia e cultura, degnamente rappresentate dalla nostra tradizione nautica e dal nostro sport nazionale, le regate. Anche se gli isolani non hanno bisogno di scuse per sfidarsi a bordo delle loro snelle imbarcazioni a vela, la stagione ufficiale delle regate va da aprile a settembre e gli eventi di maggior rilievo sono la regata Around-the-Island che si svolge il 30 maggio per celebrare Anguilla Day e le regate che hanno luogo nel corso dell'annuale Festival d'Estate la prima settimana di agosto. Per seguire le regate e immergersi nell'atmosfera dell'evento basta passeggiare lungo le spiagge dell'isola o seguire l'azione in mare su una delle imbarcazioni turistiche.

Anguilla ospita un coltivato movimento artistico molto vivace che si esprime in tantissime forme d'arte come ceramica, scultura, artigianato, pittura e lavorazione del legno. La guida "Art Tour of Anguilla" conduce i visitatori a oltre 15 gallerie e studi dove artisti da ogni parte del mondo si dedicano all'inseguimento della loro musa ispiratrice.

Anche la gastronomia di Anguilla è un capolavoro che riunisce la fusione creativa di stili culinari diversi ai sapori eclettici della gastronomia tradizionale dell'isola. L'isola offre oltre 85 esperienze gastronomiche che vanno dai ristoranti eleganti e intimi da gourmet ai bistrot casual-eleganti in riva al mare, alle allegre grigliate economicamente più accessibili organizzate per strada. Premiati chef locali e internazionali, menu fantasiosi affiancati da una lista di vini pregiati scelti con cura e il servizio efficiente e cortese si riuniscono per creare un'esperienza gastronomica straordinaria che non mancherà di essere il *clou* di ogni vacanza.

Anguilla è una destinazione esclusiva e di qualità che offre un'ampia scelta di sistemazioni. Tra queste, club vacanze extra lusso, ville private molto eleganti, proprietà di lusso più raccolte conosciute come gli "hotels de Charme" ed alcune pensioni e alberghi più piccoli. Tutte queste strutture offrono un servizio di eccellente qualità e di ottimo valore per un soggiorno indimenticabile sulla nostra isola.

Un'aggiunta interessante alle strutture turistiche dell'isola è stata l'introduzione, presso le principali località dell'isola, di alcune Strutture e Servizi Spa di classe

CHRIS MASON

mondiale. I trattamenti sono offerti in ambienti moderni e attrezzatissimi, oppure possono essere prenotati e offerti en suite o in una romantica pagoda sulla spiaggia.

L'isola offre molte attività per il tempo libero tra cui sport acquatici, bird-watching, equitazione, escursionismo, speleologia, tour di gallerie d'arte, tour d'interesse storico ed escursioni su imbarcazioni con la carena in vetro.

Ad Anguilla vivrete esperienze uniche e molto speciali. Nuotare con i delfini o guadare con le docili razze a Dolphin Fantaseas sono appuntamenti da non perdere. Se siete sull'isola a febbraio e aprile, potreste avvistare un branco di balene che gioca in mare. E sempre in questo periodo, in una notte di luna, potrete osservare le strane abitudini di nidificazione delle tartarughe di mare, una specie protetta dell'isola. Dedicate un paio d'ore alla scoperta dell'equivalente anguillese di Stonehenge, esplorate il ricco patrimonio culturale amerindiano dell'isola a Big Springs in Island Harbour, oppure calzate gli scarponi e avventuratevi nella più piccola Foresta Tropicale dei Caraibi (Sì, avete letto bene! Una foresta tropicale su un'isola con una precipitazione piovosa media di 90 cm l'anno!) E se volete vivere l'esperienza 'definitiva' del nuoto d'immersione, dovete esplorare l'affascinante relitto di El Buen Consejo, il galeone spagnolo del 17° secolo che affondò davanti alla costa nord-orientale dell'isola con il suo carico di monete d'oro, pietre preziose e artefatti religiosi destinati all'isola.

Anguilla è una destinazione di vacanza ideale in ogni stagione dell'anno ma i freschi venti di aliseo che sfiorano delicatamente il paesaggio pianeggiante dell'isola la rendono piacevolissima anche in estate. Sempre in estate Anguilla è una destinazione molto conveniente in quanto offre sconti fino al 40% sulle tariffe invernali degli alberghi. In agosto potrete assistere al Festival d'Estate di Anguilla, periodo in cui celebriamo il nostro ricco patrimonio culturale con un programma di regate uniche nel loro genere durante il giorno e musica e sfilate in costumi storici di sera. Durante l'anno organizziamo altri Festival come il Moonsplash Reggae Festival ad aprile, l'Anguilla Yacht Regatta e il Festival del Mar a maggio, l' Anguilla Night Culinary Experience a giugno, e il Tranquility Jazz Festival a novembre.

ACCESSO E TRASPORTI

Raggiungere l'isola è facile. Dagli USA, i maggiori aeroporti di partenza sono San Juan, St Maarten e St Thomas con American Eagle, LIAT, o Caribbean Sun mentre i turisti europei posono raggiungere l'isola passando da Antigua, St Kitts o St Maarten con i collegamenti della Caribbean Star, LIAT o Winair. St Maarten è a soli 20 minuti di traghetto dal terminal di Blowing Point di Anguilla; alternativamente i viaggiatori possono prendere il volo dei pendolari che in 6 minuti li porta sull'isola. Al vostro arrivo, tutto quello di cui avrete bisogno per vivere una vacanza indimenticabile è il calore, la cordialità e l'ospitalità della nostra gente. Nonostante il servizio di autobus sia irregolare, il servizio taxi è molto efficiente e su tutta l'isola ci sono molte agenzie di noleggio dove potrete scegliere tra auto, jeep, scooter e biciclette.

Anguila: Tranquilidad Rodeada de Azul

Con tan sólo unos 25 km. de longitud y 5 km. en su punto de mayor anchura, Anguila está situada a 18° de latitud norte y 63° de longitud oeste, aproximadamente 240 km. al este de Puerto Rico, en el mar Caribe. Esta islita única, con un área de 90 km², apenas sobresale por encima del nivel del mar y su punto más alto – la colina Crocus – tiene tan sólo 65 m de altura. El clima es subtropical, con temperaturas medias de 24 a 26°C en invierno y 29 a 32°C en verano. Debido a su paisaje llano, ondulado, los constantes vientos alisios la refrescan, ayudando a disminuir la humedad y a mantener una temperatura confortable todo el año, en especial durante los meses de verano. El bajo índice de lluvias, de aproximadamente 890 mm al año, es la razón por la que la vegetación autóctona se compone de arbustos, que son la característica natural de la isla, entremezclados con brillantes flores, como los hibiscos, las adelfas y las buganvillas, así como los populares cocoteros.

Anguila tiene una población de 12.800 habitantes (informe del censo de 1999), siendo la mayoría de origen africano. El idioma oficial es el inglés. Los nativos de esta isla son conocidos por su forma de ser amistosa, su orgullo, su amor a la isla y su carácter independiente,

atributos que es posible hayan florecido principalmente debido a que siempre han sido propietarios de las tierras en las que han trabajado y vivido. Hay un número cada vez mayor de residentes provenientes de Europa, EE.UU. y el resto del Caribe, que se han establecido en Anguila para trabajar, jubilarse o un poco de ambas cosas. Debido al carácter amistoso de la gente, la integración resulta fácil y los no nacidos en Anguila pasan rápidamente a sentirse parte de la comunidad en la que han elegido vivir.

En su calidad de territorio británico de ultramar del Reino Unido, Anguila tiene un gobierno de estilo ministerial de tipo Westminster. Un Gobernador británico es el representante oficial de la Reina de Inglaterra, mientras que un Primer Ministro y su Consejo de Ministros se encargan del día a día de los asuntos legislativos.

HISTORIA

Aunque fue descubierta por Colón en 1493, Anguila no fue colonizada hasta 1650, cuando se establecieron en ella colonos provenientes de Saint Kitts. Sin embargo, los indígenas de una isla cercana destruyeron la colonia seis años más tarde y durante los ciento cincuenta años siguientes, los británicos, los franceses y los españoles batallaron entre sí para obtener supremacía en la isla, destrozando tanto a la economía como a los habitantes de la misma.

Mientras tanto, la pobreza de las tierras, la irregularidad de las lluvias y la consiguiente baja calidad del azúcar y el algodón llevaron al declive del sistema de plantaciones y esclavitud en la isla. A los esclavos se les permitió buscar trabajo fuera de la isla, usando sus ingresos para comprar su libertad y la de sus familias, pudiendo así regresar, poseer y trabajar las tierras que habían sido abandonadas desde hacía ya mucho tiempo por los propietarios de plantaciones.

En 1825 los británicos, quienes controlaban la isla, establecieron una unión política con las cercanas islas de Saint Kitts y Nevis. Esto provocó un gran resentimiento

CHRIS MASON

entre los anguilanos, quienes consideraron que el nuevo gobierno los trataba injustamente.

Siguieron transcurriendo los años en Anguila, sin mayores acontecimientos, salvo por los destrozos causados por las grandes sequías de 1832 y 1890, que llevaron a Gran Bretaña a proponer la emigración masiva de la totalidad de la población, primeramente a la Guayana Británica (Guyana) y posteriormente a Trinidad. Los anguilanos se negaron totalmente a ello, diciendo que preferían morirse de hambre en su país que vivir con abundancia en otro lugar. Hubo también algo de intranquilidad política en 1875 y 1958, cuando, sintiéndose descontentos con el tratamiento que recibían como parte de la federación Saint Kitts-Nevis-Anguila, los anguilanos solicitaron a la Oficina Colonial Británica ser gobernados directamente por Gran Bretaña.

Finalmente, el asunto terminó por explotar en 1967, cuando tuvo lugar la revolución de Anguila, incitada por el Sr. James Ronald Webster. Culminó con la expulsión de Anguila de las fuerzas policiales de Saint Kitts, lo que ocurrió el 30 de mayo de 1967 y significó el final de la relación política formal entre las tres islas. Gran Bretaña se vio obligada a intervenir y mientras intentaba resolver los problemas políticos de la isla, inició un programa de desarrollo social, usando para ello a un escuadrón de Zapadores Reales. Esto tuvo como resultado que, para 1969, la isla contaba con un alumbrado público limitado, agua corriente y algunas carreteras asfaltadas. Después de muchos años de negociaciones y de una serie de cambios constitucionales cada vez mayores, Anguila fue formalmente declarada territorio dependiente británico separado el 19 de diciembre de 1980.

INDUSTRIA, TURISMO Y DESARROLLO

Anguila es considerada como un modelo de desarrollo turístico positivo por muchas de las demás islas caribeñas, quienes ven en la cuidadosa política de desarrollo de la isla un reflejo de las economías basadas en el turismo de las que disfrutaron en su día. Aunque a algunos países les gusta presumir de lo que tienen, en Anguila estamos orgullosos de lo que no tenemos. En Anguila no hay grandes barcos de crucero, ni casinos ni playas nudistas. Los *jet ski* están prohibidos, la multipropiedad o *timeshare,* tal y como la conocemos todos, no se admite en la isla y las compras, aunque pueden efectuarse en *boutiques* y tiendas únicas, son algo limitadas en el mejor de los casos. Lo que sí tenemos, sin embargo, es un ambiente de paz, tranquilidad y serenidad que atrae a la gente y la invita a relajarse, a descansar, a rejuvenecerse y a sumergirse en la tranquilidad rodeada de azul…

El turismo de Anguila está basado en sus excelentes, aunque limitados, recursos naturales: unas espectaculares e inmaculadas playas de arena blanca, acariciadas por aguas cristalinas de un azul increíble; una cadena de arrecifes, intactos, que rodea a la isla y hace que Anguila sea un lugar excelente para el buceo libre o con bombonas; las maravillosas especies de su flora y su fauna; y los esenciales recursos humanos, personificados por sus gentes cálidas y hospitalarias. Otros aspectos clave de la oferta turística de la isla son su historia y su cultura, plasmadas en nuestro patrimonio marítimo y en nuestro deporte nacional único, las regatas. Aunque los isleños aprovechan toda oportunidad de competir con sus esbeltas embarcaciones, la temporada oficial de regatas empieza en abril y dura hasta septiembre, siendo las fechas más importantes la regata de vuelta de la isla, en el día nacional de Anguila, el 30 de mayo, y la semana de regatas que tiene lugar durante el festival de verano anual, en la primera semana de agosto. Los visitantes pueden unirse a la emoción presenciando las regatas desde las playas de la isla, o bien seguir la acción de cerca, en el agua, a bordo de una aerodinámica embarcación de placer.

Anguila es el hogar de una floreciente comunidad de artistas. Hay diversos tipos de arte, que incluyen la cerámica, la escultura, la pintura y las tallas en madera. Un folleto que explica como efectuar una "Visita artística a Anguila" guía a los visitantes hacia más de quince galerías y estudios en los que pueden verse a artistas de todo el mundo siguiendo la inspiración de sus musas creativas.

Y la cocina de Anguila también es realmente una obra de arte, dado que la creativa combinación de distintos estilos culinarios con el sabor ecléctico de la cocina propia de la isla añade un toque distinto. La isla cuenta con más de 85 lugares en los que disfrutar de una buena comida, desde atractivos restaurantes para *gourmets,* de ambiente íntimo, hasta bares de playa, elegantemente informales, así como alegres parrillas a los lados de las carreteras, al alcance de todos los bolsillos. Los galardonados *chefs* locales e internacionales, la creativa oferta de platos complementados por vinos cuidadosamente seleccionados y el servicio eficaz y cortés son una combinación que hará que las comidas sean uno de los mejores instantes de sus vacaciones.

Siendo un destino turístico de primera calidad, Anguila le ofrece una gran variedad de opciones de alojamiento. Estas incluyen hoteles de gran lujo, elegantes viviendas particulares para alquilar, pequeños hoteles de lujo, de ambiente íntimo, conocidos como *hotels de charme* y toda una serie de pequeñas pensiones y casas de huéspedes, ofreciendo todas estas opciones un servicio de calidad y una excelente relación entre el precio y las comodidades ofrecidas, para garantizarle una memorable estancia en la isla.

La introducción de una serie de servicios e instalaciones de balneario de categoría mundial, en los mejores hoteles de la isla, es un interesante añadido a la oferta turística de la isla. Los tratamientos se efectúan en instalaciones modernas, de la más reciente tecnología, o bien pueden solicitarse en la propia habitación o en una romántica pagoda en la playa.

Las actividades disponibles en la isla incluyen una amplia variedad de deportes acuáticos, además de ir a ver aves en su entorno natural, equitación, excursiones, exploración de cavernas, visitas a galerías de arte y paseos en barcos con fondo de vidrio.

Una serie de experiencias muy especiales, únicas en la vida, lo están esperando en Anguila. No debe perderse la experiencia de nadar con delfines o vadear en compañía de amistosas rayas en Dolphin Fantaseas. Si está en la isla entre febrero y abril, puede que vea grupos de ballenas jugueteando en el mar. Y en esa misma época también podrá observar, en noches de luna, las peculiares formas de anidar de la población de tortugas, animales que están protegidos. Dedique algo de tiempo a descubrir el Stonehenge de Anguila, a explorar el rico patrimonio indígena de la isla, visitando Big Springs en Island Harbour, o póngase las botas de caminar y atraviese el bosque tropical más pequeño del Caribe (¡Sí! ¡Un bosque tropical en una isla con un promedio de 890 mm. de lluvia al año!) Y para la experiencia de buceo definitiva, es necesario explorar los fascinantes restos del "Buen Consejo", un galeón español del siglo XVII que se hundió justo frente la costa noreste de la isla, con una carga de monedas de oro, piedras preciosas y objetos religiosos destinados a la isla.

Anguila es un gran lugar para vacaciones en cualquier momento del año, pero los frescos vientos alisios que soplan suavemente sobre el paisaje llano de la isla hacen que Anguila sea tan agradable como una brisa veraniega. Y, además, en verano Anguila ofrece unos excelentes precios, con hasta un 40% de descuento sobre las tarifas de alojamiento de invierno. En agosto también podrá presenciar el festival de verano de Anguila, en el que celebramos nuestro rico patrimonio cultural con un programa único de regatas durante el día y música y espectáculos durante la noche. Hay otros festivales durante el año: el festival de reggae Moonsplash, en abril, la regata de yates de Anguila y el festival del mar en mayo, la experiencia culinaria de Anguila en junio y el festival de jazz Tranquility, en noviembre.

ACCESO Y TRANSPORTES

Llegar a la isla es fácil. Los principales aeropuertos con vuelos a la isla desde EE.UU. incluyen a San Juan, Saint Maarten y Saint Thomas, con American Eagle, LIAT o Caribbean Sun, mientras que los viajeros provenientes de Europa pueden llegar a la isla pasando por Antigua, Saint Kitts o Saint Maarten, enlazando con Caribbean Star, LIAT o Winair. Una vez en Saint Maarten, los viajeros hacer una travesía en ferry, de veinte minutos de duración, para desembarcar en el Blowing Point Ferry Terminal de Anguila. También pueden hacer un cortísimo vuelo de seis minutos para llegar a la isla en un tiempo record. Una vez en la isla, nuestra hospitalaria gente le dará la bienvenida y podrá ofrecerle todo lo necesario para que sus vacaciones sean memorables. Aunque no hay servicio regular de autobuses, hay un eficaz servicio de taxis, además de servicios de alquiler de automóviles normales, jeeps, motonetas y bicicletas en toda la isla.